THE ENCYCLOPEDIA MAN

Written by
Lance Russell

THE ENCYCLOPEDIA MAN

Copyright © Lance Russell 2013

All Rights Reserved

ISBN 978-0-9927841-0-2

First Published December 2013
Published by Design Marque

Printed in Great Britain by
www.designmarque.co.uk

A JOURNEY THROUGH AUSTRALIA

I HOPE YOU ENJOY TRAVELLING WITH ME

Love

Terry 2014

For Mum

Foreword
By The Author

Why has it taken me nearly twenty years to write this book? Next March it would have been twenty years ago that I returned from Australia, after spending three years and one month out there. On my return, I began to tell people of my adventure selling encyclopedias door- to- door, meeting people from all walks of life. From doctors, to council workers, from shop assistants to diplomats, I met a cross section of people that encompassed nearly every vocation on the planet. (Didn't meet any astronauts though.)

Working in the Aboriginal communities in remote parts of the jungle and deserts that were far from the tourist trail and everyday paths that people trod, I took it in my daily stride, and just thought this as my own little adventure. Telling stories and anecdotes from my travels, people asked whether I would write a book about them.

Discarding this idea, I thought it would be much easier to tell my story verbally rather than put pen to paper.   Having since travelled the world extensively, and wherever I have been, told a story or two, people have asked whether I had written a book or that I should write one. In addition to this, local people were frequently asking me to write something down.

Three years ago, I began to scribble stuff down from reading all the letters and postcards I had sent to my mother who had kept them safely for my return just in case I wanted to write a book. (Her idea, not mine.)

Handing out the first few chapters to certain local people to read, with ages from twenty to seventy plus, I was surprised that they were requesting more chapters to read.   A good friend of mine 'Willy the chip' then suggested I gave chapters to complete strangers. Living in a tourist town this was not difficult and I produced a booklet placing it in pubs and cafes around Tenby that comprised one of the chapters from the book. People then began to ask where they could purchase the novel and suddenly I began to receive e-mails on when and where the book would be available.

Anyway, I am not going to carry on as it is up to you (the reader) to judge whether these people were right or wrong with their opinions. By the way, all the blue dots on the map of the cover of this book are the places I visited. I mention this, as a few people asked when I had the booklet sitting in such venues.

All the names except from a few, who I have gained permission from have been changed and any likeness or similarities are entirely coincidental. Also, the views and opinions in the book are entirely my own.

The language I use in certain contexts is suitable to the environments I found myself in. (I really do want you to visualise the surroundings and the vast cross section of people I met.)

Right, enough of the foreword, let's get going. I hope you enjoy travelling with me.

Lance

Acknowledgements

Right, where do I start? Firstly my mother to who this book is dedicated. Every single postcard, letter and other snippet of information that I sent home to her she kept, in some hope that I would one day write a book about my travels. This in turn has let me write as accurate as possible memoir of my journey. (Some of the postcards are on the back of the cover.)

Next would have to be my fellow writer, within the Tenby writer's corner, Nicky Lloyd. This man has helped me enormously giving me his free time, guidance and help with the writing of this tale.

My fiancée Juliette who along with Nicky has proof read, edited, and given great input into the design of the cover as well as helping me with the marketing of the book.

The people that have given me encouragement to carry on writing this little story and given me input on how I should carry on writing it, all of which you know who you are.

Sarah Ray who is a designer and owns and runs a little company called 'Design Marque.' Her professionalism with helping me to publish this book, by creating the book cover and maps that you see at the start of the chapters, has aided me to produce a book far better than I anticipated publishing.

Richard Sheehan based in Leicester, who as a professional Copy-Editor and Proof Reader has helped me polish the writing up to the standard that is acceptable in today's marketplace.

To all the people that travelled with me on my great journey. Although your name has been changed, you will recognise where you are in the story and I thank you for making my trip so memorable.

Finally, my late godmother Miss Norah Rees, whom without her legacy I would have probably never had the opportunity to travel to Australia at that time in my life. Thank you.

www.theencyclopediaman.co.uk

facebook.com/TheEncyclopediaManUK

Prologue

Walking up the wide road, a slight warm breeze sent a small flurry of dust scampering across the tarmac in front of us. It was thirty-one degrees centigrade, and with a cloudless sky we were now in the depths of the Australian winter in far North Queensland. With my red-haired Irish buddy carrying our sales materials bag packed with posters, a couple of samples of the books we sold, and the little plastic money box that the families popped their coins in each day to save up their monthly instalment to pay off their books for this vast educational package, I wondered what we would be faced with next?

With the job creation scheme we had introduced for the Aboriginal people in this town going well, we were growing more prosperous by the day. The town, as far as the drunken Aboriginal violence went, was quite tame in this remote outpost town of Normanton, and we had not seen a fight for several days. This was not to last long, as before the day was out there would be more blood spilled, this time much closer to us than we had previously experienced.

Reaching a little metal gate, I pushed it aside and we sauntered up the garden path. Casting my mind back over the two and a half years I had been in this extraordinary country, little had I thought at the time about the adventure I would take, meeting people from all walks of life and experiencing moments that most backpackers, tourists and even the people that lived here could only ever dream or have nightmares about. Seeing people battered with fists, sticks and stones, waking up one morning staring up at the barrel of a gun, visiting places that no sane person would want to go to, this crazy journey of mine had surprise after surprise, and I was loving every minute of it!

Knocking on the door, it was opened by a very burly Aboriginal woman in her thirties, wearing a polo shirt in different shades of colourful blue, khaki combat trousers and a brown bushman's hat.

"What can I do for you fellas?" she asked.

"We're in town selling educational books that will help the little ones do well in school," I replied.

Looking us up and down, she paused for a moment and then said, "Well, come in."

Entering the building, we could see that the interior was very functional, containing a little kitchen table with four chairs, well-worn leather armchairs and a sofa, and a television propped up on a metal stand in the corner. The building lacked what most people would consider normal in an everyday household, with pictures and paintings on the walls, ornaments scattered around, pot plants, bookcases and usually smaller coffee tables all absent. The white tiled floor was spotless, as were the walls, and I could see they kept the place clean and tidy like the other houses we had been in over the last few days in this wilderness.

"Let's see these books then, boys," she asked.

"Is your other half in?" Terry enquired.

"He is," she responded, "but he is out for the count, if you'll excuse the fucking expression!"

"Well we can't show you the books without him being with you," I said in an authoritative manner.

"And why the fuck not, if you'll excuse the fucking expression?"

Looking behind her, outside in the back garden, I could see two other Aboriginal women talking to one another, one dressed in jeans and a top, the other in a white frilly dress.

"It is our company's policy to only show the books to both parents at the same time. My name is Terry and you are?" Terry, my diplomatic work colleague, held out his hand.

"Lucinda. Lucinda Tobias." The extremely dark-skinned lady grabbed hold of Terry's anaemic-looking white hand, and for a few seconds, black met white in a friendly gesture.

"I'm Tony," I said, extending my arm towards her.

Grabbing my hand, she shook it with a grip that made me wonder what this quite powerful woman did for a job.

"Well, he's fast asleep, as he was up until six this morning drinking with his mates," Lucinda explained.

"What does he do for a living?" I enquired.

"He works on a cattle station up on Cape York. In fact, we both do."

Cattle stockmen and women, also known as "Jackaroos" and "Jillaroos", have one of the toughest jobs in Australia. They learn the highly recognised skills of managing cattle or sheep and controlling the land in what is usually a very inhospitable and sometimes dangerous place. It was Lucinda's grip that brought home to me the demands this job put on the human body each day. It was a not a job for the weak or faint-hearted.

"Well, can't you wake him?" Terry enquired.

"Wake him? Are you crazy? If you'll excuse the fucking expression!" This saying of hers was peppered throughout her conversation with us, and I began to think of leaving the house to find another family whose husband was awake. The persistent Irishman spoke again.

"Go on, give it a go. Then we can show you the books."

Lucinda thought for a moment, and pursing her large lips together she said, "Okay, I'll give it a go. But I'm warning you, if I wake him and he gets pissed, you better run, as no one, but no one, messes with my husband Henry."

Going over to a door, she knocked gently on it and softly called out his name. With no response, she opened the door slightly ajar and called again. For a few moments, there was silence, and then we heard a grunt come from the dark room.

"Henry, there are some men here to see you."

Again, there was another grunt, followed by a passage of incoherent words that emanated from the room.

"They've got some educational books for sale that could help Eliza and Sammy." Her softly spoken voice belied this tough woman peering around the door, and I wondered what sort of creature we were awakening.

Closing the door slowly, she returned to us.

"He will be out in a minute."

What seemed like an eternity passed before the door opened again. Through the doorway came not an Aboriginal man, who we wrongly assumed would be meeting us, but a very bronzed wiry redneck of a man, in his mid to late forties, about five foot ten in height, with a mop of sandy hair and wearing nothing but a pair of black rugby shorts. (A redneck is a term for a working-class white Australian.) Rubbing his eyes and blinking so to allow his vision to become accustomed to the bright light, he squinted at us and said, "So what do you fellas want?"

"We're in town selling educational books that will help the little ones do well in school," my colleague announced.

Looking at us and frowning, he turned to his wife.

"Lucinda, grab me a beer."

With his obedient spouse walking to the fridge, he enquired whether we would each like a taste of one, to which we duly agreed. Lucinda returned to the table clutching four cans of Foster's lager in her hands, and we sat around the table and began our small talk.

Henry introduced himself, and crushing each of our hands with his powerful handshake, he informed us that he managed one of the cattle stations up north from the crocodile-infested area we were now in. Explaining that he earned extra pocket money from bare-knuckle fighting, for which he was apparently quite a formidable opponent, he also proudly told us that he'd been the first white man in this part of the country to marry an Aboriginal woman. Cracking open some more cans of beer, we got down to the business of doing our sales demonstration.

Terry decided to carry out the whole demo, so while Henry and Lucinda retreated to the sofa, I sank my body into one of the armchairs to watch the show. With their two children, aged four and eleven, absent and back on the cattle station with their grandparents, Terry decided to start off with the books for infants, where they learned the alphabet and simple words in the starter programme called ELF which was the acronym for "Early Learning Fun". Laying a colourful poster on the floor, he explained how the books and the little game worked to get the youngsters to learn their early basic vocabulary. Finishing and moving the poster behind him, he then moved onto the story books, which numbered from one to ten and increased with more difficult vocabulary, allowing the child's range of words to increase as they progressed through this hardcover set. Laying that poster down behind him after explaining their merits, he moved on to the encyclopedia, and taking the prospectus out, he knelt down on one knee in front of them and began talking them through this promotional volume. His small audience had now become completely engrossed and eagerly participated in trying to find the animals in the camouflage scene and to guess how many primary colours made up the colourful picture page.

With him finishing with the Australia and New Zealand encyclopedia and the two dictionaries, the posters now covered a large part of the floor. With his raw Irish accent explaining the methods of how the books could be paid for, he then went on to close the sale. It was at this point matters changed for the worse.

The front door suddenly burst open and in walked a bare-chested Aboriginal man dressed in black jeans and sandals.

"Where's your sister, Lucinda?" the man demanded.

"Out the back with Freda," Lucinda replied.

"She's been sleeping with another man," he shouted.

"Oh that's old news, Jacob," Lucinda said nonchalantly.

"Old news?" Jacob said incredulously. "That's my fucking wife you're talking about!"

As Jacob walked towards the back door, Lucinda shouted a warning to her sister, "Mabel! You're in the shit!"

With Terry asking them the closing questions, I looked over the heads of Henry and Lucinda and could see that the man who had stepped outside into the back garden was now shaking his finger at the woman in the white frilly dress. This was followed by several punches to her head, causing her to fall back and out of my view. Several seconds passed and she appeared again, this time clutching a lump of wood of about a metre in length, and began raining blows down on her husband's raised arms as he tried to protect his head. Moving out of my view, they very quickly reappeared, this time with him holding the wood and aiming blow after blow at her now raised arms. Then they disappeared again.

With Terry unperturbed about what was going on outside, he asked the final question.

Outside, the balance of power had shifted once again – all three appeared, with Mabel's friend now holding the wooden club, smashing it down onto the male combatant. Looking at these unfolding events, I thought of Punch and Judy and wondered whether Mabel's friend was saying "That's not the way to do it, this is the way to do it!"

With Jacob outnumbered, he re-entered the house followed by his two assailants. As he stumbled onto the posters, Terry moved out of the way as the fight continued. I could see Mabel's forehead bleeding quite profusely, and her white frilly dress was now spattered with random patterns of claret. At about that time, Lucinda noticed the wound as well. Getting up, she screamed at Jacob.

"Look what you've done to my fucking sister!"

Henry got up, and apologising to Terry for interrupting his spiel, he walked over and with his powerful arms hurled the two women to the floor before squaring up to Jacob. This muscular Aboriginal man, the same height as Henry, lifted his clenched fists and swung his right hand towards Henry's head. The champion bare-knuckle fighter ducked before delivering a right uppercut to his challenger's chin, followed by a left blow to his nose. Jacob's nose exploded, spraying blood all over the posters, and like a tree falling, he fell to the ground out cold with a thud.

"Go and get yourself cleaned up Mabel, and Terry – we'll take the books," Henry said.

With Jacob slowly regaining consciousness, he picked himself off the floor and stumbled out the front door.

"Actually Terry, I'll buy the books on one condition," Henry added.

"What's that?" Terry replied.

"You buy me a slab of VB."

The request to supply him with a carton of twenty-four cans, or bottles, of Victoria Bitter was duly met, and as Terry carried out the paperwork enabling them to apply for a set of books, I headed off to the "Purple Pub" to get the beer. On reaching the pub and entering an empty bar, the landlord informed me that he had just closed and would not reopen for another two hours.

"I'm getting the beer for a local fella," I said.

"Don't care mate, we're closed," the innkeeper replied.

"It's for Henry Tobias."

I watched as the landlord's eyes suddenly widened, and I had visions of him seeing his whole life flashing in front of him, as Henry smashed the living daylights out of him because he couldn't get his beer.

"How many slabs did you say?" he asked.

Walking back to Henry and Lucinda's house, I thought how unconcerned we had been with what we had just witnessed. Terry had carried on with the demonstration with not a care in the world as to what was going on in the garden, and I'd been taking a sip out of my can of lager as Henry had sent Jacob to cloud cuckoo land. I realised that over the past few months we had become hardened to this Australian way of life that very few outsiders had seen. We had witnessed these events many times before, and this was now ingrained into our psyche.

But, I hear you ask, this is only part of the story! How did this fella get to where he was now and into Aboriginal homes? Well, if you want to know the full story, we had better start at the beginning.

Follow me.

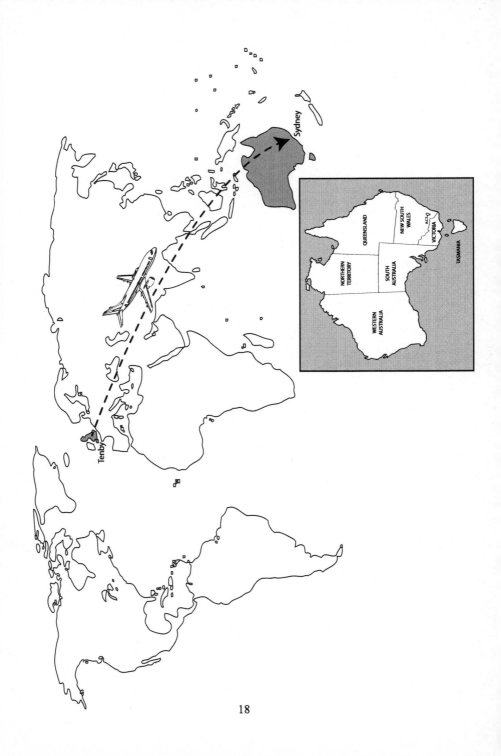

Chapter 1

It was the 2nd August 1990 – the day Iraq invaded the tiny country of Kuwait. Walking up Upper Frog Street on a glorious sunny day among the many tourists that visit my home town of Tenby in the County of Pembrokeshire and my home country of Wales, I heard a familiar voice.

"Hey Lance, we're off to Australia again, you coming this time?"
It was my long-time friend, Ian "Yobbler" Thomas, standing on the doorstep of his parent's toy shop "Clarice", which he now part managed with his sister Kerry.

"Who's going?" I asked with a trigger of excitement.

"Myself and Swalesey again," he replied. "We are flying out in February."

I had, up until then, never been anywhere else in the world except for England and Southern Ireland, and not one country really interested me enough to make plans to travel to them, except, that is, Australia.

Both Yobbler and Swalesey, another good long-time friend of mine, had travelled out to Oz in 1989 to play rugby, but, in my final year at college, I was unable to join them. This was now my chance. Having been left a legacy by my godmother, I was financially able to travel to the other side of the world and if need be stay there without working for at least a few months. This however was not the plan, as all three of us were to apply for a twelve-month working visa.

"How much is the ticket, Yob?" I enquired.

"About eleven hundred pounds as it's a multiple-stop around-the-world ticket!"

"Right, I'm up for that, count me in."

The months rolled on, and having graduated the previous year, I still had not secured proper employment to start off a career.

Tenby sits in a national park and is, in fact, the only full coastal national park of its kind in the United Kingdom. Its coastal path (a challenging a hundred and eighty-six miles in length) takes in some spectacular breathtaking views of the high limestone and sandstone cliffs, and offers views across channels of water to some amazing islands, each with their own little characters and history behind them. The beaches are sandy and clean, and many a time had been spent swimming from them during my childhood and teenage years. The park is home to wildlife such as puffins, foxes, grey seals, dolphins and hundreds of other species. It is truly a paradise on a par (some would say if not better) with many other fantastic parts of the world. It was for this reason that I was reluctant to move away.

So at the age of twenty-three, many of my mates had qualified in various disciplines, and they had either moved away to seek out their fortunes, or set up their own businesses in the area, or completed apprenticeships and started their trades locally. I needed to get out of the town soon, or the words of local character "Jimmy the sage Jones" – "If you did not get out of the town by your early twenties, you would be trapped in the town forever" – could possibly turn out true for me. I now had a goal, and that was to travel to the other side of the world and explore the one country I so dearly wanted to visit. Putting my career on hold, I worked in several local pubs to earn some pocket money until it was time to leave.

On the morning of the 11th February, I awoke to the sound of severe sobbing. It was my mother.

"What the hell is wrong with her?" I said to my father.

"Now what do you bloody think, son?" he replied.

Quite oblivious to the fact my mother was going through the emotional turmoil of her eldest son leaving the nest to disappear to the other side of the world for a year, I still had not hit the nail on the head as to why she was crying.

"What's wrong with you?" I said.

"I'm going to miss you!" she sobbed.

Thinking of something comforting to say to her, I replied, "Oh for God's sake, I'll be back in a year." These comforting words somehow made her worse, as she attempted to give me some sort of Chinese burn on one of my forearms as she tried to smother me.

The two dogs we had at the time, a Corgi and Dachshund, had their own repertoire when things got boisterous in the house. The Corgi, being the more vociferous of the two, barked and shook her bob of a tail, while the Dachshund, being quite timid, hid behind the armchair, of which they both often shared an arm each, either side of my mother when she sat by the window. My little brother Jared (who was now taller than me) was ever his nonchalant self, and was more interested with me sending T-shirts and sharks' teeth back, and not remotely bothered about the fact that he would not see his only brother for at least a year.

A car pulled up outside my parents' flat, and seeing Yobbler climbing out of the car coming to ring the doorbell, I knew it was time to grab my holdall and get ready to leave. As I opened the door, my mother became hysterical again, wailing and then attempting another Chinese burn on my arm, crying something along the lines of, "Look after yourself, and call us when you reach Australia."

Even my father put his hand on my shoulder and said, "Look son, you don't have to go if you don't want to."

Looking straight into his eyes, I said, "I'm off, Dad, see ya!"

Climbing into the car and bidding farewell, I curiously, and in hindsight now strangely, thought, Will I see the dogs again? The Corgi was now eleven, the Dachshund, ten.

So, not that bothered what fate held for my parents, or indeed my brother for the next twelve months, we headed for the nearby village of Saundersfoot to pick up Swalesey. I, Lance Anthony Russell at the time, and still am, was five foot eleven and weighed about twelve stone eight pounds at the time. Yobbler, who was slightly shorter than me at five foot nine, but far more thickset with a fuller figure, weighed seventeen stone. Andrew "Swalesey" Swales was a six foot three giant of a man and came in at just under seventeen stone with no sign of fat on his frame. The likes of Swalesey would attract the warning, "You wouldn't want to meet him in a dark alley one night", due to his size. He was a complete powerhouse of a man, who destroyed most things that got in his way on the rugby field playing for our local team, Tenby United. Having said that, you would not come across a nicer, courteous, generous, more perfect gentleman than Andy. Then again, you wouldn't want to upset him either.

So, after picking up Swalesey, the three of us, all roughly the same age, give or take a few months, set off for London. Staying overnight at a friend's place, we headed to Heathrow Airport the following morning.

On arriving at the airport, we saw armed police and soldiers, armoured cars and small Scimitar-sized tanks. The war in the gulf was now in full swing, with the capital of Iraq – Baghdad – being bombed daily, as well as the occupying Iraqi army in Kuwait taking a daily battering from the coalition air force. The land war to take back Kuwait was on the horizon, and with a possible terrorist threat to places like airports, the British government were taking no chances. As we trudged to the terminal with the ground around us covered in quite thick snow, I wondered when I would see this white stuff again.

Climbing aboard the aircraft was obviously a new thing for me. Not only was I going to fly for the first time, but I wasn't doing it by half measures either. I, Lance Russell, was going to fly to the other side of the world! Shuffling with my hand-held bag in front of me, I immediately thought how spacious and roomy the seating arrangements were.

"This looks alright, Yob!" I said, looking for my row and seat number.

"It is. In business class," replied Yobbler." Except we're not in it. Come on, follow me."

We proceeded through the plane and past a pushed-back curtain to where the configuration of the seating abruptly altered.

"Here we are!" announced Yobbler. "Economy, or cattle class as a lot call it!"

I didn't care what class it was. I got to my seat and hastily pushed my hand baggage into the overhead baggage compartment. Taking my middle aisle seat, I came across a little television on the back of the seat in front of me revealing some interesting information. This was the flight planner, and even to this day it's my favourite toy that keeps me occupied for hours when flying. While people are aboard a flight heading for some destination on the planet, they are usually asleep, reading a book (or Ipad) or immersed in the in-flight entertainment system that provides video games, pre-recorded television programmes, pop, folk, country and western music, or the latest blockbuster from one of Hollywood's studios.

I, on the other hand, am a completely different beast and although will sometimes indulge in a movie now and then, would most often be content to stare at the map on the flight planner, watching the aircraft slowly cross one geographical feature after another as we cross country after country, or watching a blue screen representing one of our oceans, waiting for another piece of land to appear – knowing the important stuff, like what the outside temperature is, the speed of the aircraft, the altitude, the time to destination, the distance travelled and how far to go, estimated time of arrival, current time of place of destination, current time of place we left, and which countries are currently in darkness and which are in daylight. I think you've got the message! As a child, and more so as I got into my teenage years, I could (and still do) ponder and study maps to a great degree, and this is probably the reason why I enjoy this part when travelling by air.

So, sitting at this screen seeing that our British Airways Boeing 747 had to fly 10,562 miles, and that it would take 23 hours before we got to our destination – Sydney, Australia – I suddenly heard the little sound to signify that the plane was about to take off. Hurtling down the runway, we very quickly became airborne, and a very important question popped into my head.

"Are the drinks on the plane expensive, Yob?"
Yobbler, taking a look at Swalesey and raising his eyebrows, said, "He doesn't know, Swalesey."

Andy, ever the deep and thoughtful figure, frowned, and raising one eyebrow said, "Shall I tell him or you, Yob?"

"Tell me what?" I interrupted.

"They're free, Lance," Yobbler said.

Free, I thought. This air travel gets better by the minute. The excitement inside me was tremendous as the speed and altitude of the plane climbed. Soon, the drinks trolley arrived and it wasn't long before we were all quite merry raising toast after toast to Australia.

Waking up over Malaysia, I could see our little plane on the screen heading for Singapore and our refuelling stop. Landing at what must be one of the nicest airports in the world, we had to disembark the aircraft, despite the plane being the same one that was to take us on to Sydney. The aircraft was to have a security check, and even though we were now halfway across the world and far away from the war going on in the Middle East, security was still very tight. A couple of hours later we were back on board for our second leg of the journey, and topping up the ale we had supped at the airport bar, we were soon fast asleep again.

Waking once again, and blinking at what seemed to be lots of activity, I quickly realised the stewardesses were serving a light snack and people were getting up opening their baggage compartments and checking their bags and removing and replacing items. With the air full of general chatter, a large percentage of the occupants on the plane seemed to be in a state of readiness

I had not detected before.

"Good news, boy!" Swalesey announced.

"What's that, Andy?" I enquired to the big man.

"We'll be on the piss in Sydney sooner than we expected!"

"How's that?" I asked, bemused.

"Tailwind! We'll be with the boys two hours earlier."

The two hours I understood, but what the hell was a tailwind? Swalesey then explained to me that a tailwind basically was a wind blowing in the same direction as the plane and that it increased the speed of the aircraft and helped the object along, reducing the time to reaching the destination. Incidentally, a headwind has the opposite effect and slows an aircraft down as it flies into it. So, ordering three more cans, we toasted the tailwind.

Landing at Kingsford Smith Airport, it was time to depart the craft and head towards immigration and baggage collection. At around 9 p.m. on 13th February 1991, my passport was stamped by immigration. I had arrived in Australia. Collecting our bags, we were met by two affable Aussie chaps by the names of "Smithy" and Gary "The Major" Newton Lourigan. They had come up on an hour and a half drive from a little town called Kiama, which was where Yobbler and Swalesey had made their temporary home in 1989, working and playing rugby in the town.

Shaking hands with them, they quickly brought Yobbler and Swalesey up to speed about what had been happening in Kiama since they had left, and the conversation was laced with characters' nicknames like "Corko", "Moat", "Snello" and a half-dozen or more aliases that splashed around in the stories and anecdotes that were bursting from their mouths. It was Kiama we were heading to eventually, but first we had a two-night stay in Sydney, and "Smithy" and "The Major" were going to give us a tour of the city; well okay, a tour of the pubs of Sydney then!

Walking towards the terminal's doors that led out onto the street, I turned to Gary and said casually, "It's pretty warm in here innit?"

To which he replied in his wonderful Aussie accent, "Wait till you get outside Lance! It's fucking roasting!"

Being inside the terminal, I was not aware that it was air-conditioned, and indeed air conditioning was an entirely new concept for me. So, foolishly, I gave a little chuckle to acknowledge what I thought was his little joke. The doors then opened, and I briefly stopped and held back momentarily as I was hit by a blast of hot air which was like opening the grill door back home on the cooker to see how the bacon was cooking.

"Fucking hell!" I said.

"See, I fucking told you!" Gary said, with a huge grin on him. "It's thirty-four degrees on the thermometer around the corner!"

Thirty-four degrees I thought. That's ninety-four degrees Fahrenheit. That's the hottest temperature I have ever felt, and it's night!

"Yep," Gary continued, "and they reckon it'll hit forty again tomorrow!"

Wow! I thought, forty degrees centigrade, that's over a hundred degrees Fahrenheit. I was not even out of the doors of the terminal yet, but, being a lover of very warm weather, I was already starting to like this place immensely. Our Australian companions had booked a couple of rooms in a hotel in the Sydney suburb of Randwick, which was a short drive from the airport. On reaching there, we had just time to throw our bags into our rooms before heading off around the city. I would love to tell you what it was like on my first night in my first foreign city, which I had travelled nearly eleven thousand miles to see, but my memories from our first night are scant at best.

The two things I do remember though are the facts that Resch's lager was the one I should drink, as it was the strongest. (This was, I soon found out in the days that were to come, quite incorrect, and despite not really liking the taste of it that much, just went with the flow that first night and threw schooner after schooner of the horrible stuff down my neck.) Secondly, getting back to the hotel at some time in the early hours, I discovered that one of my Welsh friends had decided to leave our key with the porter, who it turned out was going to bed far earlier than when we were to return and was to lock our key on a keyboard behind a steel mesh. The first night in Australia I slept on the floor, together with my mates, in the hallway outside our bedroom door.

Waking in a very sunlit hallway, I stumbled into our room to see my bag on a made-up single bed. Swalesey was sorting his giant bag out and Yobbler was in the bathroom.

"The porter let us into the room at seven, but you looked comfortable enough so we left you there," my very good friend Andy said.

Who needs enemies when I had these two as friends, I thought. It was eight thirty. Meeting up with "Smithy" and "The Major" down by the reception, we headed off to have a look around the city. Dressed in shorts and T-shirts, I had to remind myself that it was the middle of February, and while our folks were shivering back home in the northern hemisphere winter, we were now enjoying the sunshine and heat of the southern hemisphere summer.

As the temperature climbed into the thirties, we hailed a taxi that was parked on the other side of the road. The intensity of the mid-morning sun was incredible, and painful as well, as we very quickly found out. Our destination was the suburb of Paddington. Opening the back door of the taxi, we met a blast of hot air that made the one that greeted me the previous night seem like a welcoming cool breeze. The car had been parked up for some time, and the driver, standing outside the vehicle, had turned the engine off and hence the air conditioning as well. Leaping into the back of the cab, our exposed olive-skinned legs made contact with the dark-brown cracked leather seating that had been absorbing the fierce Australian sunshine while parked at the taxi rank.

Screams of agony echoed from the car as it drove off with expletive after expletive being shouted out. With the air conditioning on, the car cooled down a bit but not in time for Yobbler to avoid burning his fingers on the metal door catch. All this time I never heard a murmur from our Australian cousins, who obviously had felt the hot leather as well. I guess they're tougher than us Welsh!

With "Cooker Cabs" leaving us at our first pub of the day, I was relieved to find out that it had yet to open and that we had a ten minute wait before the eleven o'clock opening. This delay meant I had time to summon up the courage to drink more of that disgusting liquid. Entering the bar, Gary ordered five schooners of Resch's and my ordeal began. (The "schooner" is the liquid measurement that is prevalent in the state of New South Wales and is the most common measurement throughout the states and territories of Australia. It's four hundred and twenty-five millilitres, or fifteen fluid ounces; a pint being slightly more in volume at five hundred and seventy millilitres or twenty fluid ounces. However, there are measures that differ from state to state or territory, such as "the pot" and "the middy", but there's no need to expand on this subject, at least not at this stage.)

Taking a sip out of my glass, I wondered whether my brain was slowly acquiring the taste of this vile liquid, to which it instinctively sent a signal out – no. Smithy was next with his shout, but Yobbler instead asked him for two schooners of another brand of lager, called Toohey's, for him and Swalesey to consume.

When the drinks arrived, I took a sup out of Swalesey's glass, to which my brain instinctively screamed out to me – yes, yes, that's the one I want to drink next! So, having found a lager I actually liked, I only had one more schooner of the devil's potion to drink, or so I thought. "Smithy" and "The Major", it seemed, had been brainwashed by Resch's, and every time it came to one of their rounds, or "shouts" as the Aussies call it, they instinctively ordered five Resch's unless one of us was quick enough to alter the order.

Moving from pub to pub, and grabbing some pub food, we ended up at Darling Harbour, where the mercury was almost touching forty degrees centigrade. This oppressive heat was taking some getting used to, and the drinking of the alcohol helped magnify the glare of the sun in the streets immensely, as all three of us visitors possessed no sunglasses, or shades as they are known, between us.

Looking around at the hive of activity in the area, there were people of all nationalities either dressed like us, and obviously tourists, or people dressed smart casual or in business suits, who more than likely lived in the city and were either going about their work, going to work, going home, or whatever. I stood by the quayside and watched them embark and disembark the ferries that acted as a link for all these people to carry out their tasks in hand, travelling from the south shore suburbs to the north shore suburbs and vice versa. It was then I realised what a great city it was to live in. Here were all these people, and whether they were working or just on holiday, these people seemed to have fresh, contented and happy faces while they moved across this sprawling city of just under four million people. This conclusion had been greatly enhanced by the nine or ten schooners of ale now flowing through my body on this glorious, very hot summer's day, and I still had to pinch myself to remind me that I was now on the other side of the world.

The next logical step of having consumed that amount of ale was easy – we'll all go for a swim! Not just off any old beach you know, but Bondi Beach!

Picking up "Cooker Cabs" once again, we headed off for the beach, and we all realised that the Aussie lager had a unique effect – that the more you drank, the less the cab seats burnt you! On arriving at Bondi, we walked across the surprisingly gritty sand and through the hordes of people that had crammed onto it. Making our excuses, skirting around or partly jumping over people's towels, I was aware of quite a few English accents, and as I was to find out, it was to this world-famous beach most British holidaymakers made a beeline for.

Finding a spot, we stripped down to our shorts and ran into the sea. The water's edge had a steep gradient, and we plunged well over our depths in only a few steps. The initial freshness of the water was a welcome relief to what had now become a blistering hot afternoon, but the huge swell of the waves of the Pacific Ocean made me feel uncomfortable, and despite the beach being peppered with lifeguards, I soon returned to dry land.

Looking around at the packed beach, an air of disappointment crept into me. Here I was, standing on one of the most famous beaches in the world, and to be frank, I thought, big deal. The beaches back home were much nicer in the sense that the texture of the sand felt much softer on the feet, and Bondi had almost a grubby feel to it. With empty cans of this drink and that, and wrapping paper of certain foodstuffs littered here and there on the sand, it had brought an anticlimax to what I had perceived Bondi was really going to be like. Maybe it's a lot different today? (Weeks later, I was to return to Sydney and experience swimming from another beach on one of Sydney's northern shores, namely Manly. That was gorgeous!)

Heading back to our hotel, I realised I had yet to call my parents back home to let them know I had arrived in Oz safely. After grabbing a load of dollar coins, I located a phone kiosk on the corner of the street. Putting three dollar coins into the machine, I punched in (at what I thought at the time) an incredible fifteen digits, before eventually hearing a very distant ringtone emanate from the earpiece. Then, a voice – it was my mother.

"Hello."

"Hi Mum, it's me," I replied.

There was a pause and then I heard my mother say hello again.

"Mum, it's me, can you hear me?" There was a brief period of silence and then I heard her.

"Is that you, Lance?" The faint sound of her voice and the delay of each dialogue by a couple of seconds reaching each of us reminded me of those images you see on television when NASA is talking to the astronauts, but without the beep between conversations. My mother could have been on the moon!

"Yes it's me, Mum, how are you?"

"Is it hot?" I heard her distant voice ask.

"Yes it is," I replied. This was quickly followed by the same question again, as the delay had meant her not hearing my response in the time she had anticipated.

"Yes," I repeated. There was a short pause and then her voice again.

"I think this phone is playing up! Are you still there? Hello."

"Mum, I am in Australia. It takes a little time for my conversation to reach you."

Again there was a silence.

"Yes, you're on the other side of the world, isn't it marvellous that I am talking to you?"

After asking me to send a postcard, and following a brief conversation with my father and brother, I noticed the telephone was eating the dollar coins out of my hand as if there were no tomorrow. Informing her of my diminishing cash, I told her I would call in the next few days and then hung up. Content with doing my good deed for the day, I set off for the hotel and another night's drinking.

The next day we headed for the little town of Kiama. The sun was once again in a cloudless sky, but with a slight welcoming sea breeze, the day was not as oppressive as previously, despite the temperature being in the low- to mid-thirties. After stopping for some lunch at a little hamlet called Shellharbour, we moved onto Kiama. It was roughly the same size as my hometown, although, if I remember rightly, the population was a few thousand more than that of Tenby's five thousand.

Our accommodation was to be at The Grand Hotel, where we would each have a small basic room that consisted of a bed, wardrobe with a few drawers and a wash-hand basin. The bathroom was a communal one down the hallway. It was at this old colonial hotel that my two fellow travelling companions stayed when they first visited the town two years previously. The cost for my shelter was to be twenty dollars a night.

I threw my bags onto the bed as there was no time to waste; "The Major" was getting the shout in downstairs. The bar began to fill up, and Australian character after character, young and older, came over to my fellow Tenby-ites to welcome them back to the town. Although I had never met these people before, they gave me the best possible welcome one could ever hope for. The warmth, generosity, and the feeling of camaraderie among these people was nearly overwhelming, and I found complete strangers coming up to me asking what they could get me to drink. It was a fantastic feeling!

As the ale flowed, the stories and jokes did too. Gary, wearing his Akubra bushman's iconic Australian hat, and sporting his big, dark, bushy moustache and suntanned face, introduced me to his very pretty blonde other half, Leanne, who greeted me with a "How's it going sport?" Meeting person after person, I soon became confused as to who was who, and not only did I have to try to remember names, but nicknames as well. It was an absolutely amazing, memorable first night in this little town.

Over the next few days, I began to get accustomed to some of the Australian culture, and began to explore this little coastal town. The intensity of the Australian summer sun caught all three of us off-guard, and despite being given advice to put sunscreen and blocker on our exposed albino-like skins, we ignored it and all got very badly sunburnt. With my two friends back working as labourers with the builders they had worked with before, I had plenty of time on my hands and needed to find a job.

I had, in the meantime, been offered free accommodation staying with a local chap whose parents had gone off on a worldwide cruise. Although alleviating my expenditure slightly, the main problem I had was that Australia was in the grip of a recession and jobs were few and far between. Unperturbed a little by this fact, due to a reserve of cash amounting to several thousand pounds, I carried on as normal, spending the days down on the beach reading, and then drinking in the evenings with my two Tenby mates and the rest of the drinking crowd from Kiama.

One roasting hot afternoon while climbing the big steep hill that now led to my temporary accommodation on the outskirts of the town, I adjusted my newly bought Akubra hat while carrying two heavy shopping bags full of meat for the forthcoming evening barbecue. I was now beginning to get used to the heat in this fabulous country. Almost reaching the brow of this hot-tarred treadmill of a road, I momentarily raised the brow of my hat to see where I was going. In front of me, not more than three metres away, was a metre-and-a-half long snake. A fucking snake!

Frozen to the spot in terror, I watched its black slender body slithering across the road and thought, thank fuck I looked up or I'd be dead now! Backing off very slowly, I turned around and made a dash for safety, bumping into a young boy of around the age of ten with a school satchel of sorts on his back.

"There's a snake!" I said, with a tone of fear in my voice. "A snake!" I repeated.

Looking back up the road, I had now made a gap of around six metres between myself and deadly slippery Sid, who was now in the middle of the road heading towards the other side.

"It's a red belly," said the nonchalant child.

Taking his satchel off and placing it on the ground, he then proceeded to pick up some small stones and began throwing them at the reptile.

"What are you doing?" I asked worriedly.

"It's a red belly!" he repeated.

To my horror, the stones suddenly made the snake alter its course and it started heading back down the road – towards us!

"Stop it!" I said, with a heightened tone of fear in my voice. "You're pissing it off."

"Nah," said the unworried boy. "It's only a red belly."

Looking back at the snake, I could now distinctly make out that the underside of the snake was not black but red.

"But it's poisonous," I protested. "We could die from its bite."

"No we couldn't," said the kid with an air of expertise in his voice. "It'll only make you sick."

I thought for a moment about what he had just said, thinking, well that's okay then, I'll just lie in bed for weeks on end with a terrible fever, headaches and constant vomiting, and asked him once again to refrain from throwing the stones. The snake then changed course again and slid off into the grass. The rest of my way back to the house I walked in the middle of the road, preferring to take my chances with the cars and trucks rather than what was hidden in the surrounding bush.

After two weeks of drinking in the hotel or at barbecues at people's homes, I began to realise that with no income, and my expenditure for food and drink mounting each day, I would possibly have to move to a city, otherwise I would be going home pretty soon having seen very little of the country. Sitting by Kiama's geological blowhole feature that was shooting seawater metres into the air, I decided to call another person from Tenby who had emigrated out to Oz and was now living in Melbourne.

He had been back in Wales just before Christmas, and on finding out that I was heading "down under", offered to let me stay at his family home if I decided to venture down to the metropolis. I called Gary and I was relieved to find the offer still stood and that I could stay till I decided to move on. Bidding farewell to my Welsh travelling companions and all the friends that

I had briefly made in Kiama, I took the ten-hour coach ride down the Princes Highway, travelling through towns with strange names like Ulladulla, Narooma and Merimbula.

Stopping at the New South Wales/Victoria border for a break, I walked through part of the bush surrounding the café, feeling the heat of the late afternoon and taking in the pungent smell of the surrounding eucalyptus trees. While looking out for slippery Sids, I wondered if I would find employment in the state capital of Victoria. Little did I think about the job I was about to secure.

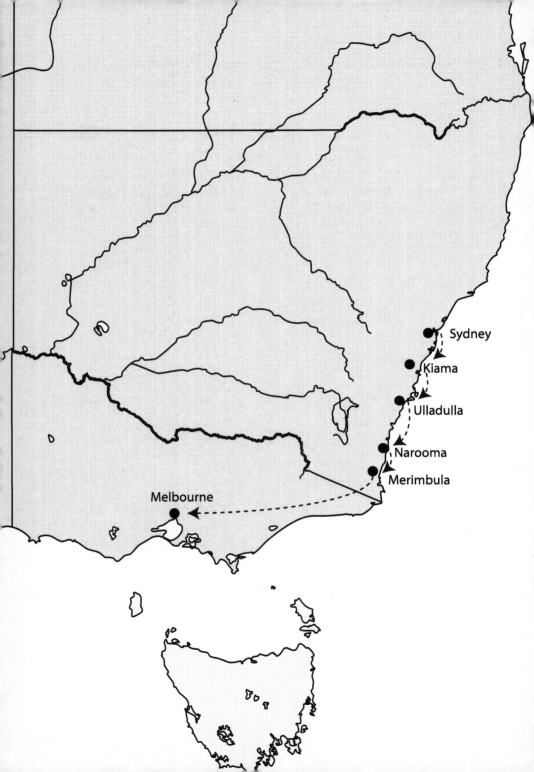

Sydney

Kiama

Ulladulla

Narooma

Merimbula

Melbourne

Chapter 2

When I arrived at the bus station in the Melbourne suburb of Dandenong, darkness had descended, and I had to find a taxi to get me to another suburb called Carrum Downs. Although I had the address, it may as well have been on the planet Mars to the taxi driver.

"I reckon it's near Frankston, mate! What ya reckon?" he said, after driving for about ten minutes.

I felt like saying, "How the hell would I know? I've never been here before!" Biting my lip, I replied, "I'm not really sure, don't you know?"

"Well I've heard of it before, but it's not on the map."

He handed me an old tatty-looking map of Melbourne. Artificial light flooded into the cab now and again from the street lamps, allowing me to peer at his streetfinder journal. Finding the suburb of Frankston on the map, I found that he was quite right and there was no mention of a place called Carrum Downs. (Nowadays, I could have used a mobile phone and rang Gary and asked for directions, but the mobile phone network was in its infancy at that time, with few people possessing such a device.)

"Can you pull over at the next telephone box and I'll give my mate a call," I asked.

I called Gary and he gave me instructions to look out for a milk bar just before a turn-off to Hall's Road. I was to get out there and walk down that road where he would meet me halfway down it. Finding the turn-off to Hall's Road, we doubled back to the milk bar where I alighted from the cab and gave the cabbie a tip and told him to buy a new map with it. Buying a cold can of Coke, I slung my heavy bag and shoulder bag about my person and walked back up to the turn-off to Hall's Road.

Despite having travelled nearly a thousand kilometres, mostly southwards, I discovered that the Aussie summer still had an enormous grip on the state of Victoria, with the late evening temperature still being in the high twenties. Being extremely warm and the bags being heavy, I stopped several times on a very dimly lit road to wipe the perspiration from my brow and to juggle the bags around while listening to all the little insects singing their hearts out in the surrounding bush. After what must have been nearly a kilometre, I began wondering where the hell Gary was, with his words ringing in my ears, "We live just down the road from the milk bar."

Australia is a vast country and you could fit the United Kingdom into this giant island continent just over thirty-one times. Because distances are so great, they tend to work to a different scale, as I was now finding out, and would do so many times in the future. Just down the road to me meant several hundred yards at the most. To someone that lived out here, it could mean many kilometres. Gary, having lived out in the country for just over two years, had now adjusted to these distances.

Just when I thought my weary legs would soon have me back in Kiama, I heard, "How's it going?"

Looking ahead, under a street lamp, I could see Gary walking towards me and clutching a couple of bottles of beer. Grabbing my shoulder bag off me, we shook hands, and cracking open the beers we chatted about what we had both been up to since we'd last met in Tenby. As we walked the rest of the way to the house, I explained about not being able to find the address. Laughing, he explained that Carrum Downs was a relatively new suburb to Melbourne and was obviously not on any of the older maps. The pace of expansion in the Australian cities I found to be amazing, especially the growth of their capital city, Canberra, where you could leave your house in the morning with no neighbours, only to return later to find your home on a housing estate.

On reaching the house, I was introduced to his Australian wife and her two children from a previous marriage. He had met her while out on a working visa, and they decided to tie the knot, allowing him to stay in the country. We cracked open some more beers and chatted till the early hours.

Waking up with quite a thick head, I noticed I was still in the living room, lying on the sofa, and that there was an empty bottle of Jim Beam standing proud on the coffee table in front of me. Rubbing my eyes and getting off the sofa, I could see Gary at the dining table reading a newspaper.

"Morning," I said.

I heard the world-famous Aussie greeting of "G'day" come back to me from the table. Stumbling over to their dining area, I asked what time we had been up till, to which he had no idea and said that he had just got out of bed himself. It was eleven o'clock.

"Where are the kids?" I asked, vaguely remembering that he had two stepchildren.

"School," he replied, without looking up.

"And you're not working today?" I enquired.

"Nope," he said, turning a page. "Not today, tomorrow or the next day."

He looked up at me, and pursing his lips said, "I ain't got a job!"

"Why?" I replied surprisingly.

He closed the paper, and getting up to walk into the kitchen said, "Lance, haven't you heard? There's a recession on. There's hardly any work out there at the moment."

A sudden wave of dread washed over me, thinking if he couldn't get a job, what hope would I have?

Opening the fridge, he took out some sausages. "Do you want some snags to eat?"

Now knowing the Aussie slang for sausages, I nodded, but my face was now blank with severe trepidation. I thought of Yobbler and Swalesey having a whale of a time with all their mates back in Kiama, without a care in the world, heading off to work each day, saving up for travelling around the country after the rugby season had finished – seeing the Great Barrier Reef, Ayers Rock and all the other fantastic places to visit in Australia – while I was now possibly going to be heading back home after only a few weeks in the country.

Opening his newspaper, I could see the job page had very little on the vocational front, and I began to wonder what I was going to do.
Over the next week we tried to get labouring work on building sites, work picking fruit, work in supermarkets – absolutely anything to earn some money. Each day we were told that the jobs advertised had been taken, and on one particular morning, we were kept on the phone for half an hour before being told the jobs had gone.

On some days, we were so disheartened we would head into Frankston, where the two of us would skull (gulp down quickly) a few beers before going to a bottle shop to take more grog (Aussie slang for alcohol) home with us. With Gary having very little money, my reserves were getting quickly depleted and things were starting to get desperate.

Opening the newspaper one day, a small advertisement caught my eye. It was a job selling door to door, but what caught my eye were the words "Travel around Australia". Obviously, this was no good for a married person, but ideal for someone being single. I called the number and almost immediately got an answer. On hearing a female with an Australian accent announce that I had got through to a company by the name of ESA, I explained that I had seen the advertisement in the newspaper and would be interested to know more about the job.

Launching into her script, she explained that the company was called Educational Systems of Australia, and that the job involved travelling around Australia selling an educational package which consisted of a set of books, including a set of encyclopedias, by using the selling technique of going door to door. Full training would be given, and on top of travelling Australia-wide, the earnings potential was uncapped, and that I could realistically earn a very

40

good to excellent wage per month. After she had finished explaining the job description, she asked if I would be interested in having an interview, to which I duly agreed.

A couple of days later, I caught a bus from Carrum Downs to Frankston where I boarded a train and headed to Flinders Street Station and the heart of Melbourne. Arriving at the very busy city railway station, I got my little street map out to locate Hardware Lane. Finding that it was tucked away off a street called Bourke, a few blocks away, I made my way through the city.

The journey took me a little over ten minutes, and during that time my senses were bombarded with city traffic and masses of people from what seemed to be from every race on the planet. The traffic was the usual for any busy city centre, with cars, buses, trucks and other commercial vehicles congested or, at best, crawling along this urban roadway. The one mode of transport that moved with a speed no other vehicle could match, though, was the tram. In existence in the city for over a hundred years and now fully electrified, the city boasted the largest urban network of trams in the world. Painted green on their bottom half and having a cream or yellow top half, you could see that they were the pulse of the metropolis that effortlessly transported commuters, tourists and other Melbournians all over the city.

Walking down Hardware and finding number seventy-seven, I climbed several flights of stairs and entered the offices of ESA.

Introducing myself, I was asked to take a seat in what was a very fresh, dingy surround, with a table full of magazines on all topics in front of me. As I thumbed through one of the magazines, a door opened and out stepped a young, slim, reddish-haired, freckled-faced lady.

"Hi, I'm Alice. And you must be Lance?"

We shook hands and entered her office. Quickly clarifying that her accent was not an Aussie one and that she was a Kiwi, she explained that she had left her home country of New Zealand a few years previously, and was now working for Educational Systems of Australia, whose parent company was Crowell International. She painted a colourful list of the places she had been to with the company, and the more she rattled off these places, that I too wanted to visit, the more eager I was to start working for them. Seeing that I had the credentials and the willingness to travel, she explained that if I were successful, then I would receive a telephone call that evening.

Arriving back in Frankston and looking at my watch, I thought I would give my parents a call back home. With the time being seven in the evening here, I calculated that with the eleven-hour time difference, it would mean they were just about getting up. It was over three weeks since I had last spoken to them. I once again heard the distant ringtone.

"Hello, Tenby 2986." It was my father with his regular reply to the start of a telephone conversation with him.

"Hi Dad, it's me!" My message crawled down the line before I heard.

"Is that you, Lance?"

Replying with a cheery "Yep", and "G'day", I then heard, "Where the hell have you been? Your mother's been worried sick!"

Slightly perplexed, I said, "Australia, where do you think?" I waited for the message to reach him before hearing my mother's voice.

"Is that you, Lance?"

Thinking that was a stupid question, and about to reply something along the lines of "No this is your early morning wake-up call", I thought the better of it.

"Yes Mum, it's me," I replied.

I could sense her relief crawl back down the phone as she said, "Thank God! I've been worried sick. Where are you now? Why haven't you called? It's been nearly three weeks since you last called!"

Taking a deep breath, I realised how worried she had been, "I'm in Melbourne at the moment, and I'm sorry, but I've been having loads of fun. I have just been for a job interview, and if I get it, I'll be able to work all over Australia."

I waited for the message to arrive in Tenby and then heard, "Well send a postcard from every place you visit if you get it, will you?"

"Yes I will, Mum," I dutifully replied.

"You promise?" she said.

"Yes," I said solemnly. (Little did she know at the time that she would eventually receive over three hundred postcards from the various places I was to visit on this giant continent during my three years of travelling.)

I spoke briefly to my brother, and he was more concerned to know where his T-shirt and sharks' teeth were. Promising that I would now call home a bit more frequently, I said goodbye and replaced the receiver.

Back at Gary's, I sat at the dining table sipping a beer waiting for the phone to ring. As the clock ticked past eight o'clock, I began to think I had been unsuccessful and wondered what my next step would be. The phone suddenly rang. Gary picked up the telephone and then passed it to me. It was Alice! I had got the job!

A feeling of utmost relief came across me, and the first few sentences of her conversation went in one ear and out the other, as I imagined all the fantastic places I would get to see in the very near future. She explained I would have to visit the Melbourne office on three consecutive days to receive some training, before being assigned to a sales team somewhere in the country.

The next day I was back in the office learning the script I was to use while knocking doors trying to sell encyclopedias to households. At first, we were to be appointment makers for the representatives that actually sold the package. The reason for this, we were told, was twofold. Firstly, it was to give us experience on knocking doors and entering homes explaining that our manager was in the area demonstrating this educational package, and we could arrange an appointment with him sometime during the evening. Secondly, it also gave us time to learn the actual sales demonstration that we were to use when it actually came to us to sell the product itself.

The script was the run of the mill standard stuff, but the obvious objective was to get past the doorway and into the house. The script was rehearsed time and time again, between two people, to get it word-perfect, and went something along the lines of the following:

1st PERSON: (Knocks on the door)

2nd PERSON: Hello

1st PERSON: Hi, you must be (depending whether adult male or female answers the door) the man of the house? (Hold out open hand as a gesture to shake hands.)

2nd PERSON: Yes, I am

1st PERSON: (Shake hands) My name is Lance. And you are?

2nd PERSON: I'm John.

1st PERSON: Well, John, maybe you can help me? You see, I've been doing some work in your area for a company called Educational Systems of Australia, and as you can see from my card this is an authorised call. (Hold up clipboard with card attached with company logo and your name written on it.) Now, I've been speaking to all the young couples and all the young families in the area this afternoon/evening. But John, it is really important that I speak to you and your other half. Is she in?

2nd PERSON: Yes she is.

1st PERSON: Great! Can I come in?

That was basically the script if you didn't receive any objections or further questions and accessed the home without any further obstacles.

However, we also had to learn a script to divert such obstacles as the following:

2nd PERSON: So what's it all about then?

1st PERSON: Well, John, I'm glad you asked. You see I'm talking to all the young couples and all the young families in your area this afternoon/ evening about a new educational programme. Surely you've heard of that? No? Well can I come in?

If the spouse or partner was not in, you then attempted to get an appointment to return to their household when they were both there. This could be as late as ten o'clock, and in one instance, many moons into the future, I actually made an appointment for midnight for a shift worker and his family. On no account, and in fact on pain of death, were you to mention the word "encyclopedias". The whole objective was (as I explained before) to get into their house, get to know the family and then get an appointment for your manager or, when you felt comfortable that the family had warmed to you, do the sales demonstration yourself. Even if they asked you on the doorstep, "Is it encyclopedias?" You skirted around the issue like a person in the legal field by reiterating the script about it being an educational programme, and if your back was up against the wall, you could then plead the fifth amendment and just walk away.

You kept on deviating from this direct question so to maintain their curiosity. Although later on, after a few weeks knocking doors, occasionally a very irate man of the house would say, "Is it fucking encyclopedias?" To which an honest reply of "Yes" would be quickly followed by a "Fuck off", as the door was slammed in your face. When I started to work the working-class suburbs of Sydney, that had had their doors knocked umpteen times before, a "Fuck off" would usually follow two seconds after the door was opened and they saw you clutching the clipboard. By the time you had said "You must be the man of the house?", you would be looking at a closed door again.

Day two at the office involved more door-knocking training and learning the art of "small talk". I have been in sales nearly all my life, and one thing about selling that is truer more than anything else, is that people buy from people. I am not talking about buying tins of beans in the supermarket, but by people buying goods that cost thousands of pounds, dollars or whatever. Consumers, or customers in this type of market, whether it's houses, cars, caravans or a set of books costing a couple of thousand dollars, will only usually buy from another person if they like them. You can have the best product on the market, but if the salesperson is not dressed in a presentable way and comes across as pushy, rude and sometimes downright aggressive, this can put the buyer off from making a purchase.

Entering someone's house can be a daunting experience for the inexperienced salesperson, but for someone letting a complete stranger into their house, it is probably more daunting for them. They are not stupid and know you are going to try and sell something to them. It's how the salesperson goes about it that is important for both parties. For the salesperson, it is to clinch the deal, and for the prospective buyer, it is for them to have built up enough trust to buy the product.

On entering a household, you had to obviously meet the other half as quickly as possible and then quickly try and build a rapport with them so as to reduce the tension in the atmosphere. At this stage, the salesperson will be rapidly thinking of what to say to diffuse this tension and veer away from the fact he/she is in their home and about to attempt to lighten their wallets and purses of a couple of thousand dollars – not literally, but eventually – if they purchased the product.

To "break the ice" you had to identify an object in their home that you could get a member or all of the family to talk about. This could be anything as long as you could get them talking – a painting, a trophy, a photograph of one of the children in their sports kit, a brand new television, a bookcase full of books – anything that would get them to talk, and more importantly make them feel proud. The painting, for example, could be of a place they had visited in the past and had fond memories. On bringing up this topic, you could build on the conversation by finding out where else they had visited. This, on the other hand, could fall on stony ground, as it could possibly be the only place of any interest they had ever visited, by which, then, you would quickly have to swing the conversation to another topic.

A trophy, for example, would usually spark up a conversation by which one member of the household would be pleased to announce they had won it and happy to discuss how that was achieved. The bookcase was something I particularly searched for in a household, as it told you that they liked books. More importantly though, you could find out whether they already owned a set of encyclopedias, on which you would then kill the conversation and blurt out, "Oh wow! You own a set of encyclopedias! That's what I'm selling!" Then you could turn around and make a beeline for the door, saving you time and allowing you to carry on knocking doors to find a family that was encyclopedia-less.

This small talk was designed to break the invisible barriers down, and to get the family to like you. Remember – people buy from people. It didn't always go according to plan mind, and you may have scenarios where Mother was still cooking the tea or Dad was watching the footy. In which case, you arranged to call back or reappoint, as we called it – preferably after young children had gone to bed. It was fatal if you carried out a demonstration to just one member of the family though, and it was for this reason that you had to get both Mum and Dad together and get their complete, undivided attention.

You may wonder why this was crucial. Well think of it this way.

Your partner sits down and watches the demonstration, and on the salesperson leaving the house, announces he or she has just spent over two thousand dollars, or a thousand pounds, of the family's income on a set of books that you know nothing about. How can you justify that expenditure if you cannot see the perceived value of the product in the first place? This in turn would lead to an argument, and as the order had a "cooling-off period" to allow the purchaser to cancel and withdraw from the purchase during a specified time, this is what usually happened if you only presented the demonstration to one person. That is not to say a sale would not necessarily go through, as some households had lots of disposable income, but it was a very rare event.

Small talk was a very useful tool to use as part of the sales process, but became absolutely useless when we started to work some of the Aboriginal parts of some of the towns in the outback. With most of these indigenous people not being very materialistic, they hardly had tables and chairs, let alone paintings and trophies. It was something we overcame though when we started working in them.

Day three, and after some more door-knocking training and more small talk practising, it was time to find out where I was going to in this vast country to start my career in door-to-door selling. There were other people who were about to go elsewhere on their new journey of direct selling, but I cannot remember a particular face or name. In fact, I know this may come across as harsh, but later on I didn't bother to ask a person's name till after a few days because of the high turnover of staff. It was not to do with the company we worked for, but the fact that door-to-door selling is not everyone's cup of tea, and the truth of the matter is, very few people can do the job successfully for a medium to long period of time.

Some of the unscrupulous managers in the company would, on meeting a new employee, ask to borrow fifty, a hundred, or even two hundred dollars, making up an excuse like, "My cash-point card is broken" or "lost and waiting for a new one to arrive". The unwitting lender would hand over the cash, and a day or so later the Manager would suddenly vanish to another state. Another common occurrence would be that after a few days, the employee would realise he or she was not cut out to do the job. On asking for their money back, which they had lent, they would be told it would be forwarded on to them in a day or so. Of course, they were never to see that money again.

As they called out the person's name, and the destination they were going to, everyone sat eagerly waiting in anticipation. I too wondered where I would be heading to and thought of all the places like Perth, Adelaide, Brisbane, or the ones in the tropics like Cairns and Townsville. Suddenly, it was my turn, and as the words fell down onto my eardrums, my brain registered the destination – Sydney. Sydney, I thought. I've just come from there!

A breeze of disappointment blew over me as I thought that bus from Kiama might as well have been a fucking boomerang!

Receiving my bus ticket, I thought of all the places I had yet to see in Sydney, like the Harbour Bridge and the Opera House, which I had missed when I was with my two chums from Tenby. I headed back to Carrum Downs in eagerness to pack. I didn't have much time as I was leaving the next day. Bidding farewell to Gary and his family the next day and wishing him the best with regards to finding a job, I headed back to the city centre and caught the bus to Sydney.

The bus was on an overnight journey, so not being one who could sleep very well while travelling by road, and with no liquor, I spent most of the night reading and watching the bus overtake road train after road train that were transporting commodities of all sorts from state to state.

Like the "ute" or utility vehicle (basically a small open-backed flatbed vehicle to carry all sorts of stuff), the road train is ubiquitous to Australia, and once in the outback it's not uncommon to see a powerful truck pulling four trailers that exceed fifty metres in length, carrying timber, petrol, foodstuffs – anything! Overtaking one of these beasts is not for the faint-hearted.

I arrived in the Sydney suburb of Blacktown at eleven in the morning, and clambering down off the bus and retrieving my bag, I looked around to see if there was anyone there to meet me.

As the other passengers dispersed and the bus pulled off, a slim dark-haired chap in his late twenties with a beard and a moustache came up to me. Dressed all in white and wearing white trainers, he flashed a wonderful smile at me and, eyes wide open, said, "Are you Lance?"

"Yes," I replied.

"Hi, I'm Todd. Todd Cartney! District sales manager for ESA. Welcome to Sydney!"

His very cheerful Australian accent bounced off me and I thought, he's a happy chappie! He picked up my bag for me and we walked over to a monstrosity of a car that looked straight out of the 1970s' American cop series *Starsky and Hutch* – the cars you usually saw the pimps driving. Placing my bag in the boot, Todd then drove us to my new temporary residence.

I was to find Todd to be one of the nicest of the people I was to meet in the company, although some of the more colourful characters I was to meet in the book business, you couldn't turn your back on for a few seconds.

Arriving outside the apartment, I could see that they were all identical self-contained units set off from an extremely long road that stretched back about two dozen units away. I had arrived at what were collectively called "The Palms".

Suddenly, the fly mesh door swung open and out bounced a roly-poly character with a big cheesy smile nestling under big blue eyes and a mop of blonde hair. He too was dressed all in white and wearing trainers, and I began to wonder whether it was a uniform of some sorts.

Thrusting out his hand, and with a slight gruffness in his voice he said, "How's it going, dude?"

This was Danny, and it was with this lovable rogue I was to have many laughs over the next few months. On entering the apartment, I was introduced to two other members of the team: a young chap by the name of David, and Danny's brother, Archie, and I was slightly relieved to see both dressed in T-shirts and shorts. David was slightly younger than me, and I quickly found out he was quite normal. But Archie, who was eighteen and quite small compared to his much stockier brother, was to paint himself like a selfish, childlike waif in a young man's body, constantly craving attention from his older brother.

Todd then explained that after lunch he was to drive the three of them to "the field", which was the term that the book business used for an area of households that a designated sales team had to knock each day. I was to have the day off to allow me to unpack and settle in. Showing me my room, Todd explained that I would be sharing with the two brothers, and that while they had bunk beds I was to have a single bed on the opposite side of what was quite a small room. Both Todd and David had a room each and it wasn't long before I threatened to leave the company unless I was moved out of what became the wailing room.

Todd returned after dropping them off and began to explain the commission structure to me. There was a retainer of one hundred dollars per week for which you were expected to make a minimum of three appointments each day for your sales manager. Each appointment that was converted into a sale generated an additional fifty dollars commission that was then added to your retainer. In theory, a sale was achieved on a ratio of one in three, so theoretically it was possible to earn fifty dollars extra a night, and as we were to work six days a week, the total earnings each week, including the retainer, could amount to four hundred dollars.

Out of those earnings, our only expenses after tax were thirty dollars a week to go towards our food. Our rent was covered, and we were not eligible to pay this expense until we began demonstrating the product itself, of which each of our sales attracted a commission of one hundred and forty dollars. After five completed sales, this would then rise to one hundred and ninety. Furthermore, he added, you could climb up the pay structure by becoming a field manager, then a sales manager and then, like Todd himself, a district sales manager.

It was soon time for Todd to pick the three up, and on their return, around ten thirty, I discovered that Archie had made one appointment and David two. Danny, who held the title of field manager, had converted one of David's appointments into a sale and also had made a sale off his own back while knocking doors himself. I had no idea what a field manager earned, but figured he must have made about five hundred bucks. Not bad for a day's work!

The next day, after a relaxing morning in and around the communal swimming pool, we proceeded to practise our door-knocking skills. This was to be my big day. At around two thirty, Todd drove all of us to a suburb called

Liverpool. Dropping David and then Archie off at different points in the area, he then drove Danny and me to another area. Danny was going to hold my hand for the first two hours (that being metaphorically and not literally), to make sure I was comfortable with the process.

Climbing out of the car and clutching my clipboard, I glanced at it to make sure my identity card was attached to it properly, though Danny's card was placed in front of mine for the moment, as he was going to do all the talking initially. Todd drove off and we approached a block of grubby flats in what was a very working-class area of the city. Knocking the first door of my door-to-door sales career, it opened and into view came a grossly fat, bald man in his mid-fifties wearing an extremely stained string vest, and grubby trousers held up by a length of cord. With the man's mouth full of food and trying to break down the contents in his mouth so that it could drop down into his overhanging guts, Danny launched into his "Hi, you must be the man of the house?"

There was momentarily a pause as we both eyed "Jabba the Hutt". Our smiles remained frozen on our faces as we waited for this overly large person to finish munching on his food. It reminded me of one of those scenes in the spaghetti westerns where the gunslingers are about to draw their guns and the camera is sweeping back and forth between the characters' faces, concentrating on their expressions. Fortunately, we didn't have to wait long for him to finish his grub, as the door was flung back into our faces. Danny just shrugged his shoulders, and moving slightly to his right, knocked on the next door.

From behind the door, we suddenly heard an Asian female voice call in pidgin English, "Who dare? Who dare?"

"It's Danny!" announced my Australian workmate.

"What you won?" the voice said again.

"Open the door and we'll tell you," Danny replied.

There was a pause and then we heard the invisible person's voice again.

"Go away."

Looking at my whitewashed-clothed colleague, I shrugged my shoulders.

"We're in the area telling everyone about a new educational programme," Danny continued, raising his voice slightly. Waiting for a response, we instead received a wave of silence.

Knocking the other two doors opposite, we found no one at home and my field manager made an entry on his door-knocking sheet. This sheet was to chart our day's work, and apart from logging down the door numbers of the street, we could enter comments abbreviated like "NI" – that being "not interested". As well as this, we could also log our appointments, or write a "CB" or "call back".

Proceeding to the second floor of the building, the process was started again. The first door, we had no response, so the adjacent door was knocked, and again we heard another Asian voice, this time male.

"Open the door and we'll tell you," Danny reiterated. There was a pause once again, and then we heard bolts sliding across and the sound of a door chain being fixed into place. The door opened slightly, and peering out over the chain from the other side of the doorway was a small middle-aged man of Southeast Asian origin.

"You must be the man of the house?" The rhetoric was delivered and then there was a pause. The spaghetti western glances were once again swapped, and the wide-eyed oriental spoke.

"No speakee English!"

Danny did an about turn and marched over to the next door, leaving me staring at what was a very bewildered man.

"You have a go," Danny said, handing me my clipboard and replacing my identity card in front of his.

Knocking the door, it was opened by a young man in his twenties. My word-perfect delivery flowed, and on his favourable response, I explained about the new educational programme we were telling everyone about. Again came the pause, and then the dreaded question was asked.

"Is it encyclopedias?"

Before I could respond, Danny blurted out the countermeasure to deflect from this question by repeating the educational programme bit. Unperturbed, the man again asked if it was encyclopedias? The next sentence that came from my able-bodied sales professional threw me completely.

"No," he said.

"Well is it books then?" the man enquired.

My roly-poly manager gave a big cheesy grin and said, "Might be!"

Looking slightly confused, the urban dweller asked, "Well are they books or aren't they?"

"Yeah, they are," my manager said, with some defeatism in his voice.

"Encyclopedias among those books?" The man probed deeper.

"Yeah, there's some," Danny said, trying to get the white flag of surrender out.

"You mean like these?" The man threw the door open to reveal a bookcase containing a set of *Encyclopedia Britannica*. Danny gazed at the display, and realising they were not the brand of encyclopedias that we sold, said, "Yeah, but better."

We carried on knocking, and after an hour with not much luck, we stopped at a milk bar for a couple of cold cans of Coke. Now used to the Australian summer heat, my skin had slowly, over the weeks, gone gradually brown, even with using the sun cream. As we quenched our thirst, Danny explained that normally we would work till ten o'clock. Todd, however, had told him that as soon as we had written an order, which was the jargon used for meaning we had made a sale, we could either give him a call or go to a pub and wait for him till he returned to get all four of us.

Picking up his bag, and myself picking up the clipboard, we carried on knocking doors and about an hour later got our lucky break. Introducing ourselves as we entered this very young Australian family's home, we sat, or rather sank, into a sofa that had seen better days. Having discovered that the husband had just got home from work and that the wife was about to prepare a meal for them and their two young children – two boys aged four and six – I scanned the room for paintings, trophies, bookcases, in fact anything to get the small talk going.

I was lost, as there was nothing tangible in view to strike up a conversation of sorts. A very brief silence hung in the air, and I knew that unless one of us came up with something sharpish to say, the inevitable question would arrive before we got the family to warm to us. That question of course being, "What are you selling?" Then the master of small talk opened his mouth.

"Those are nice fish over there, what are they?"

I looked to where Danny was pointing and could see two goldfish in a bowl.

"Goldfish," the husband replied.

Not knowing what the hell my field manager was going to say next, I eagerly awaited his response. He craned his head for a moment, frowned, and then, widening his big blue eyes, said, "Oh yeah, of course they are!"

Not knowing how he was going to get any legs out of this conversation,

I sat and listened.

"How old are they?" enquired my teacher.

"Not really sure, mate," came a very quick reply.

With the wife moving some plastic cups wedged down the side of an armchair and sitting down, her husband looked over to her.

"How old are the goldfish, love?"

She looked down at her children sitting quietly on the floor among a clutter of toys. "How old are the goldfish boys?"

The two boys looked at their mother, then at us, and then their mother again. The eldest one frowned and said, in his early days of commanding the English language, "I fink the big one is ten!"

"Ten?" my manager exclaimed. "That's really old for a goldfish, isn't it?"

Suddenly, someone who only seconds before had difficulty identifying the common goldfish had now become an expert in the field.

"Now, I don't think he's ten, Ben. You only won him at the fair last year, didn't you?" his mother kindly pointed out. The little boy nodded, and Danny started to build on the conversation.

"You won him in the fair? I love fair's, don't you?"

The little boy nodded and the mother smiled. "We take them every year and they enjoy it like we used to when we were children, don't we love?" The husband nodded back.

Then came the crucial question that had to be asked so as to qualify a potential buyer properly.

For someone to enter into an agreement with the parent company, Crowell International, and before the encyclopedias could be despatched, the company had to be sure that they could afford them. Apart from the necessary credit checks to make sure the potential buyer was creditworthy, and the fact that the household had a telephone, so an order could be verified by the head office in Sydney, one of the members of the household had to hold down a full-time job. Without this, the criteria could not be fulfilled and you could not sign up anyone for a set of books. Of course, the customer could pay for the books outright, but at two thousand, one hundred and fifty dollars a set, they were more likely to enter into a credit agreement with the company that allowed them to pay for the books at seventy dollars a month over thirty-eight months. This question had to be asked relatively early during the small talk, as you could be completely wasting your time if you found out after perhaps quarter of an hour that no one was employed in the household.

Although we had discovered that the husband had just got home from work, we had to make sure it was a full-time job. Danny very quickly clarified that the husband was a factory worker and on top of his normal forty-hour week, could do overtime as well. Happy that the family had warmed to us, and with the sound knowledge that they could possibly afford the books, the master bookseller launched into his demonstration and twenty-odd minutes later was signing up a very happy family for a set of educational books.

With the forty-five dollars deposit that was required for a credit agreement in the state of New South Wales, my new-found work colleague was investing it in the pokie machines at a nearby pub we quickly found. (The pokies are fruit machines where you can win thousands of dollars in the jackpot and are found in practically every pub or club in Australia. Also, to quickly clarify a point, before you start thinking "How the hell can he shovel a family's deposit into a gambling machine?" A manager could keep a deposit and it would automatically be deducted from his commission when it was paid.)

Heading back to "The Palms", everyone was in a very buoyant mood. Everyone, that is, except Archie. I could sense friction and possible trouble looming.

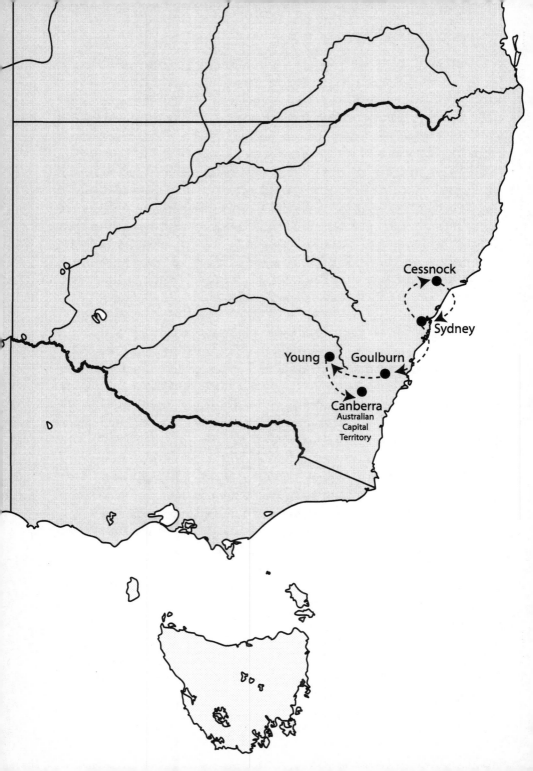

Cessnock

Sydney

Young Goulburn

Canberra
Australian
Capital
Territory

Chapter 3

On reaching the apartment, we started to prepare our supper, which was to be sausages and chips. While helping to peel some potatoes, I became aware that Todd had pulled Danny aside and that they had gone upstairs to speak in private. Not long after, Archie was summoned upstairs too. After about ten minutes, all three of them descended and Todd began to hand some beers around. The mood was jovial but, although we were all throwing the lager down our throats and chatting about our evening out in the field, Archie was strangely quiet.

Retiring to our beds at about one o'clock, I lay in the darkness wondering how well I would do in this job and what fantastic places I would get to see. As I decided it was time to get some sleep, I heard a sobbing noise adjacent to me in the bottom bunk. It was Archie.

Not sure what was wrong with him, I just lay there, and as my eyes slowly got accustomed to the darkness, the sobbing became a little louder. As I pondered what to do, I suddenly heard Danny's voice.

"Will you shut the fuck up?"

This command triggered the sob into a wail, and as I lay there I heard his big brother's voice again from the top bunk. "Will you shut the fuck up, I am trying to get some sleep, and you'll wake Lance." The wailing became louder and I began to wonder what the hell was going on. Turning on my side and facing the wall, I pretended to be asleep and then Todd opened the door.

"Will you shut the fuck up, Archie. I'm trying to get some sleep." The door slammed shut and the wail returned to a sob that continued for about ten minutes before going silent.

The next day, nothing was mentioned about the wailing, and I thought better than to bring the subject up. The morning was spent in the communal pool with Danny, Archie, David and a new recruit called Jason. Playing volleyball and generally splashing about and ducking one another under the water, Danny annoyed his brother to such an extent that he went into a sulk, and at one stage I thought he was going to begin crying again. At lunch he picked at his food and refused to speak when Todd asked if he would like seconds. This was one immature young man, I thought.

That evening I made two appointments on my first solo outing, but Danny was unable to convert them to sales, as neither potential customer could build the expense into their budget. Back to the apartment, and the same scenario was played out: the three went upstairs and minutes later descended again. After a few beers it was time for bed, and a few minutes after I turned the lights out, the sobbing and wailing began again. This time I said something.

"What's wrong, Archie?" I enquired in the darkness. His big brother's voice came back to me.

"He's blanked again, dude."

I wondered briefly what he meant as the wailing intensified, and then I asked, "Blanked? What do you mean blanked?" The wailing subsided as if waiting for the reply.

"It means he didn't get any appointments this evening!"

With the room again in complete silence, I replied to my field manager, "Well surely that happens once in a while doesn't it?"

I heard Danny get up in bed and could see the silhouette of his face and torso in the top bunk.

"It does dude, but not every night!" Suddenly I heard a feeble voice mutter something through the sobbing.

"I ... I ... I ... don't blank every night!"

Danny leaned over a bit to look down at his brother. "What? You mean you got one appointment two nights ago. That's one a week. Terrific dude! Terrific!"

Danny called almost everyone "dude", and as I processed this information, the wailing started again. "Well I can't put up with this," I said, and went back downstairs and watched television long enough, knowing that when I returned to bed he would have cried himself to sleep again.

The next morning I found out that Archie had been given an ultimatum. Either he started getting appointments or he would be fired and sent back to his hometown, which was well over seven hundred kilometres away, close to the Queensland border.

The company always paid for the unsuccessful employees' passage home, as I guess they didn't want anyone stranded vast distances away from their loved ones. Also, I guess there were no repercussions if something happened to them in a strange town or city after they had been fired. Today it would be called "duty of care".

Just before we were due to leave for another suburb, Todd informed me that if I got three appointments that evening, then I could start to learn the product demonstration the next day. That shift, I knocked on nearly three hundred doors and hit my target of three appointments, of which one was converted into a sale late in the evening by Todd himself. Archie had made two appointments, and although they were for the following evening, he was congratulated for his efforts.

Arriving back at the apartment, I was surprised to find another sales team had turned up: two young girls in their early twenties and a young lad in his late teens. One of the girls was Todd's wife and would be sleeping with him, while the other girl was given David and Jason's room. David, Jason and the young lad were then to bunk down on the living room sofa and on the floor in sleeping bags for a couple of nights.

That night we all sank many bottles of beer while playing Trivial

Pursuit in two teams, with me at a slight disadvantage as it was an Australian version.

The girl who had travelled from a nearby town just outside Sydney with Todd's wife was Amanda, and she was incredibly attractive. With shoulder-length chestnut hair, dark-brown mesmerising eyes with a crystal green sparkle, fantastic elongated sun-kissed cheekbones and cherry lips that begged to be kissed, this Mediterranean-looking beauty was a pleasure to sit next to, and her infectious laugh only increased my desire for her.

The next day, I started to learn the product that we were selling. We had large posters which were placed on a household's floor depicting what each level of the educational programme contained. The first part of the package was a little red plastic briefcase that contained books helping young children learn the alphabet and helping them to spell simple words such as dog or cat. It also contained a little game that helped them improve their basic infant vocabulary. This was called Early Learning Fun and was abbreviated to ELF and featured an elflike character on the poster. The second stage consisted of ten storybooks of different levels of difficulty in mastering the increased amount of vocabulary that took the child from the age of five to approximately the age of twelve. These were called the "Colliers Junior Classics" and had stories like *Snow White and the Seven Dwarves, Little Red Riding Hood, Tom Sawyer* etc. Eager to learn the whole demonstration at one sitting, Todd put the reins on me, saying that we were starting work earlier that day, as, it being a Saturday, more couples and families were likely to be in.

Besides, he informed me, we were all to head to the suburb of Parramatta that evening for a Saturday night piss-up at numerous pubs and clubs.

The day finished with me obtaining two appointments but no sales. As we got ready to go clubbing, I asked Danny how he got on with his brother's appointments that he had made the previous evening. He was in the shit!

Both appointments had turned out useless. One family was found to have no one working in the household and the other family had not even consented to an appointment as they had rightly guessed it was encyclopedias and didn't want to waste anyone's time. Obviously Archie could not divulge the fact that the demonstration contained encyclopedias as it still gave the seller the chance to try and sell them, but being under pressure he made up an appointment thinking the family would go along with it when his older brother turned up.

Todd had decided to leave the matter for now so as not to ruin the evening. Getting assembled downstairs, Todd was to take one car and his wife the other. With Archie in a sulk, and with hardly any money to his name and already owing money to his brother, he was forced to stay behind to watch the television. Heading off downtown to the suburb of Parramatta, I found out that Amanda was selling the product quite well, and as we drifted from pub to pub our attraction to one another increased by the hour.

Eventually, we all ended up at a nightclub where I danced the night away with this gorgeous-looking lady. On returning to the apartment in the early hours, I waited till everyone had gone to bed and for the boys downstairs to pass out, and then slipped into Amanda's room. Well, it was the wailing room or hers – no contest really.

The next morning Todd went ballistic when he found the two of us in bed together. Relationships within the company were not allowed, and his volley of words kept showering me, until I pointed out that he and his wife worked for the same company. Following my counter-attack of threatening to leave the company if I had to carry on sleeping in the wailing room, Todd informed me that Archie would not be around for long.

Later that day, Todd's wife, Amanda and the young lad left for another town in New South Wales, meaning our brief fling was over.

Returning to the apartment after work, the place was eerily quiet and there was little conversation. Guessing people were nursing bad heads from the previous night, I followed suit and said very little while watching the television.

Archie went to bed early, and when I retired I was able to fall asleep without any interruption. The next morning I awoke and the bed that Archie slept in was empty. He was gone for good.

The sales training continued and I had reached the most important part of the demonstration, where the poster was flicked open quickly to reveal a twenty-four volume set of *Colliers Encyclopedias*. Now! To sell anything successfully you need to have enthusiasm in your voice for the delivery of your presentation. If someone is standing in front of you, whether they are a singer, comedian, a politician, or just a plain salesperson, you need to have emotion in your tone of voice that will generate and project excitement about the product or service you are selling to the potential purchaser. Without that, you might as well choose another vocation.

This fantastic emotion that travels from you to your customer becomes infectious and you then have a better chance of selling your product. So the flick of the poster meant a sudden rise in the voice to announce the greatest form of knowledge at your fingertips for the family home. A sort of a little paper "Google" that could sit in the corner of your living room, bedroom, or wherever, with information at your disposal for study, general reading, or there to possibly answer any question that came to mind at any particular time.

Twenty-three volumes covered the alphabet, while the twenty-fourth contained a bibliography and index volume, where you could access information quickly by looking up a particular subject, and then find out certain pointers that directed you to a certain volume or volumes. After, the poster was placed on the floor adjacent to, or, if there wasn't enough room, on top of the other two posters. It was then that the prospectus was produced from your bag. This was basically a condensed example of what was in the encyclopedias. Laced with lots of colour pictures, this sample book had been designed to bring the wow factor to the audience. Getting up close to the couple or family, you went down on one knee, and with the prospectus balanced on top of your thigh, slowly turned the pages.

The script we had to learn, once again parrot fashion, explained what was in this educational paper paradise as we slowly turned the pages for the prospective purchaser to view. The prospectus contained two pages that involved finding animals in a camouflaged woodland scene and another in a marine environment. These got everyone involved, as they had to find creatures hiding in difficult places, such as the rabbit in the grass, and the Moray eel partially hidden behind a rock in the sea. I don't know what sort of drugs some of these families were on, but occasionally they would spy a tortoise, a bear, a whale or some other creature that wasn't even in the scene! Once they guessed correctly, or had given up, a top acetate sheet could be turned over to reveal the animals on a clear white page.

Another page in the prospectus featured a colourful bowl of fruit where the audience had to guess how many colours it took to produce the picture. Again, using acetate pages, the answer was revealed as the three primary colours: red, yellow and blue. Then again, I had some crazy answers, like one, of which was often the colour black. I mean, black? Or hundreds of colours which came as an occasional answer, which made you think that these people must see some fantastic rainbows through their superhero vision! This fun interactive enjoyment again reduced any lingering tension in the air and relaxed the recipients of these exercises, priming them for a trial close.

The trial close was aimed at getting some form of positive feedback from them, and a little commitment to actually purchasing the product. After the primary colours page, you ran the pages through your fingers and very quickly shut the book, explaining that no one volume contained as much colour in them and this was purely a sample of what was in the set of books. You then asked them what they thought of it. It was very rare where a nonchalant or negative reply came back, but if it did, then it was time to leave.

Although there were other books, the bulk of the package was the encyclopedias, and it was the profit in these that got you your commission. Besides, you could not sell the other books separately.

The next poster revealed the "Reference Service". This was a back-up augmented product to the encyclopedias. Basically, if you had a question that could not be answered by thumbing through the volumes at home, you could then write off to a panel of experts (usually teachers and lecturers that specialised in certain fields) where they would write back to you with the answer. You could ask anything from "How to build a go-cart" to "building a spaceship" and could expect to get anything from a page of information or up to a hundred pages. (Though I think the spaceship answer would have run into millions of pages and the reply from ET would have taken some time!)

The final two posters comprised a two volume in-depth *Encyclopedia of Australia and New Zealand* and two volumes of *Colliers Dictionaries*. You then told them the cash price of the package, but very quickly pointed out that the company did not expect them to pay that all at once, which led to the money box. By producing a little plastic money box in the shape of an encyclopedia, you then explained that by putting two dollars and fifty cents away every day, by the end of a twenty-eight day month they would have accumulated the monthly seventy dollars payment. After thirty-eight payments, the books had been paid for.

Making sure there were no other questions, you then had to close the sale with three closing questions that were designed to bag that sale. (Incidentally, you may be wondering why I have dragged you through this sales presentation process over the last few pages. I have, because I want you to try and actually see what we were doing, and later on when things start to get really crazy in "the outback", you will hopefully then realise why I have let you have this insight.)

Right! What were the three closing questions to make the sale?

1. Well. John and Mary. Could you see this being of an educational benefit to you and your family? John? Mary?

2. And would $2.50 stretch your budget? Bearing in mind that is only the price of a packet of cigarettes each day? John? Mary?

3. Well, John and Mary. I'd be happy to recommend you to the company, but only if it's agreeable with you both. John? Mary?

Now, very occasionally one of them might be unsure as to whether to go ahead and "sign up" for these set of books, and you really needed both of their approvals if the order had any chance of sticking and getting paid the commission. If this occurred, we would use what we called the "tennis ball' question. If one of them was unsure, we would ask the more positive of the two, for example John, that if Mary was one hundred per cent with going for the books, would he be? Obviously, John is more inclined to say "Yes", so throwing the same question over to her (like a tennis ball being batted back and forth), she is more than likely to say "Yes" as well, as she knows John would be behind her agreeing to the question. All fun and games in the field of direct sales, as us sales professionals would say. Once the order was written up and the deposit received, you skedaddled from their house and onto the next one. Having learned the demonstration, and with a bit of practise to fine tune my presentation, I could then start selling the product myself.

Todd decided we should leave Sydney and head northwards a hundred and sixty kilometres to the large industrial city of Newcastle. We would set off in two groups; the first one in Danny's pimp-mobile – the car that Todd had used to pick me up from the bus station. Then Todd would follow us in a few days with his wife, Amanda, Jason and the young lad whose name I had just found out was Jeremy. David and I would be with Danny, and we would, over the course of a week, stop at little towns on our way, to knock doors and arrange appointments for Danny to try to convert to sales. Our overnight accommodation was to consist of staying in cheap hotels and caravan parks, and by the time we reached Newcastle, I would be ready to start selling.

The first night, we stayed in one of the outer suburbs of Sydney called Windsor. Danny had taken thirty dollars off each of us for our weekly food, which would consist of basic foodstuffs like potatoes, pasta, mince, beefburgers, fish fingers, milk, bread etc. Our first night was not very productive, and the neighbourhood was not very responsive as they'd had their doors knocked time and time again by the encyclopedia fiends, and people had either bought them, couldn't afford them, or just didn't want them.

The next day we travelled to a large town called Cessnock. This time we had more luck, as Danny managed to convert one of my appointments. Stopping off at Liquorland (a nationwide chain of bottle shops, where grog was in plentiful supply and, dare I say, at the time a lot cheaper than back home in Wales), I picked up a case of VB and a case of Powers, another favourable lager I had become accustomed to. Back at the caravan, Danny was keen to get the lager down us, and when we asked what we were eating, his big cheesy grin appeared on his face.

"Tonight dudes," he proudly announced, "we will be eating my speciality."

To which we both simultaneously replied, "Which is?"

Danny gave a little chuckle and announced, "Beans on toast!"
David and I looked at one another, and then I said incredulously, "Beans on fucking toast? I'm fucking starving!" Danny's grin faded away.

"Why didn't you get us burgers or something?" David asked.

Danny shrugged his shoulders and replied, "I couldn't afford them."

David suddenly got up from the table. Although not as thickset as Danny, he was taller, with a very fit athletic build and probably had the ability to do quite a bit of damage to our field manager.

"Well, where's the sixty bucks you took off us yesterday?" David said, now menacingly pointing at our superior.

Our manager shrugged his shoulders again, and giving us a little half-smile he said, "Spent it, dudes."

Slightly puzzled, I asked, "On what?"

"The pokies," he replied.

We looked at one another with one of those spaghetti western looks again. Although, I suddenly thought, we wouldn't even be eating that tonight! Only beans on toast! Sensing the tension rising, I very quickly spoke up.

"Well there's nothing we can do now as everywhere is closed. We'll just have to have a liquid supper, and I will get some food in the morning. VB or a Powers, David?"

Turning to our gambling-mad manager, I asked him if he wanted to flip a coin to decide which brand of lager he was to drink. This in turn broke the tension in the air, and David picked up a beer and sat back down.

The next morning I realised I was in a bit of a quandary. Danny didn't have a bean to his name to pay for petrol, accommodation or food, and we still had three days before we were to meet up in Newcastle.

I figured we needed three hundred bucks, but was reluctant to lend any money to my field manager in case he felt like feeding the slot machine monsters again. Calling Todd would land Danny in the shit, but our only way out was to write two orders a night for three nights, and hope all deposits would be given in cash. With this being a very unlikely outcome, I had no choice. Telling Danny of my intentions, I called Todd back at "The Palms".

Arriving back at our Sydney apartment, Todd reimbursed my fifty dollars for the fuel we had bought on our return journey, and Danny was told he would lose his team and his manager status. No hard feelings were felt, and we all went to work as normal later on.

The next day was to be my big day; I was out on my own selling the product myself. Todd drove me to an area of Sydney called Kingswood, and as I got out of the car at my drop-off point, he told me that as soon as I had written an order, I was to call him and he would come and get me to go for a few celebratory beers on my initiation as a sales representative for ESA.

Walking to a block of flats, I decided to start at the top of the three-storey building and work down. Knocking the first door, there was clearly no one at home. Moving to the next door, I gave it a solid knock to make sure I could be heard. The door opened and I was met by a young man not much older than myself. Getting into my spiel, I quickly gained access to the home to discover that he and his young wife both had a day off from their full-time jobs. Glen and Sharon had lived in the apartment for two years and were now thinking of planning a family. On completion of my demonstration, they both agreed that purchasing the books would be beneficial for their future family, and on discovering they could pay the books off earlier than the thirty-eight months, they eagerly signed up for a set of encyclopedias. I had made my first sale!

Asking to use their phone, I rang Todd. He had just got in and found it incredulous that I had written an order so soon. My first open door, and I had made a sale, something that had never been done before, he kept on repeating as we drove to the pub. What did I think? Well, ever being the realistic one, I thought it was beginners luck. I was not wrong.

Over the next three weeks I was to bash thousands of doors all over Sydney and get absolutely nowhere. The different "walks of life" I came across were incredible, and I began to realise that this job was not for the faint-hearted. I went from extremely rough areas of the city, where unemployment was rife, to suburbs such as Cabramatta, which had a high proportion of Vietnamese that refused to open their solid vault-like doors while I listened to the "Who dare? Who dare?" coming faintly from the other side. The turnover of staff, needless to say, was high and that wasn't surprising when you were regularly told to go and have sex with someone else, or with yourself, by people who opened the door to you.

The key ingredient of getting through this abuse was to not take it personally and just let it wash over you, although the first time it happened to me, I was genuinely taken aback and momentarily thought perhaps that I too wasn't cut out to do the job. Lord knows what was going on on the other side of those doors when you were knocking them, and a person telling you to "Go get fucked!" or "Go fuck yourself!" may merely have been letting off steam while having a domestic of some sort, or having tired kids screaming at an adult that had just had a busy day at work, and the last thing that person wanted to see was someone trying to sell them something. Needless to say, it did take a very resilient person to soldier on day after day. Having said that, there were many interesting episodes. Two examples were the following:

On knocking a door at a block of flats one afternoon, a young, slight, quite pretty, dark-haired girl answered. When I mentioned the "E" word (Ssshhh, that's encyclopedias!), she told me she was living alone and wasn't interested. On her shutting the door, I crossed over to the opposite side to knock those doors only to find, moments later, the girl open the door again and enquire whether I had knocked on her's again. This time though, she had removed her clothes and was standing in a see-through white nightie that left nothing to the imagination.

Another time, a pretty blonde asked me to call back later when her husband had got home from work. On returning, I was invited in and told to sit on the sofa while she got me a beer. (Incidentally, you were not supposed to drink alcohol on the job, unless you had made a sale at the end of the shift. One of the reasons being, "How many people would let you into their home if they could smell intoxicants on your breath?") Anyway, with no sign of her husband, she then explained that he wouldn't be long getting back from work. Sitting down next to me and sidling up to me and making her ample cleavage very visible, she began to probe me about who I was and where my lovely accent was from.

After about five minutes, she revealed that her husband "not being long" meant about three hours away at midnight. Beginning to rub my leg, she told me that she was incredibly lonely. I started to think about maybe staying for an hour. That is, until I glanced at the weightlifting trophies and saw a photograph with her in the arms of a blond-haired man the size of that retired American wrestler that featured in the Rocky III film – Hulk Hogan. Asking to use the toilet, I grabbed my bag and walked into the hallway heading right out the front door. As I say, these were rough places, where drink, drugs, unemployment, marital and other social problems were not uncommon. I sometimes think about that girl in the see-through nightie and think, what if? Then again, I think, maybe I could still be there, locked in a cramped metal cage, naked, bound and gagged, with a vibrator hanging out of my rear

71

orifice. I can dream on I suppose!

Sydney was a very difficult place to go door to door and it really did sort out the men from the boys, or women from the girls. Remember, the country was in a really bad recession at the time and the places we worked were not in affluent areas. The people that had the money either had encyclopedias or private tutors. Besides, you couldn't get the same effect standing in front of a huge metal gate talking into an intercom with dialogue like, "You must be the faceless voice of the house?"

One of the more colourful characters I met in the book business was Jack. He would say he was the pizza man to get past the electric gate. If, as usual, they said they hadn't ordered one, he would say, "Well I have got two twelve-inch deep pans here that are going in the bin then." Sometimes he would get in, and on them finding out he had told them a lie as they answered the door, they would ultimately ask him to go away. I have no idea why he bothered, though he swore blind that he got into a home by using this technique once and sold them a set of books.

The police would occasionally pull you up and ask you what you were up to. The more up-market the area, the more they would soon be on your case asking why you were knocking on someone's door at quarter to ten. The rougher parts of the city were generally only allocated to males to work, or lunatics like me, and again the police would occasionally stop you, have a look inside your bag to check you were genuine, and then ask if you were crazy walking this area at night.

Entering a home in a very rough area of the city one evening, I came across a single father in his late twenties. Des had a son of nine and explained the mother had turned to drugs and had run off with her dealer. Sitting in a very spartan living room consisting of just a sofa, table and chairs, and a television sitting on a very grubby cabinet, I quickly found out that he was unemployed. Understanding that he was not in a financial position to purchase the books, he offered some good advice as I left his home, telling me not to get picked up by the shuttered shops down the road, as there were gangs of youths there with iron bars that they would beat people with, and rob them of their money and possessions. Thanking him for this information, I enquired how he knew this. Looking at me, a twinkle sparkled in one of his deep, dark eyes as he said, "I used to do it!"

Although I never suffered any violence myself, there were a couple of occasions when my instinct told me to get out of an area, when I was being followed by an odd lone individual or gangs of young lads wanting to know what I was carrying. This was done usually by flagging down a bus or going into a milk bar and making arrangements to get picked up from there. Reps did have incidents, but thankfully I escaped unscathed.

Apart from resilience, the key attribute you needed to succeed at door-to-door selling was "persistence". It could be a pretty soul-destroying job if you let it get to you. Imagine knocking three hundred doors in the pouring rain, your clipboard with your door-knocking record sheet is so wet that the ink from your pen will not write onto it. Every time someone answers the door, they see a drowned rat trying to seek refuge from the elements. On top of that you may also be cold, as contrary to belief, Australia does get cold in its winter months, and you have to travel many hundreds of kilometres into the tropics to escape the winter proper. Because of your discomfort, this, if you let it, comes out in the tone of your voice, where the enthusiasm is rapidly dwindling away, making it even more difficult to get into someone's home. By then, most would give up!

Occasionally, there would be competitions to motivate salespeople, and they obviously kept the motivation and morale going. The people that gave up were the ones that had become disillusioned with the job, or were basically afraid of hard work. You ask anyone who has been successful with what they have done or are currently doing, and they will nearly always mention the same one attribute to it – hard work! You had to keep on going and keeping motivated to achieve your goals.

Goals are one of the most important things in life, I believe, that will help you get through the everyday trials of life living on planet earth. I went on to manage teams in Queensland, New South Wales, Victoria and South Australia, and I always pushed these people, in what I found out later was a most wonderful way to achieve their goals, and that was by having fun. My initial goal was pure and simple. The more books I sold, the more of this fantastic country I got to see. In turn, I would find out what motivated the different people in my teams, and dangling a realistic carrot in front of them got the best results from them.

For example, there was to be a lad on my team in the future, who I am sure was related to Rip Van Winkle, who didn't like getting out of bed till midday or later. I would tell him to write an order, and then on doing so, let him stay in bed till two o'clock the following day if he wished. Van Winkle Junior would write an order three or four nights a week and hence we would often never see him awake till the sun was high in the sky. He loved it!

Things were not going my way and Todd had become concerned that I had not sold a set of books in a long time. To be honest, it was now worrying me. Still, with going to the pub nearly every night and clubbing in Parramatta twice a week, plus a couple of excursions into the city to see the Harbour Bridge, The Opera House, finally getting my brother a T-shirt and all the other touristy stuff, my money was being spent faster than I could earn it. On top of that I also now had rent to pay, which was about a hundred bucks a week, and apart from the commission I had been paid on my first deal, all I had left was about a thousand dollars in my bank account and five hundred pounds in traveller's cheques.

Asking me to do a demo to him, he very quickly realised I had deviated from the script and that I was now doing my own version of the demonstration. As with all successful scripts, they are written because they work. Todd asked me to revert back to the original script, and that night I sold my second set of books.

Heading inland for Canberra a couple of weeks later, we drove into the Southern Tablelands of New South Wales where the fire risk warnings on the roadside signs screamed out "extreme". Although the summer was now coming to an end, the bushland all around was a tinderbox waiting for a bolt of lightning or a careless match to be dropped on it. The speed at which a bushfire can take a hold is absolutely amazing, and although I experienced several, I was fortunate enough not to be able to label a fire as terrifying, though I met many people that had almost lost their lives or had lost loved ones in them.

Stopping at towns such as Goulburn and Young on the way, the evenings were now losing their daily heat much quicker, and a sweatshirt was now needed for you to be comfortable till the ten o'clock pick-up. Young, incidentally, was a milestone for me as it was where I wrote my first double (two sets of books in one night).

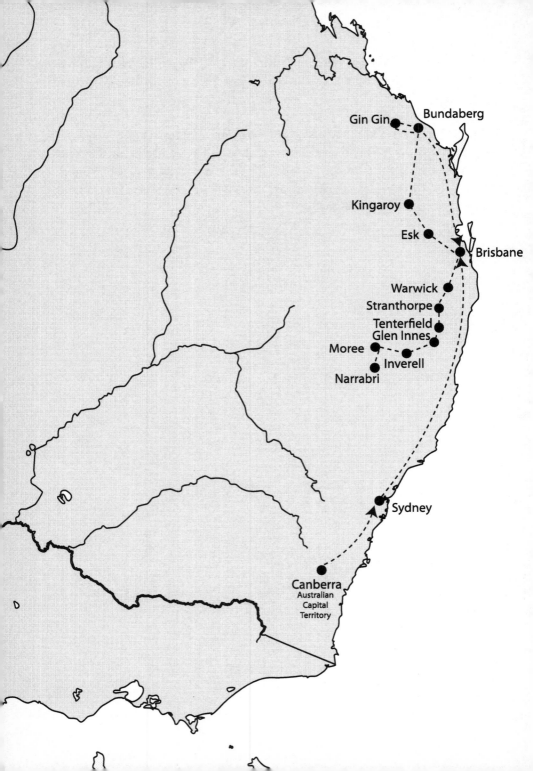

Chapter 4

The capital city of Australia is Canberra and lies in the region of the Australian Capital Territory. Australia consists of six states and two territories. The states being Tasmania, Victoria, New South Wales, Queensland, South Australia and Western Australia. The other territory is in the north of the country and hence is named the Northern Territory.

I wish I could say more about Canberra than I am about to. But to be truthful, there is not much to say, at least not from my point of view. At the time, the expansion of the city was incredible, as I mentioned earlier, and this was during a recession. With Canberra, although at the time it had a population of just over a quarter of a million people, it felt like you were working in a big town. Even arriving at the city centre, you had to ask someone where it was, as it felt you hadn't actually arrived there. The city in general though was very clean and felt almost clinical and lacked a character the other big cities had. With practically no blocks of flats once you left the centre of this manufactured urban sprawl, the rich green lawns outside people's homes were immaculately kept, and there was no feeling of grubbiness in the suburbs that you felt in parts of Sydney. Mind you, to be fair, Sydney did have a population over fifteen times the size of Canberra, and with large concentrated masses of people in one area, that filth and dirty feeling becomes apparent, don't you think?

With April nearly coming to an end, the days were often sunny, and with temperatures around the mid-twenties it was very pleasant going door to door bashing the metal fly screen doors with the metal part of the clipboard. Also, the people were much more approachable and would politely decline your offer of entering their home if they were not interested. This could have been down to the fact that a large percentage of people were employed in governmental jobs, where the bureaucratic cogs of the Australian government turned, and they had a different discipline to other working classes I had met in Sydney.

So, it was more than likely that if I eventually mentioned the "E" word, I would not get the "F" word in reply. The evenings, though, were another story.

The first day I was dropped off, I ignored Todd's warnings to put on, or at least pack, a pair of jeans in my bag to prepare for the evening chill. By nine o'clock, the temperature had plummeted into low single figures. By nine fifteen I was very cold, and working an area that it seemed had had every sales rep in the world knocking their doors in the past few months, selling all sorts of stuff like hoovers and insurance, no one was at all interested in letting me in. Not even for a warm-up!

By nine forty-five I was freezing, and with no milk bars to go in and get a drink and some shelter, I was very quickly going to get frostbitten toes on my sandal-wearing feet. I hoped that he wouldn't be late picking me up, as by ten fifteen I would begin to freeze to death and very shortly be doing a demo to the Grim Reaper and Mister Rigor Mortis.

The nights would get down to freezing, and when Todd mentioned a sojourn back to Sydney, before escaping the Aussie winter by heading up north to Brisbane and Queensland, it lifted my morale walking those cold streets at night knowing that I was going to warmer pastures on my great Australian adventure.

If you do venture to the capital city, then I would personally recommend two places to visit:

1: The Australian Parliament Building, and;

2: The War Memorial Museum. Mind you, I am very interested in military history, so the second option may not be everyone's cup of tea.

Just before we left Canberra, we met up with two other quite large sales teams with managers, reps and appointment makers from countries such as England, Ireland, Canada, New Zealand and, of course, Australia. These people were, like myself, using the company as a vehicle to get around and see the great Oz. Trooping off to a wine bar, I found out that one sales team had just returned from New Zealand and that it was an option for me in the future. I, at the time, was not in the slightest bit interested though, as I had set my heart on becoming one of the most travelled people on this huge island continent. So for the third time it was off to Sydney again.

The last night in Sydney, I decided to borrow a gnome from someone's garden. Taking note of the owner's address, he was to accompany us through many towns in New South Wales and Queensland, with him sending photos of himself (with the help of some humans of course) back to Mum and Dad of various places, including posing by the "Welcome to Queensland" sign. He was to return to his owner just over six months later having travelled just over three thousand kilometres.

We set off for Brisbane and Queensland after finishing a little earlier in the field than usual. Todd was going to drive through the night on the eleven-hour journey of what was just under a thousand kilometres. Petrol was a fraction of the price of back home in Wales, but the station wagon Todd had acquired off another sales manager not only ran on petrol, but had been converted to LPG, or liquefied petroleum gas. Autogas, as it was known, was half the price of petrol, and in Brisbane it was eighteen cents a litre, which at the time worked out at thirty pence a gallon. I figured that provided they built a few bridges between Oz and Southeast Asia, I could get back home to Tenby for less than a hundred quid. Mind you, I would have had to have been driving that truck that was driven by Mel Gibson in the film *Mad Max 2* filled with the stuff.

In the car with him were myself, Danny, and two new reps who had been with the company a couple of months and had come up from Melbourne. Mick was an Aussie and Neil was from England, travelling, like myself, on a working visa. David and Jason had quit the job days before. (See, I told you there was a high turnover of staff, didn't I?)

Crossing the Queensland border just after sunrise, we stopped to have our touristy photo taken. This was a relief as I had woken in the back of the vehicle just before dawn to see and smell a horrible sight – Danny asleep on my shoulder, looking up with his mouth open, snoring and breathing a curry breath onto me from the pie he had eaten the night before.

Stepping out into glorious sunshine, I was immediately aware of how much warmer it was, despite it only being just past seven o'clock. I was now in the subtropics and the Tropic of Capricorn was only up the road (admittedly six hundred kilometres up the road, but I too was now getting used to the Aussie distances). At just past nine o'clock we arrived at the suburb of New Farm in the capital city of Queensland, Brisbane. Working that first afternoon in glorious sunshine, the first thing I noticed about the households in Queensland was the fact that a lot were elevated off the ground several feet on stilts. This I soon learned was to keep them above the floods during the wet season.

Anyway, one of the first doors I knocked on in "Brissy" (as Brisbane is so affectionately known), was opened, and I was greeted by the first of what was to become many Aboriginal men I was to meet on my travels. Yes, I know this may sound strange, but I had up until then never come across an Aborigine in the metropolis of Sydney. Having said that, though, I never worked in the suburb of Redfern where they were predominant. On entering the household, I was wrongly assuming his wife would be an Aborigine as well. Assumption is the mother of all evils – note well! Meeting his clearly very white wife, I proceeded with the small talk.

Turning to the husband, I enquired into what his vocation was.

"I'm a bludger!" he replied.

Now, normally my inquisitive mind would have enquired into what that entailed, and indeed I should have done so to make sure the family was in the financial position to buy the books in the first place. But, and I have no idea why, I did not pursue what his profession was at the time. It may have possibly been the fact that I was in the home of the first indigenous person I had met and would have felt stupid inquiring into what a "bludger" did. Not even asking how many hours he worked, I carried out the demonstration, my mind going through dozens of professions of what a bludger could possibly do.

Flicking through the prospectus and getting to the camouflage scene, it gave me time to try to work out what a bludger did. I figured, in my naivety, that he was a factory worker that bludgeoned metal into a shape that was required for our modern industrial age. How wrong was I?

When I got to the closing questions and asked if two dollars and fifty would be a problem, he replied, "Yes," as he was not working.

I then replied, "But I thought you said you were a bludger?"

To which his immediate response, "Yes, I am" only caused me confusion.

Frowning, and with him leaning back in an armchair that seemed fit for the skip a long time ago, he said, "Do you know what a bludger does?"

My innocent spaghetti western look must have looked a picture to this couple, as my mind raced through the possibilities of what a bludger did.

"No," I replied.

"A bludger," he continued, "does fuck all!"

I could hear those maniacal laughs from those spaghetti western films echoing in my ears as I packed my bag and walked back down the wooden steps of the house. I was rapidly learning the world of door-to-door sales, and in fact everyday life. I had learned a valuable lesson, which is – if you are not sure what someone is talking about, THEN ASK!

Telling my work colleagues about it later, they all pissed themselves with laughter as Todd explained that a bludger was Aussie slang for a lazy layabout who had no intention of working but continued to live off the state. It was unfortunate that it had been an Aboriginal who had introduced me to this word, as at that time they were all wrongly (and maybe still are) tarred with the same brush, that they are workshy, which a hell of a lot are not, as I was to learn later on.

I just loved the Queenslanders. They say the Aussies are laid-back, but the Queenslanders are horizontal. These people were some of the most hospitable folk I had ever met, and there was nearly always a spare cold stubby of VB, Powers, XXXX, or some other amber nectar available in the fridge that would help you with the delivery of your demonstration. Their down-to-earth attitude was a delight to experience, and it was a pleasure each day to trudge the streets of "Brissy" and listen to the anecdotes they told about themselves, family or friends, whoever!

I had now five completed sales under my belt, which meant from now on it was a hundred and ninety dollars an order, and although the evenings were still a bit on the cool side, they didn't get down to the levels I had experienced in the frozen streets of Canberra. (That sum of money, incidentally, converted at that time, was equivalent to just over one hundred pounds.) The winter sunshine during the day meant temperatures hitting the low- to mid-twenties which was considered a summer heat wave back home in Wales. Life couldn't be better!

One afternoon, I was in one of the western suburbs of the city when I came across a husband and wife with two boys aged fifteen and seven. The father was a long-distance truck driver and was away days on end travelling interstate on his road train. Both parents were keen to get their younger son interested in the books so that it would help his schooling and were trying to instil some motivation into him to learn, something his older brother lacked entirely, apparently. In fact, just before I started the demo, the eldest went over to watch the television, albeit with the volume down low. A television switched on was a major distraction, and I often insisted it was turned off. Watching this teenager kneel in front of the set, he was that close I thought he would try and climb into it. In fact, if those beings from the film Poltergeist had been in there, they would have pulled him in there like a shot!

With his father scoffing at him to watch the television as it would not be long before he would fail all his exams and be out sweeping the streets, I started. With the youngest being seven, I skipped ELF, and went into the story books, followed by *The Science Library* and then the prospectus. (*The Science Library* was another set of books which we could give instead of something else, or as well as, after the close, to see if you could tempt a family to sign up for a set of books.)

I was pleased to see not only the child taking an active interest, but the parents as well, though the decision on whether to purchase the books would be heavily influenced by their young child.

Finishing up, I then came to the first closing question, which in case you have forgotten was, "Could you see this being of an educational benefit to you and your family?" With their young son wedged between both of them on the sofa, the mother looked down at him and asked whether they'd be of some use. The boy pursed his lips, and with his eyes looking slightly upwards I could see he was clearly thinking the question through.

"Nah!" he replied.

Looking at the mother, I could see her roll her eyes as a wave of despair washed over her, and when a slight look of disappointment appeared on the father's face, he announced, "Well, that's that! No sale for you, sorry mate."

As I began to reach for my bag to begin packing up, I suddenly heard a voice from behind me.
"I'd use them!"

The voice came from where the television was, and for a moment I thought we had made contact with our supernatural beings in the television! Turning around, I heard those magical words again.

"I would use them!"

The father got up from the sofa, and with squinted eyes said, "I'm sorry?"

The source of the voice got up from in front of the television and turned to face his father.

"I said I would use them!"

There was a brief pause and then the father turned to his wife.

"Did you hear that, my love?" he said, nodding his head as if he were a mechanical toy of some sorts. "He would use them." His spouse remained quiet and then he turned to me.

"Do you want to know something, Lance? This son of mine is so lazy that all he is interested in doing is watching television all day, or hanging around the park with his mates. In fact the only subject or course he would possibly be interested in, if they ran one, would be how to learn to become a bludger! And he probably wouldn't even finish that course, as it would mean he would have to get out of bed in the mornings to attend it."

His son scratched his head and repeated his sentence again, to which his father replied with a raised voice, "When?"

The teenager became quiet again and the father, looking back at me, continued in his broad Queenslander accent. "And do you want to know something else, Lance?"

I shrugged my shoulders, not really knowing what was coming next.

Still nodding his head like one of those toy monkeys you see bashing drums or smashing cymbals together, the dialogue flowed. "Last year, my beloved son here wanted to learn a musical instrument and eventually settled his heart on learning to play the electric keyboard. For months on end he harped on that he wanted to play the keyboard. So for Christmas we bought him a thousand-dollar electric organ." There was a pause as he turned and fixed his gaze onto his son. Taking a deep breath, the story unfolded.

"A thousand dollars that organ cost. And do you think he played it?" His head abruptly went from the nodding mode into a shaking back and forth motion. "He never even looked at it!"

I glanced over to what now looked like a very puzzled teenager, and seeing it was his turn of thinking and processing the information he had just received, he delivered the knockout blow that sealed my fate for getting a sale in the house.

"What organ?"

With his father swiping the air with his hand and replying "Exactly", I packed up and left.

I quickly found out there were other teams in the city that had come up from down south, with one team travelling from the South Australian capital city of Adelaide, which was over two thousand kilometres away. Even then, at the time I remember thinking that I would have almost been in Russia after crossing four European countries, had I set off from Tenby travelling that distance across Europe. This country was big. Really big! Some teams were heading way up into the tropics to places like Cairns and Townsville, and they were another seventeen hundred, and fourteen hundred kilometres respectively! As I say – big!

It was here that Mick and Neil left us to go to those places and even warmer climes. Todd had been told he had to return to Sydney for a two-day business meeting, and flying the next day, he gave Danny, a guy called Cotter and I a little route up to a place called Bundaberg with an overnight stay in a little town called Esk and one night in Kingaroy.

Given the reins of the station wagon, I was also given the purse strings for the fuel, accommodation and the food, and was put in a supervisory role for these two short nights. (Danny, I had learned by then, was going to lose the pimp-mobile to a finance company, hence the reason it was left behind in Sydney. Also, he was now potless from his gambling addiction, and the only reason he was still with us was the fact that he was a very good salesperson!)

I thought at the time, what could go wrong in such a short space of time? Lots! Travelling up on an inland route, we arrived at Esk just after midday and booked into a caravan park and a lovely cabin with a large glass patio door. Setting out to work at around three, we all agreed we would meet up at the pub at seven to see how everyone was doing, and if we had all written an order, we would finish early and go for a few beers.

As the town was only small, there were not enough doors for all three of us to individually knock, so I jumped into the car and drove to a nearby little town called Toogoolawah. By six thirty, darkness had fallen, and exiting a family's home clutching an order, I stepped into a warm early Queensland evening and headed back towards Esk and a cold beer. Approaching the pub, I could see Danny outside in his white shirt, white trousers and white trainers. Seeing me approach, his big cheesy grin spread across his face and he began to shake his head.

I pulled up outside the watering hole and was met by his customary salutation. Asking my fellow "dude" if he had written an order, his response came back as affirmative, followed by a little chuckle. "What's wrong with you? And where's Cotter?" I enquired.

"Nothing, dude, and Cotter's in there," he replied, pointing at the pub window.

I got out of the vehicle to have a look at what the interior of the pub looked like and wondered what new beers they might have on draught. Looking inside, I could see a typically laid out bar with the run of the mill lagers on tap and our fellow colleague bouncing around inside, waving his hands in the air in front of a small crowd of people.

"What the hell's going on in there?" I asked my blond ex-field manager. Chuckling once again, Danny gave me his thoughts of what he saw inside.

"Well, I'm no expert. But I would say he was well pissed!"

Walking into the saloon, I could see that they had carpeted the floor with the posters from our demonstration. Well, alright, Cotter had. With his back to us, and standing and waving his hands and occasionally dropping to the floor on one knee and trying to balance with the help of a hand or two, it looked as if he were playing a solo imaginary game of Twister, but without the large coloured circles. He was standing up and crouching, falling backwards and forwards; I thought the crowd had the right idea of keeping at least two metres between them and him. Just when I began to figure out what to do, out came the money box. With a garbled message from him, everyone, including us two, looked on in complete amazement at this strangely choreographed, incoherent stage act. Then someone asked how much it was for the money box? A quick one-sided bartering conversation followed, and he parted with it for ten dollars. My initial thought was to leave him in there and find another watering hole. But now I had a responsibility of sorts and we had to get him safely back to the cabin. With Danny packing up the posters and stuffing them in Cotter's bag, I made my move towards a table near the crowd where I had spied the prospectus waiting eagerly to be rescued. Picking it up, I was immediately challenged by a quite tipsy middle-aged customer. Informing me that he had purchased it for fifty dollars, I then tried to explain that it was a promotional piece of material, and that it made no logical sense as the text on one page of a subject suddenly changed mid-sentence as you turned over to an entirely different subject altogether. Giving him an example by reading a sentence on the bottom of the page about the pyramids of Egypt and turning over in mid-sentence to reveal a full colour picture of a cat, I hoped this would bring him to his senses. He was having none of it though, and then, thinking that Cotter had probably already drunk the man's fifty bucks, I let him keep it.

With one arm over Danny and the other over me, we slowly walked him back to the caravan park which was a few hundred yards away. On reaching the cabin, the one interior light I had left on for us, knowing that it would be pitch-black on our return, shone down onto the double bed on the other side of the room. Contemplating perhaps just having a couple of beers before leaping into bed, I realised the keys to the cabin were still in the car outside the pub. Leaving him with Danny, I returned a bit later to find Cotter spark out on the dusty ground with Danny trying to bring him round. "What's happened now?" I asked, wondering what was going to happen next.

Danny had momentarily left him while he'd relieved himself, and on returning,he saw our drunken colleague run towards the cabin to dive onto the bed. He would have succeeded had the glass patio door not been shut!

The next day we headed off for Kingaroy, and with Cotter having no recollection of the previous night's events, and nursing what felt like a broken nose and being extremely apologetic, we all came to a gentleman's agreement that nothing would be said when we got to Bundaberg.

The town of Kingaroy is dubbed the "Peanut Capital of Australia". As you get closer to this little town, the first structures you see are the giant peanut silos that dominate the skyline. I sent off a postcard to my mother and wondered how many she had received by now and whether she had started a collection.

Kingaroy claims to grow the best peanuts in the world, and a peanut is in fact a legume – whatever the hell that is. Anyway, with us seasoned professionals splitting up to work the town in three sections, we all agreed that we would finish early at nine and meet at the cabin we had booked for the night, and then go for a few beers.

Fortunately for Cotter I had brought along a spare prospectus, which was always useful in case one was damaged by a spilt liquid, inadvertently had a page ripped by an overeager child, or indeed sold to some drunkard in a pub! Telling him he would have to improvise with the money box bit, I also warned him to steer clear of the buildings that purveyed any sort of alcoholic substances till we met later. What a waste of time that was!

Walking along the main street of the town as dusk was approaching, I noticed a policeman looking down at a man sitting down and propped up against the frontage of a shop. On getting closer, I could see it was Cotter. He was clearly inebriated again. I explained that he was with me and made some story up that he had just received some bad family news earlier that day, hence his current condition. In all fairness the copper was good as gold, and was more concerned that he had had some reports from the local townsfolk who had been worried at the state that this door-to-door salesman was in. It turned out he was requiring "the hair of the dog" after the previous evening, and had decided to have a few drinks too many before he started knocking doors.

I looked down at Cotter. He looked back up at me and smiling said, "You mushed be the man of da house?"

The next day we headed for Bundy, as Bundaberg is commonly known, and driving right through it we headed to a place called Bargara. Todd had booked three little bungalows, where ten managers and reps were to stay for a week, and although I was sharing a room once again I didn't care as these structures were right on a lovely white sandy beach that stretched down to some fantastic turquoise wave-breaking waters.

Although Danny had blanked the previous day, I had managed to write one, so as a team over two days we had produced three orders. Not bad going seeing there was only two of us working.

Without us telling anyone, Cotter was moved to another team and so he was no longer an issue. Also, after my baptism of fire, I had now lost my temporary supervisory role and was now a mere representative for the company once again.

Bundaberg is named after the world-famous rum, and although not a city, it was then, and still is, a very large town of which I was slowly shying away from, and I wanted to work the smaller towns and hamlets that were within spitting distance of these larger conurbations. The reason behind this was the fact that the smaller the community was, the more friendly it seemed to become. It took me quite some time to adjust from large conurbation mode to small settlement mode. For example, in a large city such as Sydney or Melbourne, it was not uncommon for next-door neighbours not to know one another, especially when you were working in blocks of flats. As you moved further inland to the smaller communities, a general well-being and camaraderie became prevalent within the neighbourhood, which reminded me of home, where most people knew one another and where friendly greetings were a daily occurrence.

Many a time walking in the street of a small town would come the welcome of "How's it going?" or "How ya going?", and this would come from a complete stranger! I would quite happily sink into this mode and then be caught completely off-guard when working back in a larger built-up area, running back into my own outback routine by saying to a complete stranger, "How's it going?" You would then instantly receive a look that read, "What the fucks it got to do with you?"

So, one day, Todd asked us if anyone would like to work the little town of Gin Gin. We were now in sugar cane country, and indeed from here on northwards the mighty sugar cane fields rule the roost on the coastal regions, until you reach the areas just north of the large town of Cairns, which then turns into deep impenetrable jungle.

Gin Gin was fifty kilometres north-west of Bundy and nothing unusual stood out about this little place except that it was cursed. Well, if you dealt with books door to door you were. Over the years managers and reps would visit this little town and after finishing an evening's work would then jump into their cars for the journey back to Bundaberg. All straightforward some would say! Apparently not. On only one occasion had someone successfully driven there and back with no problems occurring with their automobile. Each had their own little story about how they had run out of fuel and the petrol gauge was reading half-full, or the electrics had packed in and they had to drive back with no lights, or they'd had multiple punctures. Anyway, based on this, most were not that keen to go to Gin Gin, due to being a superstitious bunch.

Volunteering for the town, I managed to convince a young field manager in his late teens to come with me in his old little Holden Torana. He too laughed in the face of the curse. Working the town I did two demos but blanked. On meeting him back at the car at ten though, I was pleased to see a very happy young lad who had written a double. Taking advantage of his success, I offered to drive back to where he could have a beer or two while I could get to grips with this little lookalike Ford Escort Mark one model that I had taken a shine to.

Heading out of Gin Gin, we mocked the dreaded curse and looked forward to the pizza waiting for us back at the bungalows, which Todd had promised he would cook us on our return. Laughing and joking, I changed into third and that's when the gearstick came away in my hand. The car hurtled along the road, and I was now holding a metal rod with a black plastic bulbous knob attached to it. Looking like I was holding a black microphone of sorts, my surprised passenger gazed at it in surprise. I thought at the time that if he'd had the radio on we could have played a pretend mobile karaoke

90

slot, but this was not the time to mess about.

Realising I couldn't find the hole in the gearbox where the lever fitted, I slowly brought the vehicle to a standstill. Now, I am one of the least mechanically minded people in the world, and as I would quickly discover, my passenger and car owner was like-minded. About five kilometres out of the cursed town, we tried to blindly reaffix the gear lever back into the gearbox, with just the little interior light on as an aide in the pitch-black rural night. Trying time and time again, I eventually had to access the emergency breakdown pack in the back of his car that contained four of the remaining stubbies of the six-pack of VB. Skulling the first one, I held the gearstick/ microphone in my hand, and with the plastic knob held close to my mouth and looking at my superior, spoke in my best cabaret sounding voice, "Testing, testing, one, two, three!"

Thrusting it blindly into the gearbox, it hit an invisible hole and we realised we were in a gear. Looking at the position the lever was in, I figured it was in second, so, starting the engine up and bringing the clutch to biting point, managed to get her going.

Driving the forty-odd kilometres all the way in second and jumping a red light in the process, I managed to get us home at just past midnight to cold pizza.

I was to visit Bundaberg on several occasions the following year, and did I ever visit Gin Gin again? What do you think?

Everyone staying at the bungalows in Bundy were Australian and mostly from tropical Queensland. With it now being their winter, they all thought I was mad getting up early in the morning to go for a swim in the sea, when daytime temperatures struggled to reach twenty-four degrees centigrade. People acclimatise, and to the Aussies these temperatures were a bit fresh for their bodies. It was now August and the depths of the Australian winter, but I was enjoying every minute of it. Swimming every day, I was careful not to go out of my depth and fall foul of the riptides that would gobble people up every year all over this giant island continent.

September was the turning point for the book people (as we had labelled ourselves), who would then head southwards again, to escape the tropical wet season where roads would become impassable through deep floods, and also to capitalise on the Aussie summer in the southern states. So, although I had come a fair way north, the proper Aussie tropics were to elude me for now.

Heading back to "Brissy", we were to work the city for three weeks before slowly heading back to Melbourne.

One evening, I was summoned to see one of the bosses of the company at his swish apartment overlooking the Brisbane River. (The city is named after the river, which of course was there a long time before people started building.) Over a few glasses of champagne he asked me whether I would be interested extending my visa for an extra couple of years as the company would be interested in sponsoring me to stay for that duration and to continue working for them training and managing sales teams Australia-wide. I was very keen on this attractive proposition, and as a tester they wanted me to take a team down through the outback of New South Wales, albeit a small one. Stating that I was interested, I was informed that more would be revealed when I got to Melbourne, and that it obviously depended on my performance over the next few months. I, on the other hand, had now been given the status of field manager and would receive two hundred and eighty dollars on each order.

One evening, on heading back to New Farm from the western suburbs, I came across my first bush fire. The police had blocked the highway and were turning traffic back. About five hundred metres in front and to the right of the traffic, the whole of the bush was an inferno. This fiery beast was consuming the green and brown foliage with an appetite that had no fill. Its fiery belly gorged on those helpless trees as they looked across towards their untouched relatives on the other side of the tarmac river that separated heaven from hell. Waiting for the cars to turn around in front of us, I watched as the beast suddenly threw its tongue across the highway to taste the delicious verdant virgin bush on the opposite side. Watching the fire leap from one side of the road to the other still stands in my memory today, and you could see it getting a grip very quickly indeed. With the fire services arriving in strength, I was thankful that a wind wasn't blowing towards us, otherwise it would have been a right different kettle of fish!

The temperatures in Brisbane climb amazingly quickly in the month of September as the sun heads south for the southern hemisphere summer.

From the mid-twenties they very quickly reach the mid-thirties, and I would look forward each year for the return of that heat as the Aussie spring in Queensland kick-started again.

With all the sales teams coming down from Northern Queensland and congregating for the mass migration to the southern states, I was the only team leader they wanted to take a team down south without a car. Fortunately, a field manager had quit the job and the company had acquired the vehicle. The little vehicle in question was a Datsun Cherry, and I would have use of it till we reached Melbourne, when I then had to make a decision what I wanted to do with my career in the book business.

I was given two well-established reps: one being a very likeable hippy-like chap by the name of Shane, and the other was the character who I mentioned earlier that slept for Australia – Van Winkle Junior. Both were colourful and very funny chaps, and we headed off into the wilds together. Briefly touching the Gold Coast, we bid farewell to Todd and Danny and it was the last I would see of them. (After a number of years, Todd had decided he had seen the parts of Oz he wanted to see and was settling down with his wife in "Brissy". Danny was to return to his parents, and no doubt brother Archie, to see if he could find work in his hometown.)

Heading inland, we stopped and worked the towns of Warwick, Stanthorpe, Tenterfield, Glen Innes and Inverell over the week, before getting to a place called Moree. Heading into the outback proper, I was amazed at how straight the roads were that stretched to the shimmering, scorching horizon, and even when I returned to this flat landscape many moons later with my fiancée, I would still marvel at the way the roads were just swallowed up by the sky.

Back in northern New South Wales, the little car was just ideal for the three of us and our kit, and with a little engine it was nice on my pocket for fuel as well. Apart from personal rent and food expenses, I had the maintenance of the car to look after, and though I had two reps under me, I was not entitled to any extra commission for managing them as the car had been given to me loan free.

One of the annoyances in the outback is flies. Although they are a pest on the coast they are nothing compared to their inland cousins. There are literally millions of the little bastards! Although I eventually got used to them, they are around you from dawn till dusk landing on your face, exposed hands, arms, feet, legs and food, seeking out moisture wherever they could find it. If you had an open wound from a scratch or mosquito bite, they were at it continuously, playing who can infect the human first.

Moree was quite an eye-opener for me at first, as it was the first town I'd been to with quite a large Aboriginal population. With this fact, and now seeing kangaroos daily – hopping around the water-starved, brown, flat, never-ending horizon-grabbing bushland – it offered a unique Australian flavour that you could not savour on or near the coast. We were now over three hundred kilometres inland, and that was barely scratching the surface of this abyss-like feeling the outback projected to you.

With one of the bosses already in the town with two other well-established teams, we decided to stay just one night before heading south to Narrabri.

Walking through the town centre, I came across a group of Aboriginal men and women that were clearly all drunk, and stepping into the road and skirting around them I heard a male shout, "Hey bro! Ya gotta dollar?"
Not wanting to make eye contact with the source of the voice, I quickly carried on walking with my little bag on my back. That question, and "Hey bro! Ya gotta smoke?", I would hear hundreds of times in the future when I really started to go native!

As I mentioned earlier, mobile phones were in their infancy in the early nineteen-nineties, so the company had armed me with a pager, with which they could send a message to me to contact them. On reaching Narrabri the next day, one such message came up on the luminous green screen of the little hand-held device, stating that I needed to contact the Melbourne office. Speaking to Alice, who had originally hired me, she explained that she was sending me a new recruit up from the city. Now that was all well and good, except I didn't really have enough room for another person and their luggage.

She mentioned that he was a Canadian, and I was to pick him up from a much larger inland town by the name of Dubbo the following afternoon at one o'clock at the bus station. With my protest being largely ignored, she announced it was too late as he was already on the bus and that his name was Steve Boulder. Getting out the map, I found Dubbo was just down the road, as Alice had mentioned – two hundred and forty kilometres down the road. My round trip was going to be nearly five hundred k's and was the equivalent of me driving from Tenby nearly to Scotland, just to pick someone up!

Giving Shane and Van Winkle Junior a map of the town, I told them to split the town into two of the places we had not worked the previous day, and see how many orders they could write, while I went to collect our new recruit. As an incentive I promised to buy a slab of VB for anyone that wrote a double, and if Van Winkle won, he could also have a long lie-in the next day.

All around Narrabri, and indeed from Moree down, it's cotton country, where the stuff is grown and picked in an abundant amount. Anyway, hurtling down to Dubbo in my little "Dinky" car, I arrived at the bus station just as the bus was pulling in. Watching the people disembark from the vehicle, I noticed a mountain of a man six feet something high and four feet wide, with black curly hair and clearly of an Afro-American origin, exit the bus in a T-shirt and shorts. Looking at his darkened skin, I could see that his upper arms were almost the girth of my thighs. He was one big chap!

As the crowd dispersed, I scanned the area to find the lost soul that would be looking for me. The hugs and kisses from friends and family that were meeting the occupants from the bus singled out this giant of a man who stood alone with two quite largish bags. Looking at him, I wondered that surely he wasn't the guy I was expected to pick up? The spaghetti western look became apparent as we both realised that David and Goliath would soon be travelling in the tiny Datsun Cherry chariot back up to Narrabri together.

Walking over to him, I asked the question, "Are you Steve?"

He replied in his native North American accent. "And you must be Lance? Hi!" With a massive smile and engulfing my hand in his, we shook our hands until I thought he would take my arm out of its socket.

"Can I help you with one of your bags?" I enquired.

"Yeah sure."

Reaching down to pick up a leather holdall, I found I could barely lift it off the ground. "Hell! What have you got in here?" I asked.

"My weights!" he replied.

Carrying the bag over to the car with both hands, I placed it into the little boot, and doing so, heard the suspension creak as he threw his other bag on top of it. Driving back, my mind raced as to how I was to get everyone into this little craft to take us southwards, and I thought of maybe buying a vehicle like Doctor Who's Tardis, one that was probably the same size outside but could accommodate a guy the size of the Norse mythological creature "The Kraken" inside!

Each time I changed gear from first and into second and then from second into third, Steve would have to lift his bulk up slightly to move his leg away so that I could complete the operation. On returning back to Narrabri, I now realised I had an appointment maker and two reps to look after. The team was expanding, in more ways than one.

Offloading his gear at the caravan I had booked for the couple of nights, I decided to give my new recruit an initiation into the book business. What an initiation he had! Driving out of the town earlier that day, I had noticed about twenty houses on the outskirts. Knowing Shane and Van Winkle would have not walked out that far from town, I decided to take us out to this little satellite community to see if I could write an order or two. With me and the Canadian monster driving into the vicinity of these houses, I suddenly heard noises from something pinging onto the roof of the car. It was our welcome from the Aboriginal community of Narrabri, which was basically, "You're not welcome here, piss off!"

The stones hurtled down onto the little vehicle as the giant of the man next to me said, "Let's get the hell out of here!" I glanced at his size, and sensing he was worried, I figured I should be worried too. Watching two more young Aboriginal lads exiting a house and picking up more stones to join in, I turned around sharpish and we headed back to Narrabri central. Reaching our accommodation, Steve was anxious to discover what was on the menu for the evening as he was in need of a good feast, having not had a decent meal since Melbourne. I, on the other hand, was more preoccupied with the big question of how the hell we would all fit in the car along with our luggage and work materials.

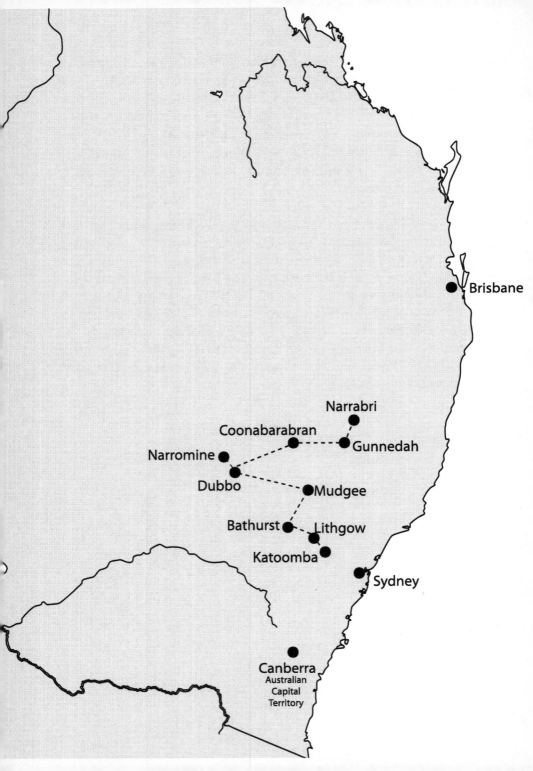

Chapter 5

The next day was incredibly interesting, and I was contemplating contacting the Guinness World Records for them to record the highest number of animate and inanimate objects you could put into a vehicle of the size I now commanded. Thinking back to it now, I should have bought a roof rack, but not one of us came up with that amazing idea at the time.

Putting Steve's holdall, his leather bag full of weights, my holdall and our bags full of sales materials, into the boot, I had the boot rammed to capacity. Steve, being much larger than my other two reps, who were both around five foot ten and with a slight build, had the front seat pushed right back onto Van Winkle. In fact, it was that far back that it looked like they were both almost in the front seat, with Van Winkle peering over his suitcase rammed up to his chest.

Likewise, Shane sat behind me, but not in such a cramped position, with his quite largish bag on his lap and his precious glass "bong" clutched safely in his hand. (A "bong", for those of you who don't know, is a pipe of sorts, that you smoke stuff with, that you can't buy in high street shops.) It was his friend and mentor and he would not let it out of his sight, relaxing only when he knew it was safely put away in a cupboard. Oh, and he'd also be relaxed when it was out and chatting to him with those strange smoke signals that "bongs" do, but we won't go into that.

So, heading out of Narrabri, I now had to carefully watch my speed around corners as the back wheels had acquired a tendency to rub against the wheel arches. Thankfully the outback does not have many corners on its roads. Hurtling along, we looked a bit like the "Anthill Mob" from the cartoon The Wacky Races, and I think if the little engine could have spoken, it would have asked us on frequent occasions to stick our legs out and run to help it along.

Again, because the roads were flat and straight, I didn't need to use the lower gears so much, which meant Steve didn't have to lift part of his body so much, where each time he did it looked like he was about to fart.

Heading towards Gunnedah, the flatlands began to disappear and the landscape began to become more undulating, meaning more and more gear changes. With Steve shifting up and down each time I changed gear, he looked like he was doing an exercise from a "Jane Fonda" workout routine.

We found some accommodation at a caravan park and then decided to work the quite largish town for two nights before moving onto the next town of Coonabarabran. During the evening we experienced some rain, and to the north we could see a fantastic electrical storm taking place, but we were too far away to hear thunder. From Moree down, they had not experienced the wet stuff for the last six months and obviously it was a welcome arrival!

The next morning, I awoke at seven to hear the clanking of metal hitting concrete at intermittent times. Looking out the window, I could see Steve "The Kraken" Boulder, working out with his weights. Watching him lifting, squatting and throwing them around as if they were tiny fishing weights, I noticed that through parts of his vest several dubious scars could be seen on his exposed body. My inquisitive mind started to whirr, and I thought I'd have to ask this mighty fellow where he had got them from.

Doing a quick shop at the local supermarket, I bought eggs, snags, bacon, bread and tomatoes for the team to have a good breakfast, though it would be lunch for Van Winkle. With it hitting nine o'clock and with Shane still asleep as well, I told Steve to cook himself some breakfast as I wasn't hungry. (In fact I have never been much of a breakfast man.) Leaving him to it, I walked the short walk back into the little town to do some reconnaissance and to pick up another postcard to send home.

I had recently spoken to the family but apart from, "Thanks for the T-shirt, and have you got any sharks' teeth yet?" there was nothing eventful to report.

The town of Gunnedah is a coal mining town, and again was steeped in its short Australian history. I could tell you more about it, but won't! In fact, if I told you just a little history of the towns, hamlets, cities and all the little places that lots of people don't even know exist, that I had up until now and over the next two and a half years visited, this book would be the size of an encyclopedia itself. So, you will just have to find out the stuff yourselves, although I will let you know some points of interest at certain places if I can remember!

Returning to the caravan at around ten, I found Steve washing his plate up and Shane just getting out of the shower. As I was reading the newspaper, I heard Shane ask if I had been shopping.

"Yes!" I replied. "There's a mountain of snags and bacon and eggs in the fridge."

Shane opened the fridge and took out some plastic bags that I had put in earlier that contained the meat.

"There's not much here," he sounded gloomily.

Looking up, I replied, "There should be?"

Holding the plastic in his hand as if it were a set of weighing scales, he opened up the wrapper inside the bag.

"Just two sausages and two strips of bacon here, Lance."

As I got up from the table and walked over to him, Shane rummaged around inside of what was nearly an empty fridge, to see if he had missed anything.
"And no eggs either?" he said, sounding surprised.

Completely perplexed, I called out to Steve who had gone back outside and was dismantling his weights to put back into his bag.

"What did you have to eat this morning, Steve?"

With his bold Canadian accent, he read out his breakfast list, "Four sausages, some bacon, six slices of bread, the tomatoes and six eggs!"

I looked over to my hippy colleague, and as he looked back at me, the Canadian's voice boomed again.

"Do you want me to go and get some more food?"

I looked at the tiny food cooling device in the caravan and thought of that line in the film Jaws, where the character Martin Brody turns to the skipper of the boat, Quint, and says, "You're going to need a bigger boat!" In our case, it was a bigger fridge.

I had not yet asked Steve for his weekly thirty dollar food allowance, but knowing he would have already been told that, I wondered how I would address the issue? Fortunately, he had realised that his food intake was much greater than ours, and presenting me with a hundred-dollar bill, asked if that would be suffice for his weekly allowance.

Ready-cooked chooks (Aussie slang for chicken) and chips were on the menu that evening from the milk bar. Steve's chook, though, was in the plural.

The next morning he was at it again with the weights, and as I returned to the caravan with a string of sausages that would have stretched back to the local library a few blocks away, I decided I had to ask him about his scars. It transpired that he used to be a doorman at a very rough nightclub in a large city in Canada and the wounds consisted of four stab wounds and a bullet wound. I left the conversation at that!

Gunnedah was kind to us, as over the two days we all wrote orders, though my two were to be cancelled before the ten-day cooling-off period. This could be a right kick in the teeth at times, as you initially assumed when leaving the happy family's home that had signed up for the books that everything would be "hunky dory". Remember! Assumption is the mother of all evils!

Also, the two cancellations were converted appointments that Steve had made for me. And the poor fella didn't have much beginner's luck, as other appointments in towns later on that I tried to convert into sales were to fall on stony ground, with people not prepared to commit to purchasing the product.

One of the reasons that the ten-day cooling-off period existed was to allow the purchaser/s to think things through after the salesperson had left the home and after the hype had died down. Remember! A good salesperson will lift the atmosphere and generate a feeling of well-being in the household, and amid the euphoria the family may momentarily forget about the realities of whether they can afford it or not and make the purchase regardless.

Another reason it existed was to combat against the salesperson that had adopted the "hard sell" tactic and coerced a family to buy the product that they did not necessarily want or need. Although I never once adopted that stance, nor tolerated any of my sales teams doing it, there were many people that would do, and hence some other teams had copious cancellations. A succession of cancellations, which could be as many as five or six in a row, could finish a salesperson mentally, and if starting out as a new recruit, financially as well! Hence the pushy salesperson did not last very long.

You may wonder how it can affect someone mentally. Well, after so many cancellations, or let's call them rejections, a person can start to question their ability and whether they can "sell" or not. It's a bit like dating for the first time where you pluck up the courage to ask the one you are attracted to, to go and see a film with you or go for a bite to eat. The first time you get rejected is usually hurtful enough. But more than once! Their self-esteem and self-belief begins to be eroded until they lose all the will and determination to carry on with the job. It could be just sheer bad luck that they are experiencing, but it plays heavily on their minds and before long you have someone "throwing in the towel".

Once the recession really started biting, I had, on a few occasions, four cancellations on the trot. Then, not only do you have to stay positive yourself, but you also have to lift the morale, in some shape or form, with the people in your sales force who are getting their heads kicked in mentally as well. As I say it takes a very resilient person indeed to stay in this game.

Setting off the next day, we headed for the small town of Coonabarabran, which is a must for any astronomers. "Coona", as it's affectionately known, is the closest town to the Siding Spring Observatory, which has the largest optical telescope in Australia. It peers out into space with its brothers in this region – which is quite mountainous – looking for comets, meteors, aliens, space dust and all sorts of intergalactic stuff. It's definitely worth a visit, even if you're just slightly interested in space.

Anyway, arriving in town I must have caught the two middle-aged ladies at the tourist information centre on a bad day. Asking them what there was to do in the town and area, they replied, "Nothing!"

I was astonished. "Nothing?" Knowing full well I was in the right place to find out what there was to do.

One turned to the other and said, "What's to do in Coona?"

With a big beaming smile her fellow informant replied, "Nothing!" This was quickly followed by, "You better drive on to the next town."

Leaving the building with a little street map, we booked into some accommodation and after lunch started working the town. By seven, Steve, Shane, Van Winkle and I had knocked the whole town, and with no further appointments and just one order, decided to call it a day. Heading back to base and feeling a bit cheesed off, I offered to "shout" some beers in one of the pubs. Van Winkle and Shane were up for it, but Steve declined the offer as he wanted to carry on reading his book on sales techniques. Dropping our kits off, the three of us headed to the pub, leaving the giant behind.

On entering, we found a few people around the bar and a gang of lads in their late teens playing pool. Van Winkle loved playing pool, and leaving myself and Shane at the bar, sauntered over to the table to see if he could get a game. Winkle quickly found out that at the pool table, it was winner stays on. So putting his coins on the table, he was soon facing the current champion. As he set the balls up, the winner enquired whether he would like to place a wager on who would win. Agreeing on twenty dollars, Van Winkle broke up the little pack of coloured balls.

Now, at the time I considered myself a more than average pool player, but Van Winkle was in a different league. In next to no time he had cleaned up and had lightened the lad of his twenty bucks. A quick shake of hands and the next combatant came up to face the pool shark. Agreeing on another twenty bucks, he was very quickly stuffing another similar amount of coinage into his pocket.

With the previous competitor returning to the table and agreeing once again on a score of Aussie dollars to win the frame, Van Winkle very quickly won a third consecutive frame. He came over with his winnings and bought the three of us a drink before returning to the table. At this point, we decided to join the master and watch his skill at moving the balls around the baize to where he wanted them to be, before sinking them in the pots. The fourth frame involving the two consisted of a double or quits frame, where if Winkle won the frame, then his opponent would then owe him forty dollars. Ten minutes later, it was a double or quits for eighty bucks. Everything was going well for our bookselling colleague, except his challenger was getting more irate and aggressive because of the frustration of not being able to beat the guy that never saw morning. Sensing this tension, I suggested to Van Winkle that maybe he lose a frame deliberately. Standing to lose eighty big ones, he understandably refused. Minutes later he had once again destroyed his enemy.

Asking for the eighty bucks, the quite well-built player asked our colleague if he would go one more round of double or quits, to which Winkle reluctantly agreed. Eighty dollars was a lot to lose if "Van" lost that frame, and he knew there was quite a possibility of that happening in the world of pool, and he would have to start from scratch again. The frame started and both Shane and I were getting acutely aware of how the teenager's body language had changed. Van Winkle had to lose, or else.

Oblivious of what the outcome may bring, Winkle brought the game to just the black ball for him to pot, while four other balls belonging to his would be assailant remained on the table. Suddenly his opponent snapped, and smashing the pool cue against the side of the table, almost breaking it, he accused Van Winkle of cheating.

With a sudden "stand-off", Van Winkle Junior quite rightly protested his innocence and said he had been playing fair and square. This only infuriated the challenger and with of volley of words that threatened violence, I realised that not only was Van Winkle much smaller than his fellow player, but we were also outnumbered by just over two to one. With the now menacing pool player not only making these accusations but also demanding his initial twenty bucks back that he lost in the first frame, things were not looking that good. With his six friends suddenly all getting up, in what I could see was about to be a one-sided gladiator battle, all three of us simultaneously thought of running towards the pub door.

Turning towards the door, I saw it being flung open and a colossus of a man walked into the bar. It was "The Kraken"! Time stood still and then slowly unfolded like a Quentin Tarantino film, with each frame of the film showing the giant beast slowly entering the bar. As he spoke, his dialogue was slowed down to match the pace of the film that was now running in slow motion. His mouth opened and the slow, drunken-sounding voice penetrated my eardrums.

"What are you drinking, boys?"

My head slowly turned back to my drinking buddies, and I could see the mob that was about to launch itself at us abruptly stop in its tracks. With "real time" quickly restored and everything running at normal speed, I turned once again and said to Steve "our very best friend" Boulder, "Three bottles of VB please, mate!"

Turning back to look at the insurgents, I realised that although we were still outnumbered, I figured Steve could take at least four of them on, and hopefully the biggest four at that. For a brief moment, everything came to a standstill while everyone weighed everything up. With Steve completely oblivious as to what was about to happen, he had gone to the bar to order the drinks.

106

With our enemy suddenly realising that this aircraft carrier of a man was on our side, they very quickly had to come up with a "Plan B". Fortunately, this was a very sensible plan that involved leaving the pub through another exit.

As Steve came over clutching the four stubbies that looked like thimbles in his hands, we all made a toast to the greatest country in the world – Canada!

The next day we headed south again to Dubbo, the large town I had picked Steve up from initially. With me not wanting to work such a large town personally, I left the two lads to work the town themselves, and with Steve, we headed off for a nearby much smaller town called Narromine. Working the town together, we took it in turns of doing the "You must be the man of the house?"

At nine o'clock and with only having done one demonstration and no orders, I decided to knock it on the head. Walking back towards the car, Steve noticed a light on at a house that had previously been extinguished.

"Let's knock that one, Lance!" he said keenly.

Walking up the path and knocking the door, it was opened by a quite well-built bearded chap. Entering his house, and offering us a welcome beer, he very quickly realised that his "Sheila" (wife in Australian slang), had gone out without him realising. With the beers already cracked open, we decided to have a little natter before making the drive back to Dubbo. With our men talk getting well under way, our host asked us what our hobbies were. With Steve replying "Weightlifting", and myself "Weightlifting" as well, albeit while fixing the weight onto a fishing line, we in turn asked what his interests were.

"Guns!" he replied.

Steve's eyes raised a little as he repeated the word "Guns!"

"Yeah!" the guy said, suddenly giving us a crazy sort of look on his face, "and I've got a shitload as well!"

With the smile turning to a devilish sort of grin, his voice lowered as he said, "Do you wanna see them?"

Before I could reply, Steve had blurted out a "Yeah sure!"

Taking us to the back of the house, he asked us to sit down in a small living room. Returning very quickly, he held a cluster of guns in his arms that could have equipped those lot in that western, *The Wild Bunch.*

Putting the weapons on the table, he began to explain what each one was called and what each was capable of doing. Frankly, you didn't need to be a rocket scientist to work out that each and every object on that table could kill something!

Rifles, hunting rifles, shotguns, pump-action shotguns, revolvers, more rifles, more shotguns; he kept on retrieving more from his personal arsenal at the back of his house, until he had an assortment of seventeen variations of killing machines. Picking up a very shiny silver revolver, he explained that it was a .44 Magnum, and aiming it at Steve's very large torso, he activated a red laser beam onto his body. With the little beam dancing all over "The Kraken's" body, Steve enquired whether the pistol was loaded.

Momentarily turning the piece onto its side and studying it, he replied, "I'm not sure."

It was time to leave.

The next morning it wasn't the clunking of dumbbells that woke me, but the little pager bleeping away with a message from one of the big bosses on its little screen. The message read: "Work in Dubbo one more day and tomorrow I will meet you in Raymond Terrace."

Straight enough, I thought. Apparently not!

At the end of each evening, I also had to use the pager to send the results of the day, to notify my superiors how many orders we had written on that particular day. It had been a bad day, with all of us "blanking". Sitting in the chalet I had booked at the caravan park, I sent the dismal message of "Nil orders", and then proceeded to scan the street map of Dubbo to find Raymond Terrace. With Van Winkle and Steve cooking dinner, Shane and I, together with "the bong" attempted to find the street. With all four of us eventually poring over the map, looking through the puffs of smoke coming from the glass object and Shane's mouth, we all drew a blank as to where it was. Giving up, we drank a few more beers through the whirling wisps of some weed that was going up in smoke, and strangely, we all slept incredibly well that night!

The next morning everyone had a lie-in, and although only Shane had been actively speaking to "Mister Bong", we had obviously gathered up some of his gossip during the evening. With Steve commenting that he had not missed an early morning weight-training session for many sunrises, and telling us he felt that there was a giant cloud floating in his head, I grabbed the street map to try and find Raymond Terrace again. I was at a loss, and at eleven o'clock decided to call the boss.

On him answering, I asked where he was.

"Raymond Terrace," came his reply. Explaining that I couldn't find it, he replied very vehemently, "How the fuck can't you find a fucking town?"

I stopped and thought about what he had just said – town?

Before I could answer, he came back asking, "Where are you?"

Still a little confused, I replied, "In Dubbo!"

There was a pause and then a tirade of words were hurled down the phone line along the lines of, "You stupid bastard, that's nearly four hundred kilometres away. Why didn't you drive here this morning, like I told you to?"

It suddenly dawned on me why we couldn't find Raymond Terrace on the street map of Dubbo. They didn't have one!

So, admitting my mistake, the voice on the other side of the line calmed down. It was too late for us to leave as we would lose a day's work in the field, so it was decided that we stay in Dubbo for another three days so our mail could be forwarded from the head office in Sydney.

Raymond Terrace was indeed a town just north of the large city of Newcastle, and after three days in Dubbo I wished I had gone there. Over those three days, not one of us wrote an order, and the appointments Steve had got me, though very good ones, I failed to convert into sales. The recession was beginning to bite deep, and although we had people interested, that seventy dollars a month was just a little too much. Steve was on the verge of quitting and the other two had become somewhat disheartened with the job. I needed a plan.

Picking our mail up from the post office, my mother had sent a couple of editions of our local newspaper that had gripping headlines like "Burst Water Main" and "Garden Gnome Stolen". (They couldn't have me on that one, I thought, as I was on the other side of the world gnome-napping one of his antipodean cousins in Sydney.) Along with those exciting titbits came a letter, and a sticker of a Corgi dog to stick in the car window.

Calling the boss, I asked him if there were any towns not far from Dubbo that had not been worked recently. "Try Mudgee," came the reply. The town was literally in spitting distance in Australian terms and was just over a mere one hundred kilometres away. The logic of trying to find a place that had not been worked in recently was that people's circumstances constantly change, especially financially. So, someone knocking on someone's door twelve months or even two years ago might have found a family that wanted to buy the encyclopedias but at the time could not afford it, but were now in the position to purchase them. The books we sold were not available in the shops and this was in the days before the internet and armchair shopping.

Travelling to Mudgee, I promised Steve I would now begin to train him to do the demonstration. This lifted his morale, but I desperately needed orders from all of us to get us more upbeat again. Mudgee, and the region it's in, is renowned for its fine wines. In fact the area is peppered in wineries, which meant that if it all went horribly wrong on the sales side, I could sell the car (which obviously wasn't mine) and we could all guzzle down a river of red, or white, of the stuff, before I skedaddled to Sydney and flew back home to Welsh green pastures! What a plan, hey?

Arriving in Mudgee and booking into yet another caravan site, we all went into a four-pronged attack on the town. Steve had made three appointments within two hours, and from them I managed to convert one into a sale, where the family paid for the books in full by writing a cheque for two thousand, one hundred and fifty dollars, which meant practically a guaranteed commission.

On meeting up with the lads at ten, I found that Van Winkle had written an order and Shane had two. We were back on track again! Sensing it was now time to tell Steve of the two cancellations that had occurred in Gunnedah, and hoping that the cash deal I had just done from his appointment would cancel out that negative message, I was not surprised to hear the big fella announce he wanted to quit. He'd had enough! Then again who wouldn't? If you'd had a .44 Magnum pointed at you in someone's house, you'd want to leave, wouldn't you?

I called the Melbourne office and informed them of Steve's decision. I was to drive him back to Dubbo to put him back on a bus to Melbourne and wait for another bus to arrive from Sydney with another new recruit, this time a girl. I momentarily thought that, surely, there was no girl the size of "The Kraken"? How right I was!

Shaking the big man's hand, he climbed aboard, and sitting in the back of the bus, prepared himself for the journey back. I then had to wait a couple of hours for the bus that was bringing Laura who would join "The Bong Team". I had been given a good description of her and what she was wearing, so when she stepped off the bus, I greeted a young, red-haired, very pale-skinned, slight, pretty female. Loading her fairly light bag into the boot, I guessed the little Datsun was glad to get rid of Steve's big bag of weights. With her dressed in a bright yellow sweatshirt and a small little black skirt, I noticed I could now change gear quite easily, as her fairly long legs were quite a way from the gearstick, which was a shame.

I got back to Mudgee and introduced her to the lads, then we loaded their kit aboard and headed off to the next town of Bathurst. We now had a bit more room, where three of our bags and the sales materials fitted in the boot, and with Shane and Laura in the back, her quite handy luggage was squeezed between them.

The road that took us there was the roughest I had experienced since being in Oz. Leaving the sealed tarmac road, we were now on a very rough, unsealed route, with rocks the size of footballs, which every now and then I hit due to the sheer numbers of them.

Climbing ever higher along the side of a mountain, I thought, one mistake and we're goners! Reaching a plateau, I thought we had made it, but then disaster struck! Puncture? Engine breakdown? Brake failure? No, it was much worse than that.

Shane let out a scream and cried out "Oh my God!"

As he was behind the front passenger seat, I turned to look around and nearly drove off the road and off the mountain as well.

I stopped the vehicle, turned and said, "What the hell's wrong?"

Shane looked at me as if he was going to cry.

"I've left the bong behind!"

Sixty kilometres and halfway there, he now wanted me to turn around on this hellish track and go back and get his little glass pipe. I was having none of it.

"But you don't understand, man. Me and the bong go way back. Please turn around," he pleaded.

I thought for a moment. "I'll buy you another one, Shane."

There was a quick pause while he thought this offer through. "No, man, that bong is special to me. Let me out here, I'll hitch back and then hitch to Bathurst and meet you there later."

Just over an hour later and we were back in Mudgee rescuing his beloved friend.

Bathurst is a city and the oldest inland settlement in Australia. It was where some explorers from Sydney said, "Hey let's go and start exploring this great country!" and this is where they first stopped. It is, among other things, home to the Bathurst 1000, where motor racing fanatics descend on the city and the Mount Panorama circuit to see V8 supercars hurtle around the track to win the thousand kilometre touring car trophy each October.

With us camped here for two nights, I dropped the boys off at two separate areas of the city and took Laura out into the field for her initiation into the book business. Taking it in turns to do the door-knocking spiel, I found she was incredibly confident, and getting into houses, I was aware how at ease she was to be in some strange family's home, often taking the lead with the small talk. Her home was in Perth, which is the capital city of Western Australia, and I thought at the time that her description of the city, and the attributes it had, made it sound as if she was selling Perth itself. In fact, if it had been for sale, and had I had billions and billions of dollars in my bank account, I would have probably bought the whole city. This was a potentially good salesperson in the making.

After writing an order in the third household we had got into, we stepped out into a chilly evening. With the summer proper descending on New South Wales, it should have been very warm, but Bathurst is over six hundred metres above sea level and the mountains around it receive snow on them in the winter. Yes, snow!

113

So, with us still in our summer togs of sweatshirts, shorts and skirt, we headed back to the car and picked up Shane and Van Winkle, who had written another two orders. The next night all three of us blanked, and this is generally what the sales pattern was all about, with its up and downs, as we inched our way down the map of the fourth largest state of Australia. It had dawned on me quite quickly that the "three appointments a night equalled to one sale" theoretically was correct as a typical conversion rate. In practice, it was a different story, and on some nights, though rare, you would be unable to carry out a single demonstration.

One demonstration a night was not that rare, mind, but the more doors you knocked on, the more chance you had of finding a sale. It was a pure numbers game which generally it is in sales. Many would give up after four or five hours of rejection, but instead of sitting in a milk bar waiting for the pick-up time to arrive, I would still be out there in all weathers bashing away. I honestly couldn't tell you how many homes I got into between quarter to ten and ten o'clock, but that persistence usually paid off, as someone letting you into their home at that time would genuinely be interested to see what you had to offer and would usually end up buying the books.

With instructions to head towards Sydney, we stopped on our way in towns like Lithgow and Katoomba, which are in the incredibly beautiful scenic Blue Mountains. Only just over an hour's drive from Sydney, it's definitely worth a day trip if you are visiting Oz and just stopping in New South Wales' largest city. It boasts the world's steepest railway and the Three Sisters rock formation with its stunning backdrop that just begs every camera in the world which arrives there to take a photo of it. The local Aboriginal legend attached to it is interesting as well, so pop up to this geographical feature to have a look!

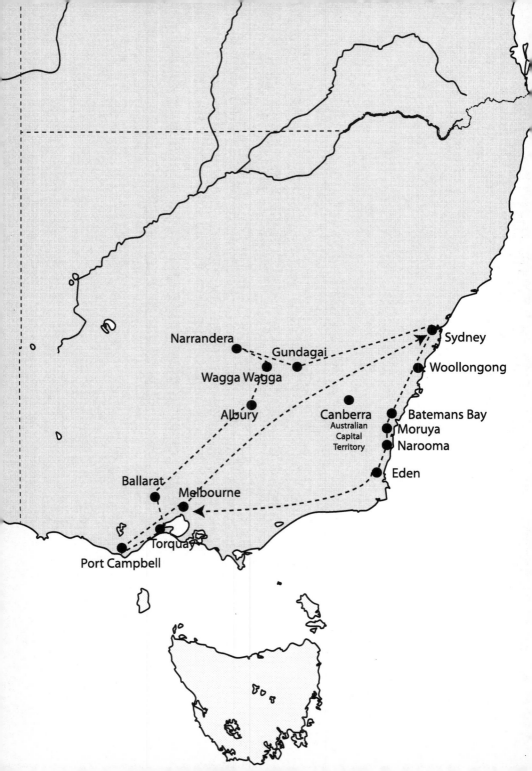

Chapter 6

Well, there are no fictitious names in this next little part of my story, because I am mentioning no names at all. Reaching the suburb of Windsor, I received an invitation to a party on my little pager. It was to be that evening in central Sydney at an apartment owned by an employee of the parent publishing company, Crowell International. I had met this successful middle-aged lady, who had excelled in sales throughout Australia, in Brisbane, and she loved throwing a party now and then at her home. The boss had informed her that I was in the city and hence I received the invite. The venue will remain anonymous for the simple reason that, after the party, I still to this day cannot remember the exact location!

In fact, after getting into the swing of things at this social gathering, I could have been anywhere in the world. Leaving my team in the outskirts of Sydney with a night off work, and warning on pain of death that if either Shane or Van Winkle shagged Laura while I was away on my sojourn to the big smoke that they would be sacked, I headed off to this little party. Stopping briefly in the suburb of Parramatta to return the gnome I had gnome-napped, I quietly put him back into the garden home he had left months ago, with a little note on his hat saying, "I'm back!"

Parking the little Datsun in a side street in the city, I located this quite large apartment and found a host of very smartly dressed people at many different levels of inebriation. Dressed like a tramp compared to the other guests, and finding my host, she offered me a glass of champagne and introduced me to a number of people, some of whom worked in the publishing business and others who worked in a range of other professions. As I chatted to my new friends, it became evident that all of them had well-paid jobs, and you could smell the money in the air as the champagne flowed. With my host explaining to these people that I was possibly going to be sponsored by the company to stay on in the country for an extra two years, and meeting someone who had originally been sponsored from England who had just applied for permanent residency, I skulled champagne, beer, vodka, and numerous other tipples. My host showed me the bedroom I was to sleep in that night, and she then led me into the kitchen where I could see a young man and woman snorting a line of white powder each.

"Do you want some coke, Lance?" my host enquired.

Realising she was not on about the liquid stuff that you mixed with vodka, and having had a lot of that already, I thought, what the hell! I took a line of it, and that's all I remember of the party. The next thing I knew I was waking up in bed in the chalet on the caravan park in Windsor the next evening.

Apparently I had returned to my troops mid-morning after driving back, and in a state of euphoria suggested everyone go knocking doors that afternoon – naked! Now not even "Mister Bong" would suggest that, Shane later told me. When the team returned to the chalet after going to the field without me, they all had a good laugh at the state I was in when I had arrived back, with Laura commenting that my eyes had been larger than saucers. Not a good example to set, and I never touched the stuff again.

The next part of the plan was to slowly make our way back down to Melbourne, and it was suggested to me to take the coastal route. I had, however, formed a mental bond with the outback and decided to go back inland.

On frequent occasions, I would bring a team in from the interior dressed in rags, and they'd meet smartly dressed teams that would ignore us or comment at how shabbily dressed we were, with me usually wearing a dusty T-shirt and cut-off jeans and sandals. On one particular day, a sales manager said to me, "How the fuck do you sell books dressed like that?" Before I could reply, one of the directors of the company, who was present at the time, replied, "They sell more books in a week, than you lot do in a month!"

Presentation is everything, but charisma, charm, a nice personality, and a good sense of humour can be powerful attributes in the world of sales. That is my philosophy anyway. Besides, the outback was much more accommodating with regards to what you could wear, and providing you were courteous and pleasant with that laid-back attitude that was prevalent inland, you couldn't fail to get into people's homes.

The next morning we set off very early, as I wanted to get as far inland as possible and work some of the towns that had not been worked for a while. Setting off just after six, I drove four hundred kilometres until we reached the little town of Gundagai, which is just north of Canberra. Summer was now on our doorstep, and afternoon temperatures hovered in the mid-thirties.

Gundagai made its money from gold mining and the original town was built in a flood-prone area, against the advice of local Aboriginal people in 1838. In 1852, the inevitable happened and the great Murrumbidgee River decided to pay a visit to the town taking the lives of eighty-three of what was then a two hundred and fifty population. There is a lot to be said for listening to people who know what they are talking about, whether young or old. When I visited the little town of Menindee in the far north-west of New South Wales just over a year later, I was surprised to see their brand new school three feet under water. The authorities had decided to build it in a dip in the land where the older folk of the town had remembered flooding decades ago.

Against their advice they built it, and three years later here came the water again, looking to have a good long rest in its favourite dip. Although there was no loss of life this time, the school was crumbling into the water in blazing semi-desert temperatures from the condensation build-up inside the building. History certainly repeats itself!

Just outside Gundagai is the little statue of the "Dog on the Tucker Box" (Aussie slang for lunchbox). It's a memorial to all the pioneers that entered into this harsh land to discover what this great country was hiding in its interior, driving cattle and doing all sorts of other tough, bushland stuff. The statue is about a mythical dog that guarded his master's grub and comes from a poem of that very same name.

Moving onto the slightly larger town of Narrandera the next day, the land became very green and trees were a common feature, unlike in the northern part of the state. The roads were still those long ones that stretched to the horizon, but instead of parched grasslands, we now had orange trees and grape vines among other crops by the side of the road as we hurtled along. Oh, and our friends "the flies" had returned en masse!

We set up camp, and over the next few days the boys stayed in and around the town, while Laura and I went off to the town of Leeton and a little place called Whitton, which only had a population of fifty at the time. The girl had a knack of getting good appointments quickly and this was followed by orders for books.

The four of us had a scream at this inland town, and Laura was occasionally persuaded to chat to "Mister Bong" in the evenings. Although Van Winkle and I didn't speak to his glass brother directly, we might as well have, as from the gossip he was emitting and thus us breathing it in while swigging beers, we were all in a more than merry mood.

Having fun and lots of laughter generates a good feeling in any sales team, and it usually makes that team more productive. As a result, we very quickly gathered together a little pile of orders to send back to Sydney in the postal courier bag for processing.

The last night in the town we all got steaming drunk, and back at the accommodation, Van Winkle and Shane decided to retire to get some sleep while me and my appointment maker sat chatting and finishing off our beers.

Suddenly putting her hand on mine, she suggested that now the other two had gone to sleep we could both head to the double bedroom where I was sleeping and that she would return to her bedroom before they both woke. Alarm bells started ringing and two little imaginary characters appeared on each of my shoulders, where the proverbial angel and devil conflict began. The little devil was jumping up and down screaming at me, "Now's your chance!" while the angel calmly gave me a lesson on the warnings I had given my two trusty booksellers and the consequences it would bring if I proceeded with her offer. The devil was having none of it though as he screamed, "You're the boss, they can't fire you! Go and shag Laura!"

I thought for a split second and remembered that the golden rule was no relationships within the company as things could get really messy – as I would find out later on in my bookselling career. I smiled at her and thought momentarily, with the devil leaping up and down and screaming, "For crying out loud, they are both asleep!" Removing her hand from mine, I politely declined, explaining that it wouldn't work, and making my excuses I went to bed on my own, quietly kicking myself for being so disciplined. Lying alone in my bed, I watched as the devil hopped over onto my other shoulder and began twelve rounds with the angel.

The next day, as if nothing had happened, we steered our little troop carrier southwards in the direction of Melbourne. Obviously, being a city, I was reluctant to go straight there, although the summer of '92 turned out to be an amazing time in Melbourne, where I got to know the place like the back of my hand and met characters galore!

Calling the office, I asked if I could stay away from the metropolis for a little longer. As we had reached more than our target of orders, this was granted, though I had to be back in the city by early December to start training new appointment makers into sales representatives and to execute our plan of attack on the city.

Getting out a map of the state of Victoria, I asked the team for any preferences. All three of them had the inclination of going places on the "Great Ocean Road", whose existence at that time I was unaware of. This road, they told me, apparently had some of the finest coastline on the continent. And they were not wrong! Heading down and taking in overnight stays in the towns of Wagga Wagga and Albury, and then a fairly long trip over the Victorian border down to the city of Ballarat, we arrived four days later at Torquay and the start of this great road.

The scenery from this road is indeed truly breathtaking. Giant sandstone cliffs with a coastline that features the stacks of "The Twelve Apostles" and what was then the iconic "London Bridge" make this drive a truly memorable one.

Right. Three little stories now. Are you sitting comfortably?

Firstly, the two hundred and forty-three kilometre road that runs from Torquay to Warrnambool (try saying that after a few beers), was built from 1919 to 1932 by soldiers who had returned from World War One as a memorial to all their dead comrades. It is reputedly the largest war memorial in the world.

Secondly, this story has to be about one of the unluckiest couples in the world (depending on how you look at it, and the story is apparently correct according to local gossip). On the 15th January 1990, a couple had decided to park their vehicle near the main road, and walk over the two sandstone arches that stretched out to sea, seventy metres above the great Southern Ocean. This amazing geographical feature was then known as "London Bridge" as it looked like the one that used to lie above the River Thames in the eponymous city. It was sold to an American oil baron in 1968, and he had the entire structure shipped bit by bit to the States. Anyway, crossing the first arch and then the second, they looked out at the big blue that led right out to the horizon. Everything was going to plan, and they then decided to return to their mode of transport.

Crossing the first arch, they came to a surprising obstacle, notably the bridge crossing the next arch had suddenly absconded. In layman's terms, that meant about thirty metres of rock had crashed into the sea after Mother Nature had instructed it to do so. So now we had two people trapped tens of metres up on a rocky outcrop unable to reach the mainland. What happened next was probably the most unusual cliff-top rescue by a helicopter in, if not Australia, then maybe the world! Anyway, they got rescued and were brought to the mainland. In the meantime, not only had the local press got wind of this, but a major television channel as well. When they were eventually safely dropped on Terra Australis proper, they were met by a multitude of journalists wanting to get a story. It later transpired that they were both playing away, and again, in layman's terms this means they were having an affair. With all the television coverage, they must have cursed "London Bridge", which now, incidentally, is known as "The Arch".

And finally the third story, for which the family, even to this day, must be kicking themselves nearly as bad as I had, when I left Laura to retreat to my bedroom alone. "The Twelve Apostles" are an amazing stack of rocks that over the years were probably joined by bridges from the mainland like "London Bridge", and when each bridge fell, a "stack" was left in the ocean. On the 4th July 2005, a family on holiday from Sydney were taking photos using the backdrop of the stacks behind them. They momentarily stopped the camera, and it was then that one of the giant foremost stacks decided to fall and crumble in front of their very eyes, after thousands of year's erosion. If they had timed it right, they would have caught this million to one chance on film.

Incidentally, there have only ever been nine apostles, which are now obviously eight! (Just in case you get the question in a pub quiz.)

Anyway, arriving at Port Campbell, and before detouring and working the inland towns of Colac and Camperdown in-between this scenic drive, I realised that over the last few days we had written very few orders. We had been having fun and I had "taken my foot off the gas", starting later than usual in the afternoon, and letting the team finish earlier. Van Winkle was even allowed to sleep till midday, despite having not written an order for nearly a week. Meanwhile, the angel was constantly fighting off the devil. Now with Laura's ever persistence in the evenings, and now even the afternoons, after dropping the boys at their locations, she had en-listed another devil onto my shoulder. This meant the angel was outnumbered. It was only down to my stubbornness and the fact that the angel was indeed a very strong one, that I could keep this pretty thing at bay.

Incidentally, the main reason for making these detours was because the coastal habitations had many holiday homes, which meant the towns were half-empty residentially. Reaching this touristy town, I realised that we had all made very little over the last few days. In fact, our performance had been so dismal I might as well have put "Mister Bong" in charge, with his army of weed. So, returning to Melbourne, we booked into a little caravan park in the suburb of Footscray. As we settled in, unpacking our stuff, the little pager sounded instructing me to call the Melbourne office.

By early evening, I was boarding a bus and heading back to Sydney once again to pick up yet another car with two sales reps and two newly trained appointment makers, leaving Laura, Van Winkle and Shane behind. It was the last time I would see Shane because he soon decided to leave the company along with his odd glass "friend".

On reaching "The Palms", I was introduced to my new team by an Irishman a little younger than me called Terry. This pale-skinned chap with a mop of red hair had been working for the company about six months longer than me, and had been recruited in Laura's home city of Perth, in Western Australia, commonly known as WA. It was this Irishman I was eventually to travel with to some of the most inhospitable, remote and quite occasionally dangerous places on the continent. We would experience the Aboriginal life that no outsider could and probably ever would be able to experience, unless they actually ate, drank and socialised in their communities, as well as in their own family homes.

Leaving Terry behind with another team and this time travelling down the coast, we stopped at the city of Wollongong, and the towns of Batemans Bay, Moruya, Narooma, and Eden, before a fairly big drive to Melbourne. The two weeks it took us to get there brought us up to the festive period. There is little point telling you the names of this team because by Christmas they had all quit, despite two of them doing quite well. Door-to-door sales certainly had more than its fair share of casualties.

Arriving in the city, I was instructed to pick up Laura from the recruitment office and take her to the caravan park in Footscray to pick up her stuff and drive her to the bus station. She had written ten orders in just over two weeks, which was quite some feat, but had now decided to return to Perth and her family. On reaching the caravan and glancing at my watch, I realised she had nearly three hours to get to the bus station, which was half an hour away. Suddenly, the little devil appeared on my shoulder, then another, then another, and then another, until both shoulders were covered in devils with not an angel in sight.

"Do I get a kiss goodbye, Laura?" I asked cheekily.

She stopped packing her stuff, and walking her slim, slender body towards me, she wiggled her forefinger at me.

"I thought you couldn't have encounters with your staff, Mr Russell?"

"Yes," I replied. "But you no longer work for the company and hence are no longer one of my staff!"

Nearly three hours later, with the devil and his pals winning a victory, we got to the station.

Christmas was looming, and it seemed strange walking through shopping malls with Christmas trees and decorations adorning the interior of the buildings, and then walking out into, not a snow-covered winter wonderland, but baking sun-bleached streets with a giant orange sun blazing and beating down on you.

I had moved to a large set of apartments on Beaconsfield Parade in the suburb of St Kilda just a few kilometres to the east of the city centre. This was to be my home on and off for nearly six months. In these apartments were an assortment of field managers, representatives and appointment makers who were from all over Australia, of which some of these going through the mincer wouldn't last more than a week. (The book business was certainly a mincer, as it minced more employees in such a short length of time than I could ever keep up remembering!)

Having said that, there were some very experienced battle-hardened salespeople among them. These included Mike, the young lad whose car gearstick had come away in my hand in Gin Gin back in Queensland a few months ago; Jack, the guy who would use the pizza delivery line to get past those electric gates; and Luke, who was the typical hat-wearing, sunglasses, surf shorts and shirt, wave-riding dude. Van Winkle had quit, but, quickly missing the nomadic existence we all lived, decided to return to the company only to be posted to another sales team in Canberra. It was to take him three months to get back with us because I had no openings in my team and no one wanted to leave or be transferred elsewhere. With the new recruits, we numbered around a dozen people spread out among these buildings.

Jack's career in the book business was all over the place. One minute he would be a sales manager and then he'd get busted back to a field manager for some misdemeanour like shagging some pretty little girl who had not been in his sales team for five minutes. Then he would be busted back to sales rep after perhaps spending his sales team's food kitty money for the week on the pokies (another Danny), or borrowing money from a new recruit and then denying he had done so, and then threatening the lender with violence if he asked for his money again. And he even got demoted to appointment maker level once, but I can't remember what he had done to get back to the bottom rung of the ladder. Each time I met him over the years, I would ask him what position in the company he was and each time it would be different from the last time. Mind you, this man, who was several years older than me, and a scallywag and a half, could definitely sell books.

Christmas came and went, and apart from the surreal feeling of walking on the beach at St Kilda in T-shirt and shorts on Christmas Day, saying "Merry Christmas" to a cosmopolitan array of people, it was pretty uneventful.

The call to home was brief, and apart from their questions of "What's the time there?", "What's the weather like?" and "Where's my sharks' teeth?", the news from back home was pretty much the same in the time capsule of Tenby.

January 1992 and it was time to train new sales teams. Still with no car, I had been given the use of a beast of a machine, namely a Holden Commodore which had under its bonnet a very powerful V8 engine. It belonged to one of the directors of the company and this car had been a special edition, with the engine tweaked to provide more power and hence was called the "Brock Commodore", after Peter Brock, the racing geezer who had won umpteen races at the Bathurst 1000 in New South Wales. The conventional dashboard of the normal Commodore had also been ripped out and replaced with a racing driver's surround. It would leave most other cars standing, and I was amazed how the fuel gauge would flicker back and forth, heading for the empty level in next to no time, and emptying my wallet in the process. I would have to sell lots of books to keep this monster on the road.

Getting established in the company and the directors realising that not only could I sell books but manage people as well, I was given the task of training and motivating the new recruits. As I said before, having fun generates good productivity in a sales team. So the first thing I did was change the door-knocking script. Well, not so much to change it, as it worked perfectly well in the field, but to create a bit of madness when we were rehearsing it in either the training office, or on the way to some suburb of the city in the car.

Now my newly recruited appointment makers would meet characters, and not just John or Mary. Two such door-openers they were faced with was the fictional boxer "Rocky Balboa" from the *Rocky* films and the dreaded "Terminator" from the film of the same name. The scripts went something like this.

SALESPERSON: (Knocks on the door)

ROCKY: (In his Italian stallion accent) Hey! How's it going?

SALESPERSON: Hi you must be the man of the house?

ROCKY: Yeah sure am!

Rocky would then make that iconic sound of "Huh huh, huh huh" as if he was pulling sit-ups or some other physical exercise, while weaving his head and shoulders about expecting to receive a punch from the salesperson. He was usually played by me, but once the recruits realised we had deviated from the script a little and had learned it, the roles could then be switched.

SALESPERSON: My name is … and you are?

ROCKY: Rocky. Rocky Balboa.

(Again, he would make the physical exercise noises, sometimes to the extent where the appointment maker could not get the next line out and would crack up laughing.)

SALESPERSON: Well, Rocky, maybe you can help me? You see I've been doing some work in your area for a company called Educational Systems of Australia and as you can see from my card this is an authorised call. But Rocky, it is really important that I speak to you and your other half. Is she in?
ROCKY: Uh, not sure. Hang on I'll find out.

Rocky then turns around and bellows out his wife's name.

ROCKY: Adrienne (A short pause). Adrienne (Another pause). I don't think she is in but my trainer is. (Bellows out again) Mickey. Mickey. Uh he's a little deaf I'll go and get him for you.

The "Terminator" script would be with my best Austrian accent, and when this killing machine enquired what it was all about and received the normal salesperson response, this in turn spurned the cyborg on, to ask whether there were any Uzi 9mms, or a Phased Plasma Rifle in the 40 watt range, in this educational programme. With the door-knocker still being stubborn and trying to gain entry in to "The Terminator's home", this programmable assassin would utter his memorable line of "Fuck you asshole!" With my head moving like a mechanical doll, I would then say that immortal line, "Hasta La Vista" and slam the door in their face.

Now at this stage of the book you are probably thinking that the writer is a complete and utter lunatic, and you would not be that far wrong. However, it was this craziness that made it fun, and although these comedic sketches were played out daily, it left the person who was going into the field to knock dozens or hundreds of doors in better spirits than if I had carried out the normal mundane but practical script that was normally used. It was not long before I soon had other salespeople asking if they could be transferred to my team, or teams, especially when we did little trips out into rural Victoria or into South Australia.

Actually, thinking about it, I needed to have a screw or two loose to work with some of these young people, who I am sure had left the childbirth assembly line before the finishing touches were applied, leaving the finer tuning of the brain behind. On one occasion, we were an hour into a trip from the city to a place called Traralgon, in rural Victoria. One of the newly recruited appointment makers, a young lad who had arrived from Egypt with his parents several years previously, suddenly announced that he had left his Egyptian food back in one of the apartments. Big deal I thought, he could eat something else.

This was not the case, however, as it was special food for his unique diet. Well this was no glass bong we had left behind, and with his moaning and groaning that he would starve to death, I was not going to turn around. Heading for the nearest railway station to ship him back to the city, my surf-dude colleague, Luke, questioned him on his favourite foods, going through every vegetable, meat dish, fish dish, fruit and every other foodstuff you could think of, but he just kept drawing a blank. We arrived at the station and the boy announced there was only one other food he would eat apart from Egyptian. We all sat in the car in silence, and I realised we were saved when he announced another special brand of food he ate ... McDonald's!

Back in St Kilda, I was slowly getting to know the city and had built a good core of people to work with. With my rep, Luke, I had four great trainee appointment makers, of which one each day would travel to the field with Mike and his team, as I could only accommodate five in the car. These were: a dashing young blond-haired Australian chap, James, who very quickly became a rep; a lovely guy called Trevor, who was from the island of Tonga, over four thousand kilometres away in the middle of the Pacific Ocean; Tracy from Melbourne; and Anna, an incredibly attractive young girl from Sydney, who had settled in Oz from Russia with her parents quite a few years ago. It was this girl who was to really break down my barriers and get to the heart of me.

News had arrived that the company, Crowell International, had decided to sponsor me to work for them for the next two years, and hastily filling in the application form for their solicitors to file to the immigration department,

I realised I probably wouldn't see my parents or brother for some time yet. Some people would have been glad to have had the one-year working visa, but not me. I still had a hell of a lot of country to see, and besides, I was having a ball.

Like all big cities, you have nice and not so nice areas. The suburb of Heidelberg was considered one of those not so nice, but I loved it. Within this suburb was the Olympic Village and it was here the company didn't let females work alone after dark. It was full of houses and blocks of flats that were built for the athletes when Melbourne hosted the Summer Olympics in 1956. By 1992, they had become very run down and were not a desirable place to live in at all. The majority of these homes were owned by the housing commission (a state-owned government body that provided affordable housing that people could purchase if they wanted), and hence there were quite a few of the unemployed living in them.

Despite that, it was good territory to sell books, as the logic behind the people who worked and bought the books was to enable their children to get the best possible education, get better-paid jobs than their parents and get them out of the suburb and onto better things.

One day, my sales manager informed me I was to take a representative of my choice out into the field and hide a tape recorder in my little rucksack containing the sales materials. One of us would do the demonstration, while the other secretly taped it, stopping and starting it if the presentation got sidetracked, as sometimes it did. The outcome was hopefully that it would end with a sale and the tape could then be used as a useful training tool in the future, enabling trainee representatives to listen to and hear how a sale was made out in the real world. My choice of rep was Luke, and the choice of location was the Olympic Village, though I would later regret my choice of the latter.

With "the village", you had to sometimes knock a lot of doors to find someone who didn't already have a set of books, and, more importantly, had a job and could afford them. This was, in turn, a gamble, as with so many unemployed in the area, we could draw a blank and finish without a sale.

With James having the car to take other reps and appointment makers to other parts of the city, he dropped us off earlier than usual as we wanted to maximise our time in the field to achieve our task. Bidding us good luck, and not hanging around before the car was up on bricks with the wheels gone, he drove off. Once we had written an order, we could grab a tram home. With Luke adjusting his shades in the mid-afternoon sun, we set about knocking doors. Within an hour, we had got into three homes with each of them containing unemployed people. Unperturbed, we soldiered on in this concrete jungle, walking past a burnt-out car and rubbish of all sorts discarded on the pavements and in the road. Knocking on a door of a house, we realised there was no one in, and then, heading back down the garden path, we saw a taxi pull up in front of us.

Climbing out of the back and walking towards us was a blond-haired, muscular, thickset man in his early thirties, carrying a slab of VB under his arm (a "slab" being a twenty-four carton of either bottles or cans). His other half emerged from the front passenger seat – a stocky woman with blonde raggedy hair, sporting several tattoos on her arms and again of a similar age.

"Hey Gareth!" she called out to him in a gruff voice while lighting up a cigarette. "Ask those boys if they are selling those fucking books!"

Turning back towards us, he asked if we were selling encyclopedias, and following a positive response announced he wanted to buy a set. Bingo! I thought, we're going to be able to tape an actual sale.

Walking back up the garden path, I introduced ourselves and found out that his wife's name was Sue. Quietly, I instructed Luke to turn the tape on, but on entering the house asked Luke to turn it off again, after Gareth asked where he had to sign to get his educational package.

Normally, we would have just signed them up, but we needed to get the sale recorded. So, making up some bullshit that although they had seen the demonstration before, they still had to see it again as it was company policy, Gareth handed us both a beer each. They were typical working class, and the conversation from them both contained more foul language than you could poke a stick at. To say these were a rough and ready pair was an understatement. Then again, all they wanted to do was to do the best for their children. The small talk was chopped down in size as they knew what we were selling, so after clarifying that he was employed and that they had two boys aged nine and eleven, and after informing us that they had not been in the financial position to buy the books the last time they had seen them, I decided to start the demonstration.

With Luke secretly pressing the record button on our hidden recording buddy, I began.

Within two minutes, I knew this recording was doomed when Gareth asked, "Do you want another beer, boys?"

Bearing in mind that drinking in people's homes was not encouraged and that new recruits would be listening to this masterpiece, we both replied, "No", with Luke adding, "We don't drink on the job", thinking that somehow people would miss the word "another" in the dialogue. This caused a little confusion from our prospective book buyers, especially as we both silently took a can from him. At the time we thought we were both being clever, though little did I know that later on you could hear the cans being opened on the recording.

"Do you wanna smoke, boys?" Sue enquired, holding a packet of cigarettes towards us.

Although, I was a non-smoker, Luke, who normally liked a puff or two, declined as well.

"What about some weed then?" Gareth piped up. "I got some really good shit here."

With Gareth unravelling a little leather pouch and producing some leaf of some kind, Luke's eyes lit up.

"I'm okay," I replied, and glancing across to Luke with my eyes wide open to telepathically remind him of the recording taking place, his response was thankfully similar.

Luke, being Luke though, was a clever surfer, and fumbling in the bag, located the pause button on the tape recorder and pressed it.

"Actually, I don't mind having a toke on it, if it's good shit!"

I looked alarmingly over to him following this response, not realising he had actually stopped the tape. His quick wink at me from under his Ray-Ban shades perched on his head immediately reassured me.

"I'll roll you one now, mate," the leaf distributor announced.

With the children too old for ELF, I had started the demonstration with the story books and a set of books called *The Science Library,* before introducing the encyclopedias.

As I reached for the prospectus, I was aware of a key being inserted into the front door of the living room. Looking over to Luke sitting on an armchair, he instinctively felt around in the bag to stop the tape once again. The door flew open, and in came two young lads in their school uniforms and school bags. They momentarily stopped to take in the scene that was in front of them. Looking at Luke puffing on a big reefer and me on one knee on the floor in front of their parents holding a big black book in my hands, the eldest of the lads spoke.

"What's going on here? Mum? Dad?"

The parents quickly took stock of the situation and the father replied, "Will you two get in and fuck off upstairs!?"

"Why? And who are these people?" persisted the eldest again.

"Why? Because we are trying to do something for your education, and it's got fucking nothing to do with you at all!"

"Can we watch?" the youngest asked with interest.

"No you fucking can't! Now fuck off upstairs like your father told you!" the mother snapped back.

With their children hurriedly climbing the stairs, I continued with the demonstration, which became a protracted affair with more offerings of cans, chatter, and more weed being rolled. Needless to say, Luke was starting to get stoned, and the tape recorder just carried on playing, picking up Gareth's voice when he asked Luke what he thought of the weed he was smoking, to which Luke's response of, "It's good shit," confirmed to the listener of the tape that he was smoking more than your average cigarette. Getting to the camouflage scene in the prospectus, I asked them if they could find where the rabbit was hiding.

As quick as a flash they both lunged towards the book, almost knocking me off balance, and like two big kids attempting to knock one another's hands away from where the creature was, argued with one another about who had found it first, the language again being peppered with expletives.

Opening another can, I asked them where the stick insect was. He was a right bastard to find and made the rabbit stand out like a sore thumb. After about a minute, they both gave up, with Gareth remarking that there was no fucking stick insect in the scene and that I was taking the piss. Pointing out that it was on a log in the foreground, both of them then launched into a tirade of expletives which included the "C" word.

Finishing the demonstration with the closing questions, I nodded to a semi-comatose Luke to switch the tape off. Mission completed, we signed them up and left the house.

Waiting at the tram stop, we played the tape back and literally cried with laughter. Handing the tape to the sales manager the next day, I explained to her that it may not be the sort of material she was after, to which her reply was, "As long as it ended with a sale, I'm not that bothered." As we sat in the office with her, I noticed her eyes widen and eyebrows rise, as she listened silently to the dialogue. With the tape finished, I asked her what her thoughts were. She used my surname. I knew she wasn't that happy.

"Well, Russell. When we play this in future to trainees, not only are they going to think that the people they are going to sell these books to have the vocabulary of a sewer. But also, they will think that while doing the demonstration, they can get fucking pissed and smoke as much pot as they want!"

I never got asked to do a special task again.

This next story is amazing, and even to this day I cannot believe the odds of finding this lady in all the millions of people in Melbourne and it was an absolute coincidence it happening at all!

As I explained earlier on in the book, door-to-door selling can become one of the most soul-destroying jobs in the world if you let it.

The mind must be focussed on where the next sale is coming from, and even if the last hundred, two hundred, even three hundred doors knocked has produced not even a remote bit of interest in what you are doing, you still have to push yourself to carry on and remain in as positive a mood as possible. You have to visualise that the next door you knock could have a family or young couple behind it looking to purchase a set of encyclopedias. Having said all this, even the best of us could become disheartened with the job, especially if over the past week you had knocked on a couple of thousand doors and had failed to make a single sale.

Occasionally, I would go out into the field with disillusioned sales reps that were on the verge of quitting, with the intention of making a sale to show them that they had only slightly gone off the path and were still capable of selling books. Half the problem was that they started the day with a negative attitude, because they constantly thought of the previous days that had delivered no results, and straight away this came out in their tone of voice. A monotone delivery of the opening script would put people off continuing the conversation with the salesperson, let alone letting them into their household.

I myself have a dark, wacky, wicked sense of humour, which you probably now realise, which I used in the field to stop myself going down the path of insanity. (Though some would say I went down that path a long time ago!) I would bring this sense of humour to these people's doors, and I only knew a handful of other people in the business that could do it as well. I often implemented this fun element when working in Melbourne, as it not only kept my spirits up but also brought a bit of cheer to these city dwellers who often led mundane lives.

Anyway, one day James decided he'd had enough and wanted to return to his hometown of Queanbeyan in New South Wales. He had made quite a bit of money, not only for himself but the company as well, and it was for this reason that they didn't want to lose him. So, taking him out into the suburbs of the city, we began knocking doors on a beautiful summer's day.

About an hour later, a door was opened by a lady who I would say was in her mid-sixties. Now, from experience, the elderly did not buy encyclopedias, and in fact I only ever sold one set to an elderly gentleman who decided to purchase a set for his great nephew's children. So on meeting the older generation, I would tell them outright what I was selling and move on quickly. However, on some occasions my humour would rise and I would announce that I was selling "Dead Sea Scrolls", or that I was doing a survey to find out whether people wanted Australia to stay in the Commonwealth or become a republic.

Basically, something stupid along those lines which had nothing to do with disclosing what I was really doing. With James telling this inquisitive sexagenarian what we were doing, I suddenly remembered watching the pop star Kylie Minogue on television the previous night in a pre-recorded concert, which, if my memory serves me well, was at Wembley Arena in London. She was scantily clad in some sexy lingerie, and I thought I would have a bit of fun by mentioning it to the occupant of the house who's door we were now standing in front of.

"She was wearing practically nothing and might has well have been naked," I said with a hint of feigned disgust.

"Well that wouldn't have bothered me," she replied in her weathered Australian accent.

"No?" I said, acting surprised

"Not really," she continued. "I've seen Kylie naked many a time!"

"How come?" James enquired.

She smiled at us and then the next sentence made us both look genuinely surprised, and then slightly perplexed. "When I used to wash her in the bath, when she was little." Her smile became the shape of an upside-down half-moon, and a little sparkle shone in her eyes as she delivered her knockout blow as she said, "I'm her grandmother!"

We both looked at one another, but James was the first to reply with a quick, "Yeah right!"

She could see we didn't believe her.

"Wait here a moment," she said. Walking back into her ordinary little house, she returned clutching two photographs.

Handing one to me and one to James, I could see I was holding a picture of the famous pop singer in her school uniform at the age of about twelve or thirteen.

"That's Kylie when she was in school," said an incredibly proud grandmother, pointing at the photograph I held.

Then, pointing at the photograph James was holding, she began naming the people in what was clearly a family portrait. Pointing out Kylie and herself, she also pointed out Kylie's parents and her younger sister, Dannii, who at the time was just making inroads to becoming an international celebrity, like her older sibling.

James, being a typical young Australian lad, then delivered a very straightforward question. "How come you live in a shitty old house like this when your granddaughter has got millions of dollars in the bank?"

Taking the photographs back from us, she once again gave us a little smile. "I don't ask anything from Kylie, as she has done well from working hard herself. Although …" she paused, and we held our breath in anticipation of what she was about to say next. Her smile widened once again, "… she always brings me a very nice present at Christmas."

Walking to the next house, we were both at a loss of what to say to one another. I was thinking what the odds of that encounter was, bearing in mind I had up until then, and indeed after that, never mentioned the near-naked Kylie concert, and that the coincidence was absolutely incredible. James suddenly started blabbering about the odds I was thinking about, and his conversation was peppered with expletives.

"We'll have to tell the guys when we get back to the apartment," he said.

"They'll never believe us," I said, chuckling back.

"Yeah, you're probably right," my fellow bookseller replied.

On returning to the apartment at a little after eleven o'clock, we had some pizza, and with our colleagues, cracked opened some beers. After about an hour, James turned to me and said, "We gotta tell them, Lance."

I smiled and said, "You tell them.'

James began to tell of our encounter and our close brush with a superstar's grandmother. After he had finished, do you know what they all said at once?

"Yeah right!"

Incidentally, though we never sold any books that day, that little episode raised James' morale and the next day he wrote a double. Also, Kylie's grandmother did not live in a shitty house as James had mentioned but in fact in quite a nice neighbourhood. I think he would have visualised this lady living in a mansion, in a place like Beverley Hills.

As I say, some people could bring some cracking humour to these doorsteps, though Jack would go a little too far at times. He had now decided he didn't want to manage any teams for the moment, so he was now a guerrilla in the urban jungle.

Bumping into him in a very working-class area of the city, we decided to work together for an hour or so just for a bit of fun. Knocking on the metal mesh fly screen door of a house, the wooden door behind opened to reveal an Asian-looking man.

"You speak English?" Jack asked, to which a quick nod of his head and a "Yes" triggered Jack into his next movements. Opening the outer door, Jack flashed his company badge on the clipboard and announced he was from immigration. (Our badge did have an outline of Australia below the letters ESA, which is what the recipient would have briefly seen.)

Pushing past the man, he walked into an open-plan living room/diner and kitchen and staring back at him were a woman and two small children sitting around a very grubby table. Seeing a packet of cigarettes on it, he opened the packet and proceeded to empty half a dozen into his hand before stuffing them into his shirt breast pocket.

"How long have you been in the country?" he asked, with an air of authority in his voice.

"Two year!" came the reply from a very startled man.

"Where are you from?" he said, firing another question at him.

"Vietnam," the man replied, squinting his eyes, trying to figure out what the hell was going on.

Jack, walking over to the fridge, opened it, and seeing some cans of VB, took two cans out, slammed the door and walked up to the man.

With now two frightened children by their mother's side, Jack looked the man straight in his eyes.

"We're watching you!" he said menacingly.

Before I knew it, he was back outside thrusting a cold can of beer into my hand and beckoning me to follow him back up the garden path. Looking back at the family, I could see they were speechless and one of the little children had started to cry. I was too dumfounded to say anything, and shaking my head ran to catch Jack up.

"What the fuck are you doing?" I asked him.

"Why? What's wrong, Lance?" he said, lighting up one of his newly acquired cigarettes.

"What's wrong?" I said incredulously. "You just walked into a family's home and nicked fags and booze in front of their very eyes. They're bound to call the police." My voice quivered, mostly through anger at what he had just put this family through.

"No they won't," he replied nonchalantly.

"No? And why not?" I enquired.

"Because they think I'm from the immigration department, and if one of them ain't an illegal immigrant, if not all of them, then they probably know someone that is and won't create a fuss. The last thing they want is getting the police involved. Besides, I've done this loads of times before."

He was right. At the time, Australia had more illegal immigrants in the country than they could handle. Something I was to find out first hand in the future.

Right! I better finish off this chapter, because if you are like me, you're probably reading in bed at home or on holiday somewhere, and will start thumbing through the pages to see how far it is to the end of the chapter. So, either go and grab a drink at the hotel poolside bar or switch the light out. On the other hand, here's chapter seven.

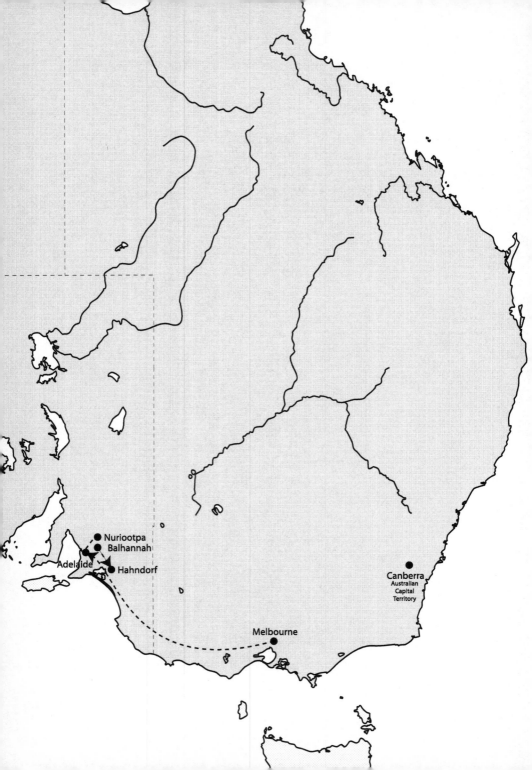

Chapter 7

It was now the end of January and almost a year had elapsed since I had entered this fantastic country. As I drove back to the apartments, the pager sounded in my pocket, and reading the message to contact the boss, I noticed the word "urgent". Going over to the telephone kiosks opposite the wine bars, milk bars and other assorted businesses on the drag that was St Kilda, I called to find out what this pressing matter was.

It transpired I had an early start the following morning at 5 a.m. I was off to Sydney yet again, but this time by plane. My application had been lodged with immigration, but without my passport and a signature missing on the paperwork it could not be processed. Faxing pages of my passport (which these days you would scan and send by email) was not sufficient, and an original signature was required in the presence of a solicitor who was responsible for my applicable documents.

Furthermore, due to the red tape that often comes with these bureaucratic processes, it all had to be done by midday the next day or the whole thing would become void, and I would indeed be heading back home after my working visa had expired. So, the next morning I boarded a plane, and instead of the usual twelve-odd hours sitting on a bus, the plane touched down just over an hour later.

I went to the solicitors, surrendered my passport and signed the legal document required for my application for sponsorship for another two years. Then I headed back to the airport, hopped onto another plane and was sitting in Monroe's wine bar back in St Kilda by seven o'clock.

We had all adopted Monroe's, and would end up in there in the early hours drinking shots, slammers, and my favourite: Carlsberg Elephant Beer. Served in bottles, it had a wonderful taste and a sting in that elephant's tail of 7.2 per cent alcohol. It was run by a Greek family, and if my memory serves me well again, the two guys that were there to serve you were the very accommodating Jimmy and Spyros. At the end of the evening, whether you had a dozen drinks or just one, Jimmy would not let you leave until you had a drink "on the house", usually a shot of Metaxa, which is a distilled spirit made from brandy and wine that originates from Greece.

Between the small beach of this suburb and our apartments was the park. From Monroe's, we would sometimes go back, and collecting some glasses, a box of wine and some bread, head to this green little pasture and lure the possums down from the large palm trees that dominated the area. This was sometimes well after two in the morning and we were the only ones there, apart from the usual homeless Aborigines sleeping off their daily grog ration. Possums are like … little furry squirrel creatures, with sharp teeth and claws that like crawling all over you, and they loved bread. Look them up on the internet as it will be quicker than if I attempted describing my non David Attenborough version to you.

I sold my return flight ticket back to the travel agent, and decided to prematurely celebrate my sponsorship by taking the team to Monroe's for a massive piss-up. As I say, there were other teams in the apartments, but the other managers, including Mike, had a tighter rein on their teams and usually retired far earlier than us or didn't let their reps go out at all some evenings. (This was another reason why other reps would be constantly looking for a place on my team.)

Anyway, the following morning I had to drive Anna to the bus station as she was going back home to Sydney for a week to see her parents. The bus left at 10 a.m. and was a good twenty minute to half-hour drive in the heavy morning traffic into the city. As the clock ticked past 3 a.m., and yet another shot went down our throats, it was the least of our worries. Back at the apartment, I vaguely remember finishing off a bottle of wine at around five-ish, and then waking at nine thirty. NINE THIRTY!

Rushing into Anna's room, I woke her and we frantically rammed all her clothes into her suitcase.

"We're not going to make it, Lance!" she said worriedly.

"Yes we will," I replied uncertainly.

Climbing into the superfast chariot I now had under my command, and setting the volume on the awesome sound system that filled the cockpit of this racing car to an almost deafening level, we headed off towards the city centre.

Weaving in and out of traffic and hurtling through intersections at breakneck speed, my only thought was to get the girl to her bus on time. Speeding closer and closer to the city centre on the freeway, I momentarily glanced in the mirror and noticed an unmarked police car right behind me with its little blue flashing light attached to the roof.

Thinking I had better pull into the left lane to let it pass, I approached another intersection to see a marked police car coming down the road to the right of me with its blue and red lights aglow as well. Seeing the main traffic flow from that direction had been stopped by red lights, I suddenly realised the police vehicle had no intention of stopping and slammed on the brakes. Being a high performance car, it had the brakes to match, and screeching to a halt, we found ourselves staring in front of a now stationary chariot of the law with a policeman staring right at me.

The unmarked vehicle quickly stopped adjacent to us, and following a very quickly executed reversing manoeuvre, I was now clearly blocked in.

Now, in the United Kingdom it is customary to get out of the car as a sign of good manners. In a country where the officers of the law carry guns, this is not such a good idea. As I opened the door, I heard the command, "Stay in the vehicle!" Shutting the door and operating the electric window, I watched in the mirror as two policemen got out of the car behind me with their hands clearly on their gun holsters. At this stage most people would have been shitting themselves. Me? I didn't have a clue what was going on. With the older of the two, a man in his late forties, approaching my window, I heard the first unforgettable question.

"What bank have you two just robbed?"

"I'm sorry?" I replied, still not having the foggiest what he was on about.

"We have just clocked you doing a hundred and forty in a sixty zone," he said in a very stern voice.

"Oh, I'm sorry," I said in my best apologetic voice, "but I'm trying to get this girl to the bus station as she's running late!"

"Well she's going to be later still now," I heard the other officer of the law say.

Seeing the other uniformed man was much younger and barely in his twenties, and noticing the older one wave at his colleagues to indicate they were no longer needed, I wondered what was going to happen next.

"Why didn't you pull over when we started chasing you?" the eldest asked.

"I didn't realise you were chasing me," I said with a puzzled frown.

"Didn't realise?" the younger one said incredulously. "We have been after you for well over a minute. Didn't you hear the siren wailing?"

"I've had the music on," I replied, still not realising the trouble I was in.

They both shook their heads and the youngest asked for my driving licence. Removing my paper licence in its transparent plastic cover from my wallet and handing it to him, he then, from his next question, obviously noticed the smell of alcohol on my breath.

"Have you been drinking?"

"No," I honestly answered, giving him a little half-smile.

Looking at me through his sunglasses, he suddenly screwed my licence up in his hand. "You're in big trouble!"

He walked back to their car and got into the driver's seat to carry out all

146

the necessary checks. The senior of the two walked around the car, looked it up and down and returned to the window.

"How long you been in the country for?"

"Almost a year, officer," my reply came, addressing the law properly.

"And when do you go home?"

Now, my next answer was spontaneous, as I could have launched into the fact that I was seeking to stay in the country for an extra two years, but at that point in time, I had really screwed that up. So rather than bore him with a lengthened story, I replied, "Thursday."

With it being a Saturday, that was just five days away. Walking back to the car, with the light still flashing, he climbed in next to his colleague. With their window down I could hear their conversation taking place. The younger one informed his partner that I was clean and had no outstanding warrants for my arrest; he then proceeded to enlighten him as to what he was going to charge me with, which was basically everything you could get charged with, with regards to driving a vehicle wrongly in the eyes of the law. Listening intently that I was going to have the book thrown at me, along with being breathalysed, I turned to Anna to apologise to her that she would now miss her bus, to which she replied something along the lines of, "That should be the least of your worries!"

Still not grabbing the magnitude of the trouble I was in or perhaps that I was still pissed, I carried on listening to the lawgivers. It was now the turn of the eldest to say his piece. His sense of reasoning suddenly made me think that maybe I was going to escape unscathed. His argument being that his young colleague would carry out a mountain of paperwork on the driving charges I was about to receive, and that by the time the court proceedings had been issued for me to attend the court to face these traffic offences, I would be back home on the other side of the world. It was then very unlikely that I was going to jump back on a plane to come back to face my punishment, which would probably have been a fine, as points or a driving ban would have made very little difference, with me holding a United Kingdom driving licence.

I watched as the young police officer got out of the vehicle and walked back towards me. With my screwed-up licence in the palm of his hand, he attempted to smooth it flat with his other hand before handing it back to me.

"Try not to drive so fast in the next few days," he said, in the way that only men of the law can say.

Reaching the bus station and thinking that her bus could possibly still be there, we arrived to find an empty bus bay. Anna went into the ticket office to find out when the next one was leaving and returned with a big smirk on her face.

"What's wrong with you?" I asked. "You'll probably have to sit here quite a few hours before the next bus."

"No I won't," she replied. "The bus is running late!"

She was right! The bloody thing WAS running late. Getting her case out of the boot, she gave me a peck on the cheek promising to buy me an elephant beer in Monroe's when she returned.

Up until now, I had not been really interested in languages of the world, and apart from learning a bit of French in school, which I could barely use in a conversation, I was only able to speak English. With our Tongan friend, Trevor, aboard my team, I decided we should all learn his lingo, albeit on the way to driving to the field with the team. So, in-between the door-knocking script, meeting "Rocky", "The Terminator", "Indiana Jones" and God knows who else, we had a language lesson. I based it on the old Sesame Street style, where today we would learn the letter "j", "k", or whatever. Instead, I would announce an English word or a sentence, which he would translate for us, and we would repeat it time and time again so we could remember it.

The Tongan language I found easy to learn, and within a month or so could have got by in very basic communication with the Tongan people. In fact, later on when I was in the very far north of Queensland, I came across a Tongan family. Realising where they were from, I said "Malo-e-lelei" which means "Hello". It completely freaked them out, and then I turned to the children and said "Fe-fe-hake?", which means "How are you?" We all burst out in laughter at the chances of a white non-Tongan man being able to speak to these islanders who originated from an island in the middle of the greatest ocean on the planet.

I now needed to buy a car of my own and was advised to call a medium-sized garage that sold reasonably priced used cars. This particular garage and small sales ground had, frankly, cars that had seen better days, and it was where most managers of the company acquired their cars, as a good deal could usually be struck, apparently. At the car sales ground, you were met by the owner and his German mechanic called Helmut. Now, the northernmost city in Australia is Darwin, nearly four thousand kilometres away from Melbourne. The owner had this habit that when you asked what any car was like, he would, in turn, look to Helmut and ask him what the car was capable of.

Obviously, he, being the mechanic, would have worked on the car in preparation for getting it ready for sale, and would also know its capabilities. Helmut's response would be to walk over to the applicable car, and holding his arms wide open with his palms outstretched, as if you had just won the vehicle on a television game show, announce in his broken German accent the unforgettable catchphrase of "Dis car vill get you to Darvin and back!" and that it would get you from the bottom of this giant continent and back, whatever.

It didn't matter what car the owner pointed to, it was the same answer from Helmut each time. He might as well have been one of those action men toys, where you pulled the cord, and from his throat, he repeated the same few sentences all the time. I could picture it – a doll looking about sixty years old with a grey beard and moustache, dressed in grubby overalls, holding a spanner and a road atlas of Oz, wrapped in plastic transparent packaging, and labelled "Achtung Helmut!"

Undecided what to buy, and by the fact that I would have needed at least a few thousand dollars to buy a half-decent vehicle, which at that moment in time I didn't really have at my disposal, I asked if I could keep hold of the petrol-guzzling monster for the meantime, and this was granted.

This was to be a bad move from my end though, as, eager to see more of this great land, I was asked if I wanted to take a team to the South Australian capital of Adelaide for a fortnight. There would be one appointment maker and three reps for which I would get an override of eighty dollars for each sale that each rep completed. Ever being the positive one, I jumped at the chance, but this little venture was nearly to break me financially.

Most large countries of the world have different time zones, and usually they are broken down into hourly intervals. South Australia is an anomaly, as it sits in what countries call an offset time zone and is only a half-hour interval behind that of Victoria, New South Wales, the Australian Capital Territory and Queensland, and is in an area known as Central Standard Time. (The Northern Territory shares this unique time zone with South Oz, and with regards to time zones we will leave it at that for now, as it gets more complex depending on which seasons are current.)

With Luke, James, and a young man from Melbourne with an appetite for a laugh by the name of Tony, along with an eighteen-year-old from Sydney called Phillip, who had emigrated to Australia when he was very young, this time from India, we all headed off on our six hundred and fifty kilometre journey to yet another state capital. With my crazy mind going into overdrive, I warned my team that our vehicle was in fact a time machine, and we were going back in time and to strap ourselves in. I was crazily trying to re-enact the scene from the *Back to the Future* films.

With Luke and James already knowing how mad I was, and with Tony joining in with the mayhem, we all thrust ourselves back in to our seats and rocked our bodies up and down and back and forth, as if being thrown around by an invisible vortex as we crossed the border. With our Indian chum not knowing how to take all this in, we synchronised watches to make sure we had travelled back just the half hour, and instructing the team to look out of the car for dinosaurs in case we had gone too far back in time, we headed to Adelaide. (I was to do this trip back and forth, Melbourne to Adelaide, on numerous occasions, and always having a seasoned sales veteran with me, the other new recruits would think we were nuts most of the time. One young girl, who lacked a complete sense of humour, once commented what all the fuss was for, as we had only gone back half an hour? Again, this madness kept my sanity and hopefully others in this very unusual job.)

I had booked a little ground-floor apartment in the delightful suburb of Glenelg, which was a "hop, skip and a jump" to the beach. Still being summer, the temperatures were constantly in the high twenties to thirties and even the occasional forties.

Being further north, the weather in Adelaide was much more stable than Melbourne's, and on this point I have to touch on the weather that Melbourne receives. They class it as temperate and variable. VARIABLE!? They ain't kidding. This urban jungle can receive four seasons in one day. Really! I have been in the city where at midday the sweltering heat has taken the thermometer to forty degrees centigrade, only for it to plummet to sixteen or seventeen degrees in mere hours. It could sometimes be raining one minute, with terrific gusts of wind, and next, the hot sun reappears and has the ground baking hot again in next to no time. To say the weather is fickle is definitely an understatement. I was thinking of finding a reason, but there are far too many variables, so you can do the research yourself!

From fickle weather, I will jump to speech and accents and how people speak and pronounce words, sentences, phrases, whatever. Being in a country for a length of time can have some bearing on your native accent, and without many people knowing, they slowly become accustomed to pronouncing words in the way people that surround themselves in their everyday life do. Some people, though, tend not to be influenced by the change in accent and return to their country of origin with very little difference in the way the sound of their speech comes across.

After three years of living in Australia, my accent had changed very little, which was pointed out when I returned. I was conscious of certain words that I pronounced with that certain Aussie twang, like the iconic phrase of "No worries", and indeed the country's name itself where I now emphasised the "trail" in the word. During my time in Oz, I was made aware that I was retaining my native accent quite well, but I did not realise how well. Working in the suburb of (and again if my memory serves me well) Port Adelaide, I entered the boundaries of a house with a tree full of a summery blossom of some kind.

Knocking the door of the household I was met by a "digger" of a man, which is basically an Australian man well into his final years of life. (The term "digger" comes from the Australians that fought during the First World War and from the fact they were originally miners.)

Well, realising he was not encyclopedia material, I quickly informed him of what I was selling and turned around to face a huge industrial plant belching smoke out into the stratosphere about a kilometre from his home. Bidding farewell to this fellow, I walked back down his pathway until my curiosity got the better of me. Spinning around, I shouted at the old fella still standing in the doorway.

"What does that factory make over there?" I asked, pointing in front of his very colourful garden tree.

"Flowers," his croaky old throat replied.

My brain very quickly analysed the answer and caused my face to convulse into a very strange shape.

"Flowers?" I said, surprised.

"Yes, flowers!" he replied once again.

Turning back to face his garden gate, I began walking towards it and again heard his voice.

"Oi, mate!"

Turning back around once again, I peered at the old chap peering back at me.

"Did you say factory?" he enquired again.

"Yeah!" I replied.

"Sorry mate, it's your accent." His ancient voice hit me again. "I thought you said fat tree."

I looked at him as he pointed to his wonderful tree in his garden and thought, it ain't my accent mate, it's your fucking hearing!

Adelaide is known as the city of churches as they are all over the place. What struck me though was how quiet the city centre could be for a population of just over one million at the time. You could walk down any street in the heart of the place during the evening in the midweek, and it would be like walking in a town with people few and far between.

For years I pondered why this could be and I eventually came up with two possible reasons. Firstly, because it was a typical Australian city and spread out over tens of kilometres of space, no sod could really be bothered to drive into the nerve centre from the outer suburbs unless they really had to.

Also, the lack of tourists was noticeable, where you would notice them in abundance in Sydney, Melbourne and indeed "Brissy". Not sure how the city does with tourists these days, but it seems to be mostly left out when you see the normal holiday routes of Cairns, Brisbane, Sydney, Melbourne, Perth and, of course, Ayers Rock advertised in newspapers and magazines. That's a shame as it really is a lovely city and worth a few days' stop, where you can build in a trip to the fantastic Barossa Valley and its wonderful wineries, as well as nip over to Kangaroo Island, which escaped me over the years. The fortunate ones that have visited the latter tell me the island holds a fantastic arena of flora and fauna, and the opportunity of seeing Koalas – little marsupials I never saw once in the wild in all my time in the country.

Working the suburbs, we found it hard going and after five days had only produced two orders. For some reason it seemed to me that the recession was having a more acute effect on this state than the others I had worked in up until then, but then again maybe it was just me. With the boss screaming down the phone at me and saying how useless we all were, morale in the team started to dip. With my money dwindling away, making sure I could keep the thirsty "Brock" beast on the road, I had to think up something or I was in the shit.

On a sunny Saturday, I announced we would be starting slightly earlier than normal and decided to launch a two-pronged attack at the Adelaide Hills and the Barossa Valley. Again, the logic was that these smaller towns had not been worked for a while, and we would now find people who were in the market for the books. Dropping Luke and James off in the valley at a town called Nuriootpa (pronounced Newry-ute-pa), I warned them not to expect me back till early evening and that without any orders from the both of them we would be heading back to Melbourne a lot sooner than anticipated. Heading off to the hills, I dropped Tony at a smaller town called Stirling and then proceeded with Phillip to the heavily German-influenced towns of Balhannah and Hahndorf, with its little population of, then, just over a thousand.

Dropping Phillip off at Balhannah, I asked him to make appointments from four o'clock onwards, pointing out that if he had to, he could make them as late as possible so to accommodate a time that would suit some prospective buyers. The other three of my team would have to wait for as long as it took to get an order. Hahndorf's little shops were full of ornamental clocks and windmills and trinkets that people buy on holiday, and reminded me of all the stuff some shops back in my hometown sold to the tourists during Tenby's summer months.

Knocking every accessible home I could, I achieved one demonstration but no sale. Heading back to Balhannah, I picked up Phillip, who had made just one appointment. This was good for him as his track record had been appalling, and getting no appointments on frequent evenings, I suspected he was only knocking a fraction of the doors that he was actually recording. We met a very young family who decided it would be a good investment, and I wrote my first order in nearly a week. With early evening approaching, I decided to head back to the car, stopping at a milk bar to pick up two cold drinks for us.

It was in this milk bar that Phillip scored his first own goal, which was to eventually to see him kicked out of the bookselling league. A woman queuing in front of us turned, and instantly recognising Phillip, gave him a cheery welcome. I thought nothing of it as he'd probably met her earlier knocking doors, but she then proceeded to tell him of her disappointment at not being able to see the demonstration as her husband was not due to return home till eight o'clock. Watching the blood drain from his face and his deep Indian complexion turn to almost match my tanned face, I quickly interrupted and offered to wait until that specified time.

"Oh no," she said, smiling, "I've spoken to him in the meantime as he came home earlier than expected, and with him knowing you didn't make appointments after six, he went off fishing and will now probably end up in the pub."

Without a mobile phone, which nearly everyone has today, there was no way we could contact him. Walking back to the car, I angrily quizzed Phillip as to why he had not made the appointment for eight, to which his feeble excuse that we had to pick the others up only annoyed me more.
My anger only subsided when I found that Tony had written an order, and on reaching Nuriootpa found that my other seasoned reps had written one each as well. Getting back, I reminded Phillip that we were a team and that his idea of finishing early didn't do any favours for the rest of us. Deep down I guessed he was a lazy person and not cut out to do the job. The next misdemeanour that he committed, though, surprised even me with its audacity and was to see his exit.

Two nights later and trying again in the city, I picked Phillip up to find he had arranged one appointment. Sending him back out to see if he could arrange another appointment or more between seven and nine o'clock, I headed off to the one he had arranged. On reaching the house, I was pleasantly welcomed by the husband and wife who immediately informed me that they knew it was encyclopedias I was selling as he had told them so, and that after a quick discussion after he had left, decided they did not really need them. Understanding this decision, they then asked if they could be reimbursed for the telephone call that Phillip had made while in their home.

"Telephone call? What telephone call?" I enquired.

"He asked us if he could call his parents back in Sydney as he had something urgent to tell them, and having had no money on him to call from a kiosk and it being too late to give them the message by the time he was picked up by his manager, we let him use our phone," the husband said.

"How much do I owe you?" I asked.

"A hundred dollars," the wife replied.

"A hundred dollars?" I blurted out.

"Yes, a hundred dollars, he was on the phone for nearly an hour."

"Nearly an hour?" I said incredulously. "What was he talking about for nearly an hour?"

"We don't really know," the husband said, shrugging his shoulders, "he was talking in Indian!"

I stopped to take all this information in, and frowning, pointed out that a call to Sydney for an hour would not cost a hundred dollars.

"Well, Lance, you're right," the husband continued. "But after he left the house we got a little suspicious and decided to call the operator to find out if he had indeed called Sydney."

"And did he?" I probed deeper.

"No," the husband said, shaking his head.

"Well where?" I asked, trying not to let the suspense kill me before I received the answer.

"Bombay!" a now wide-eyed husband said.

"Bom-bloody-bay!? Bombay in bloody India?" I blurted out again.

"Yes," they both replied, nodding.

Handing them a precious hundred dollars, I left to pick up our international speaker.

At first he denied the call had ever taken place, and then, with me threatening to take him back to their home, he very quickly crumbled and spewed out a sob story of not being able to speak to his grandparents back home in India for quite some time, and that it was too expensive to do so anyway.

By now I was absolutely livid, and pointing to his door-knocking sheet, insinuated that he had not knocked half the doors he had recorded, with him vehemently denying that that was the case. Pointing at an entry on his log that revealed he had been in a house where he had found out that the people were unemployed, I decided to call his bluff by suggesting we knock the door again and tell the so-called people that they had just won a set of encyclopedias in a draw. Panicking, he quickly confessed that he had not knocked the door, as I had guessed, and then burst into tears. This now pitiful person suddenly reminded me of Archie when I had been back in Sydney almost a year ago at the start of my bookselling career. The next day I put Phillip onto a bus and sent him back to Sydney.

With the bus ticket I had to fork out for, along with his phone call, I was well over two hundred bucks out of pocket – two hundred dollars that I could not really afford. The day after, we were travelling forwards in time back to Melbourne!

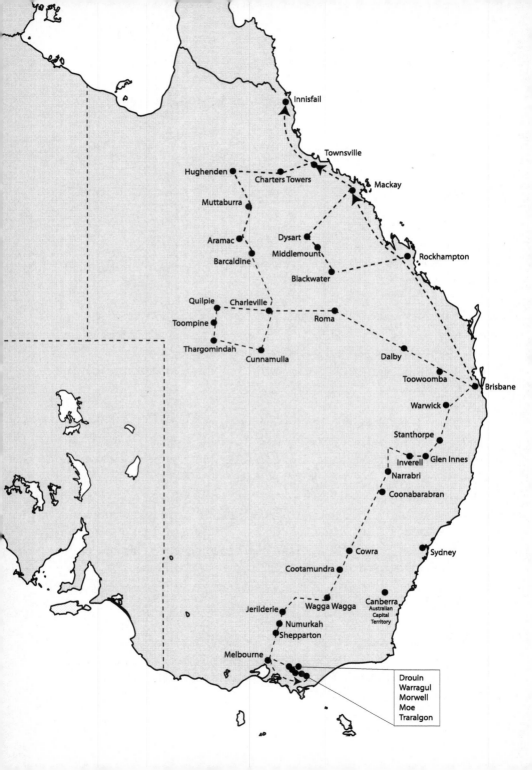

Innisfail

Townsville

Hughenden Charters Towers

Mackay

Muttaburra

Aramac Dysart

Barcaldine Middlemount

Rockhampton

Blackwater

Quilpie Charleville

Toompine Roma

Thargomindah Cunnamulla

Dalby

Toowoomba

Brisbane

Warwick

Stanthorpe

Inverell Glen Innes

Narrabri

Coonabarabran

Cowra

Sydney

Cootamundra

Wagga Wagga Canberra
Australian
Capital
Territory

Jerilderie

Numurkah

Shepparton

Melbourne

Drouin
Warragul
Morwell
Moe
Traralgon

Chapter 8

I was back in Melbourne and summer was gradually floating away. The trip to South Australia had been a disaster financially for all of us. Both Luke and Tony's only orders had cancelled during the cooling-off period, and although my order and James' had completed and we would be paid our commission, I was well out of pocket as I had missed the overrides from the two lost orders and expenses had gone through the roof, what with paying for Phillip's bloody bus ticket and phone call as well as a few hundred bucks for fuel, not to mention my share of rent for the accommodation and food.

The boss decided to move Luke and Tony to another team in Sydney and gave them an advance in their wages which they would have to pay back with later commissions. This was sometimes done to boost a rep's morale as having no money only created a negative person in the field. With them gone, Van Winkle could now join the team, and he turned up on the doorstep three days later. Introducing him to Monroe's, I was thankful they didn't have a pool table and hence he couldn't put his "shark" potting skills to the test and piss some unsuspecting person off.

With a trip out into rural Victoria to places like Drouin, Warragul, Morwell, Moe and Traralgon, my fortunes turned yet again and with myself and Winkle working the appointments that Trevor, Tracy and Anna were setting up, as well as the results from our own door knocking, the orders started coming in once again and my finances started to look healthy again with only one cancellation from a total of eleven orders.

The last three towns mentioned are in the La Trobe Valley in an area called Gippsland. It has heavy industry, like power stations, and the area provides many governmental and administrative jobs which are usually a lot safer during times of recession, hence the low cancellation rate.

It was on this trip that I found the devil once again on my shoulder whispering naughty ideas into my head. This time it was my growing affection towards Anna, who I found had a similar sense of humour to me, and with her attractive, photogenic looks, she was becoming more irresistible by the day.

She had approached me before in Monroe's on a couple of occasions, but the angel on my other shoulder was obviously a teetotaller as my resistance kept up while the devil got hammered on Metaxa most evenings.

With the Aussie winter approaching, it was time to make plans to head north to warmer climes again. The car now had to go back to the boss, and I found myself asking Helmut at the car sales ground what car would get me to Darwin and back.

Finding a little red Datsun, I parted with a couple of thousand dollars and bought it. A lot slower, it was also a lot more economical and that would help my wallet on the long two thousand kilometres plus trip back up to Queensland. Besides, I thought, the other Datsun had been reliable enough!

Only able to carry three people with me, I had to choose who was to make the trip with me. It turned out to be an easy one, though as the result of circumstances I would have preferred to have been different. Van Winkle decided he wanted to switch to a team that had room for one more rep and was heading north up through South Oz and into the Northern Territory. This middle route via Alice Springs would give him an opportunity to visit the giant inselberg and the world's largest monolith: Ayers Rock.

This was not an option open to me as I had instructions to go to the Sunshine State via Sydney. With Winkle gone, I still had to decide who would be the one not to travel with me. Unfortunately, it was Trevor who made the decision for me, suddenly informing me that he had to leave the country as his mother had succumbed to cancer and her death meant him returning to his island in the Pacific. I was never to see those two great guys again. Van Winkle eventually quit for good once he reached Queensland, and Trevor, once he had returned home to Tonga, stayed to look after his younger brother and sister.

So, leaving Melbourne with James, Tracy and Anna, we headed northwards, which, it being the month of June, was indeed quite cold at night in the state of Victoria, with the thermometer on low single figures while we knocked doors.

Reaching the quite large town of Shepparton and booking into accommodation at a caravan park that had very cosy chalets and lodges, the devil in his woolly coat popped up onto my shoulder. With no angel in sight (probably looking for another woolly coat.), the devil asked me why I should be traipsing around in the freezing cold when I could drop James and Tracy in the next town up the road and then take Anna back to a nice warm bed in the chalet and have some fun playing games till it was time to pick them up at ten. Dropping them both at a smaller town called Mooroopna and heading back to the caravan park with my Russian lovely, I heard the devil announce, let the games begin!

These initial games lasted a few days, and apart from the both of us hardly doing any work, we had to be careful not to let the other two even suspect what we were up to. If it was found out later on up the line that we had become more than just work colleagues, there would be a real danger of the boss splitting us up.

Heading up and working our way through the towns of Numurkah, Jerilderie, Wagga Wagga (pronounced Wogga), Cootamundra and Young (again), we arrived at Cowra where we received fresh instructions. Very quickly I realised I had to find a balance between work and the games with Anna before I became skint, otherwise someone would begin to suspect something was up. With no need now to head for Sydney, we were to leave this medium-sized town and head northwards inland to meet up at Coonabarabran (again).

Before we leave Cowra though, there is a little history lesson about it. This medium-sized town lies three hundred kilometres due west of Sydney, and it was where one of the largest prisoner of war escapes of World War Two took place. Australia had acquired prisoners of war from a number of countries, including, among others of course, Japan. This camp contained our fellows from the rising sun, a load of Koreans who had fought on the Japanese side, and some Italians. It was guarded by Australian veterans too old for service, some disabled, and young men not deemed fit for frontline duties. Surrounded by barbed wire and manned with rifles and machine guns, the Italians and Koreans were willing to sit it out till the end of the war. The

Japanese on the other hand had other ideas.

Very early on the morning of 5th August 1944, a bugle sounded and over five hundred of the Japanese made a dash for it armed with knives, baseball bats, clubs and any other weapon of sorts they could get their hands on. Throwing blankets over the wire, dozens of the Japanese were cut down in a hail of bullets, but despite this, the sheer numbers against the guards allowed over three hundred to escape. Many committed suicide or allowed themselves to be killed rather than face recapture, and after ten days all the ones on the run had been taken back to the camp. This pointless episode was to cost them two hundred and thirty-one lives and four Australian men's lives as well, who probably only wanted to sit this dreadful war out.

Arriving at "Coona", we met up with the boss and another sales team outside the pub where I earlier nearly got my skull cracked with a pool cue. His plan was for me to swap cars and take a team to "Brissy" for three nights before driving up into the far north of Queensland and the town of Townsville. This was a total distance of over two thousand kilometres.

I looked in horror at the only vehicle that was parked outside the pub – the Brock V8 Commodore! Surely he didn't expect me to drive that gas-guzzling beast all that way funded from my own pocket? Suddenly another vehicle turned the corner, and instantly recognising the station wagon that ran on the extremely cheap LPG, I hoped it would be that chariot I would be commanding up into Queensland. I was right!

That evening after work, all twelve of us headed to the pub (yes the one with the pool table), and seeing none of those pool-playing lads around, we relaxed and laughed as we swapped stories about the book business and some of the homes we had been in over our period of time employed by ESA. Meeting all sorts of weird and wonderful members that make up the human race, the stories flowed.

One guy working in an outback town with a sizeable Aboriginal population had been in the middle of a demonstration when the police turned up to speak to the father. Apparently, this typical white, very patriotic,

162

Australian had got home from work one afternoon and had noticed the Aboriginal flag flying higher than the Aussie one in the courtyard of the school. (This flag represents the indigenous people of Australia and it is divided in half by a red lower region and an upper black region with a yellow disc superimposed in the centre.)

Apparently seething with rage, he entered the building, and on finding the head teacher (who was also white), threatened to kill him unless he lowered it to the same height as the Aussie one. Racism was an issue I often encountered in the outback but I will return to that later on in the book.

Another interruption during a demonstration was where the father had to momentarily leave to tend to his four-year-old son who had awoken restless, and he went to tuck the young mite back into bed. While leaning over and tucking him in, he suddenly felt a very sharp hot pain in his foot. Removing his foot from under the bed and putting the light on, he could see a deadly funnel-web spider attached to it. (These little bastards can kill you very quickly unless you seek medical help.) Needless to say, the salesperson did not get to the closing questions to secure a sale!

One young girl who had been with the company for three months had recently sold a set to a family who already had *World Encyclopedia* and *Encyclopedia Britannica*. What they wanted another set for was anyone's guess.

Jack was the first person to hand back a commission to the company after a family sent the books back. Already owning a set of *Collier's*, he offered some different books we had available, and on getting to the encyclopedia bit, he told them that this set was completely different. The family signed up for them, only on delivery realising that of course they were identical. Gullible people were at the mercy of Jack, but as I say, he certainly knew how to sell.

Mike had recently sold a set to, as he described it, a strange little and probably very eccentric middle-aged man who must have had pots of money as he already had three identical sets of our brand of books. And the boss had another story about Mike which had nothing to do with selling. He had recently purchased a new car through a loan with the company, and deciding to drive down to a Liquorland bottle shop very late one evening to replenish the grog supplies, wrapped the car around a lamp post.

Climbing out of the vehicle, he headed to a telephone kiosk to tell the boss what he had done. To the question of how he had managed to do this, his reply was that as he had turned a corner, he had been momentarily blinded by the ... MOON! And that it had nothing to do with the twelve bottles of beer he had already consumed before getting behind the wheel! He was now without a car and had returned to sales rep status, where he was to accompany me with a new team to Townsville.

The next day I headed for the capital of the Sunshine State (which Queensland is known as) and the city of Brisbane once again. I had all reps on board. This time we stayed in the West End suburb (which for cricket fans is just down the road from the "Gabba"). Staying in a very large house that was to be the home to about a dozen reps and appointment makers, we were off northwards again three days later. On board I had some very experienced members comprising James, Luke, Mike, Jack, and an Englishman by the name of Dan, who had acquired the job, like me, through an advertisement in one of the national newspapers.

Anna and Tracy had gone ahead in the boss's car with another appointment maker, and our bedroom manoeuvres had been curtailed for a while.

Again stopping for a moment in this scribe I am writing, you may or may not be wondering why these two girls are still appointment makers and not now reps selling the books themselves? Very quickly the book business discovered who was capable of doing what.

There were people who could make appointments but could never make the transition to be a sales representative of the company, where you had to close a sale. This was down to either a lack of confidence and not being able to take on board the technique of being a salesperson, or just not wanting to progress up the chain for some reason or other. I tried my best to train my Tongan friend in the script for the demonstration, but he kept forgetting it. Whether it was down to the fact he knew his mother was dying and couldn't really concentrate, or just could not remember the script through his train of thought, I don't know. Both girls, though, were now learning the demonstration in earnest and would both be reps by the time they hit Townsville.

Anyway, with all our bags comfortably stashed in the back of the wagon, four of the lads were squeezed into the back seats, while Dan and I, he being the biggest, sat in the front for what was to be the longest journey I was ever to drive in one complete run, with only quick stops for fuel and snacks.

Taking the evening off and grabbing a few hours snooze, I picked the team up from the field at ten. Grabbing some drinks, pies and a couple of cooked chooks, we headed off.

Arriving at Rockhampton, which sits on the Tropic of Capricorn, at just after 4 a.m. to refuel, I got out of the car, with the five occupants inside now snoring heavily away. Filling her up with both gas and petrol to give me a range of nearly seven hundred k's, I was surprised how chilly it was. This was the depths of the Aussie winter, and although now in the tropics I could still feel the awesome effect that the season of winter brings.

Heading off onwards and upwards, the next large town, Mackay, came onto my scope just after sunrise. It was here I was to find the "Holy Grail" that I had been searching for ever since arriving down under, but it would have to wait as I ploughed ever further north.

Reaching the town of Ayr with the sun high up in the sky and the vehicle now alive with Aussie and English chatter, Dan offered to drive the last part of the journey. I had by then been driving for almost twelve hours and had covered over twelve hundred kilometres. (Nearly the same distance from one tip of Great Britain to the other.)

With all of us getting out of the car in glorious, very warm sunshine, we walked around an orchard of orange trees like a bunch of geriatrics trying to get the blood flowing around our lower limbs once again. The town thermometer read twenty-seven degrees and I had escaped the winter once again.

Townsville was to be a base of sorts for nearly ten weeks. The boss had decided to return to Brisbane to run some teams from there, putting me in charge of two field managers and now nearly a dozen reps who had come up from Sydney and Canberra. As an acting sales manager, my pay had also risen, and Anna was now back with me as a rep which meant the clandestine sexual manoeuvres could continue. From this headquarters, I could send teams up to large towns like Cairns, which then had a population of just over one hundred thousand, for several nights, or back down to Mackay, holding another sixty thousand human beings or so, with options for them to work the smaller towns in-between. I was careful not to constantly keep Anna by my side but to send her off with other people on occasions, and this kept the suspicions to a minimum.

Taking a team down to Mackay for a few days, I came across a family whose husband's occupation was as a fisherman. Asking him what he generally caught, I listened intently to his daily catch, until the word "shark" suddenly registered in my brain.

"Do you have any sharks' teeth?" I enquired.

"Yeah mate, what teeth do you want?"

Shrugging my shoulders and explaining that my little brother back home wanted some teeth of sorts, he disappeared and then returned. He put two extremely whiter than white devilish sort of teeth into my hand and asked if they were okay.

Examining the teeth I could see they both had a very sharp pointy bit, but what amazed me more than anything else was the fact that the teeth were serrated along the sides like a sort of kitchen knife.

"What shark are these teeth from?" I asked

"Tiger!" he replied.

Okay, it may not have been the "Holy Grail", but at least I had found, after over eighteen months, some sharks' teeth for my kid brother!

Brushing my finger against the serrated part of a tooth, I did so again, applying a little more pressure. This resulted in my skin being split apart and blood being drawn. I remember thinking what a killing machine this fish must be, and the wonder of the way nature made this beast to survive in our vast oceans.

Returning to Townsville, I showed the teeth to Anna, who did exactly the same as me and soon had blood pouring from one of her dainty digits. Heading for the telephone and calling home, I was amazed to find that my mother had now accumulated nearly a hundred and twenty postcards from the different places I had visited, and informing her of the teeth find, I then had a very pleased brother on the phone wanting to know when I would post them.

My mother came back on the phone and there was a tinge of sadness in her voice when she heard my reply to her question, "When are you coming home?" It had now been over a year and a half since I had last seen my folks, and I still had no intention of returning in the immediate future, despite having still to hear from immigration as to whether my sponsorship application had been successful. In fact, I was beginning to think I would be out here those two extra years before I'd receive a reply.

One morning in a town called Innisfail, I woke feeling a little jaded and had begun to sweat. By mid-morning my mouth had become very dry, and along with a constant thirst, perspiration was now cascading from my body. Feeling ever weaker, I now realised I had a fever of sorts, and asking one of the field managers to do the training and to drop the reps off out in the field, I went to have a lie down. By mid-afternoon my bed was soaking wet with sweat, and with Anna back in Sydney visiting her parents, I now felt very poorly and wanted someone there to care for me. Getting up to go to the toilet, my entire body ached and I moved like someone with severe arthritis in their hips and legs. I felt like the *"Tin Man"* from *The Wizard of Oz*, without his oil to lubricate his limbs.

As I returned to bed, the door opened and the field manager came in without knocking on the door. Oblivious to my state of degenerating health, she then began to moan about all the trouble and strife she was having with her career in the book business; this was often her general gripe. Now normally I would have sat her down and listened to her problems, but I was now not in a fit state. Trying to raise myself out of bed, I told her in no uncertain terms that if she didn't go back out in the field and write an order, then on her return I would kill her.

The evening seemed to last a lifetime, and now even too weak to reach for a glass of water by the bedside cabinet to quench this insatiable thirst, I began to wish I hadn't said those awful words to her. Just then I heard a little knock on the door, and I saw a familiar face peer around it; it was Dan. The boss, having received a telephone call earlier from a very tearful field manager with the news that I had gone off the rails and made homicidal threats to her, had decided to get Dan to drive down from Cairns to see what this abnormal behaviour from me was all about. During the evening I had heard the pager sound several times, but with it being about ten feet away from me, fatigue had reached a level where I couldn't get out of bed to retrieve it, and to be perfectly honest didn't really care what the message was or who was trying to reach me. Dan took a good look at me.

"Come on mate, we gotta get you to a doctor."

I had acquired a very nice mosquito-borne infectious disease called Ross River fever. This virus is endemic to Australia, Papua New Guinea and the South Pacific, and it is like a very severe bout of flu magnified a few times again. You don't want to catch it. Trust me.

Getting a dose of drugs, I spent the next few days back down in Townsville resting up and slowly getting my health back. I was quite fortunate to get back on my feet quite quickly as it can take months to get better in some cases. It's also a bit of a bugger as well, as it stays in your system until the day you die and has the habit of a recurrence every now and then. I had it again thirteen years later back home in Tenby, where my body ached and played up for nearly six weeks.

Heading back down to Rocky (Rockhampton), I asked if I could take a team into the Queensland outback. Working the coal mining towns of Dysart, Middlemount and Blackwater, this was another learning curve in the book business. It was the opposite to the likes of the Olympic Village back in Melbourne. Here, everyone had a job, and the households earned megabucks, where a set of books would be a week's wages. Here, you had to bash hundreds of doors in these towns specially built to accommodate the families, just to find occupants who didn't own a set. Also, being in a very affluent area, they had door-to-door salespeople knocking their doors selling stuff all the time, which meant sometimes you got the "F" word shouted at you when a door was opened.

Having said that though, once you found a family that had recently moved to these purpose-built towns and did not own a set of books, many would write out a cheque for the full amount, which meant you could spend that commission mentally in your head as it was a done deal. It would amaze me the number of times they would say, "Do you want a cheque for the lot now?" But, as I say, they all earned very good money and it was in these towns, because the employees that mined these worldly deposits worked shifts, that we worked double shifts starting at ten in the morning to catch as many miners, engineers and managers at home as possible.

The machinery that carves and scoops up the coal would blow my mind as well, as everything was enormous, with the draglines (giant excavators) having buckets the size of houses. This jaw-dropping experience would return as you watched the length of the trains that transported the mineral out of the area, with many of them exceeding a hundred trucks full of the black stuff.

With mining towns like this, only seasoned managers and reps worked them. There were two main reasons for this. One being that you had to work long hours and continuously maintain a positive mental attitude. You could knock three hundred or four hundred doors and get nowhere and then three houses in a row would each buy a set from you. This, I guess, was something to do with the housing allocation or something, and looking back at it, what I should have done was ask someone in charge, like the accommodation manager, to mark on a map where all the new families in the town lived. It would have saved a lot of time and bother.

The other reason was the cost of living there. No tourists came to these towns, and because of the wealth in the region everything was expensive. A beer was nearly one and a half times more than back on the coast, and it would cost two hundred bucks a night for a one bed room as only employees of these mines (again with loads of money or paid for them by their company) stayed in them, while visiting these huge operations on business. Hence, you had to write at least two orders a day to keep your head above water. However, if you kept at it for the few days you worked these places, it could become quite lucrative and you could easily earn well over a thousand, or even two thousand dollars, in the time you spent there.

Right, it's time to digress again. Working in sales, as you probably have worked out, is a very up and down business. You can have good or bad weeks, months and even years in what is an ever-changing economic climate. What used to amaze me, and still does, having sold all sorts of stuff over twenty years of being in this business, is the fact that some salespeople can never ever save any money for the leaner times. A typical salesperson would have a few average weeks, and then during a certain week land a bumper pay packet, only to spend the lot on shopping, gambling, drinking or whatever, to become broke again in a very quick period of time.

Take, for instance, Jack, who would outperform many other salespeople in the book business but was constantly skint. His mega pay packets would be swallowed up by the ever-consuming bottomless pits of the pokies, for which he clearly had an addiction. There was also a girl who was a shopaholic who couldn't resist spending her hard-earned cash in high street stores. On one particular week she had a pay cheque of fifteen hundred dollars. Dropping her off in the centre of Brisbane one morning in cut-off denim jean shorts and a T-shirt, I returned to retrieve her at lunchtime to find her dressed in a designer label dress behind a mountain of shopping bags with a lot of similar labels on. She looked like Julia Roberts in the film Pretty Woman, where she has been given free rein spending Richard Gere's character's money. In a wild spending frenzy, she had even spent her rent money for the week and had to get an advance to pay for her accommodation. Also, most of the stuff she had to post back home as she had no room for it in her medium-sized suitcase when she went back on the road again.

Admittedly, there are a lot of businesses around the world that encourage this sort of behaviour by encouraging their staff to get into debt, either through acquiring large mortgages, or expensive flash cars, or anything to keep them hungry. It is this hunger that drives the salesperson on to earn even more money and in turn drive the bottom-line profit of a business ever higher. Mind you, a driven person in sales will relish this, as it keeps them focussed towards their goals. My main weakness is visiting far-flung, often isolated, unspoilt parts of the globe, where my hunger and drive for them has taken me all over the world. However, it's always nice to have a bit of money put aside for that rainy day.

Anyway, back to the travelling. From these mining towns we headed back to the sugar cane lands of Mackay and Townsville where I was reunited with Anna again. Word had somehow got out that we were more than just buddies, and I soon received instructions to take a team back down to Brisbane with her not on board. With winter now over and the sun heading back into the southern hemisphere again, it was time to head back down to New South Wales and Victoria. It was also wise to leave this region before the wet season returned, where floods can block roads and shut down towns and cities for days, weeks and even months.

My car was also back in "Brissy", and the sales manager whose car I had been using now wanted her car back. If you are wondering why she would have swapped her car for mine, when the little Datsun was not as comfortable and ran on the more expensive petrol – well the reason for this was that she was needed back in the city to train up new recruits, and this suited her more as she had grown tired of the constant travelling after three years of being on the road. She had also been given a cash incentive to lend her car to the teams that were out on the road, while she obviously had use of mine. Her car at this stage was pretty intact and in good working condition. This was to change though, as I had other ideas as to which way we were going to return to the capital of Queensland.

Wanting to see ever more of this country, I studied a map and plotted an inland course where several very long roads were classed as "unsealed". With these having no tarmac, they varied in condition enormously, as I was to find out. With the journey just over two and a half thousand kilometres, we were to head westwards to the towns of Charters Towers and Hughenden, before turning southwards down to Barcaldine via Muttaburra, and on reaching the very inland outback town of Charleville, heading even further inland to Quilpie (pronounced Kwil-pea). From there we would drive via a very tiny place called Toompine, then turn and go to Cunnamulla, before returning back up to Charleville, then eastwards for the big smoke of Brisbane. With overnight stops it would take us around a week.

The first stage of this little adventure was easy, but on the third day we found ourselves on an unsealed road that made the hellish one back on that mountain near Bathurst seem like heaven. The camber on this road was so steep it only really suited four-wheel-drive vehicles. With our low-slung suspension, the car occasionally acted like a snowplough, pushing devilish melon-sized rugged rocks aside to carve a path forward as the engine heaved and screamed as it struggled to propel our craft. This road to Muttaburra was over two hundred kilometres, and as it attempted to destroy the car, I began to wonder whether this inland route had been a good idea?

Without the option of turning back, we hurtled along; the radiator grill was torn off and the rocks and little stones that were being hurled up put a hole in the exhaust and a crack in the windscreen. Very shortly after, the passenger wing mirror casing was smashed, leaving it hanging by its internal wires, while somewhere along the track an indicator light was taken out. We could have been driving one of those clown cars you see at the circus, where it disintegrates in front of your eyes.

This road also had another weapon in its arsenal, and that was the fine red dust being blown at us that, incredibly, started to penetrate and enter our vibrating sealed cabin. With a film of dust settling on the dashboard and our clothes, skin and hair, we soon began to look like clowns anyway, with a light coating of powdery red dust.

Reaching Muttaburra and carrying onto Barcaldine, I was relieved that the road had returned to tarmac. Dropping three of the team in this town of a thousand people, Dan and I headed back to Muttaburra and another tiny, though slightly larger, settlement just before it called Aramac. Writing an order in each, we headed back to the town, and picking up the other three who managed to produce another two orders, we booked into a typical outback hotel.

These dry and dusty isolated communities had not seen rain for over a year, and the sight of cattle carcasses on these barren water-starved surrounds made me wonder how long you would survive out on them with little or no water.

Right! Here's a little treat for any dinosaur fans.

In the little town of Muttaburra stands a full-size replica of the Muttaburrasauraus that was one of the largest dinosaurs found in Oz. The bones, discovered near the town in 1963, revealed a lizard that measured twelve metres long and around two metres high. Now, if you are wondering how the hell something that big could survive in these harsh conditions, you only have to find out the translation of the Aboriginal word for the town, which means "the meeting of waters". This region around Muttaburra once contained a giant inland sea and was obviously drinkable; "Ol Mutty" found it a lot easier to survive all those years ago. Much easier than the current dead bovines that now littered this now predominantly redundant grazing landscape.

Heading off down this inland road to Charleville and doing a bit more research of the area, I realised that Quilpie was not large enough for a full team to all work at once. So, changing the plan slightly, I left three of them in this town of three thousand, telling them that they only needed to write an order each and they could finish, while me and Dan, leaving at nine on a very hot sunny Sunday morning, headed off inland. Dropping Dan at Quilpie, I headed southwards to the far-flung town of Thargomindah.

Between these two very isolated small towns is Toompine, which has a population of two, who are the landlord and landlady of the one building there, which is the pub. It was about a kilometre from here that the car had another blow to its body to add to the ever-mounting repair bill ... a puncture! Nursing the car into the empty pub car park at just past noon, I changed the tyre and popped in to get a pie and a drink.

Apart from the odd cattle station, the nearest towns to this place were roughly sixty kilometres equal distance. Remarking this fact to the landlord and saying how quiet it was, his only remark was, "You oughta see this place at night, mate!"

Writing an order in Thargomindah, I nipped into the shop to buy some chocolate and another drink. Talking to Thargo's shopkeeper, I found all the newspapers four days behind the current date. Questioning this, I was told that this was always the case, as they came by road from Brisbane and took that time to get there. Mail was not that much better either, with just two deliveries a week. This region had become a completely different world to the Australia that the everyday tourist saw, and the nearest coastline was now over a thousand kilometres away.

With dusk now approaching, I headed back to pick up Dan. Driving at night in the outback is not recommended, as with all the emus, kangaroos, the occasional camel and whatever else that can inadvertently smash into you, they can easily cause some serious damage and even write off a vehicle. The station wagon had no bull bar which is a very effective barrier for any animal that chooses to run in front of your vehicle and take out anything that the engine needs to keep it moving, like the radiator for example. By the way, you did read that right ... camel.

From 1860 till the invention of the motor car (early 1900s), some ten thousand camels were imported to use as transport. As time went on they were no longer needed and were let loose to roam the outback. Suited to the inhospitable dry conditions of the interior, they thrived. There are now an estimated one million of them in the deserts out there.

The roads again between Thargo and Quilpie were unsealed but were now corrugated and these ripples in the road caused the vehicle to vibrate and rattle every bone in your body. Getting used to this sensation, these tracks would suddenly change into rivers of deep, red soil that slew the forward motion of the station wagon from side to side like a rattlesnake in the sand. These conditions tested the mechanics constantly, but strangely enough it was this rough and tough environment that drew a certain fondness from me for this region.

Driving at night in the outback is like playing a video game where, driving your on-screen car, you kept your eyes out for hazards that attempted to knock your vehicle off the road. In the pitch-black you watched out for potholes, thick unexpected red soil, strewn bushes lying in your path, Kangaroos and emus coming at you from all angles. On top of that, if you were thirsty and needed to keep the laughing gear moist, you had to hold a beer or a box of wine between your legs while pouring it into your plastic glass from the little tap. It ain't easy, I can tell you!

On the subject of drink-driving, I am afraid to tell you, and by no means condoning it, that this practice was rife in the outback. On reaching Toompine again at just past seven, I was amazed to see the pub car park rammed with all sorts of vehicles. Having no alcohol on my person, I thought I would nip in and grab a few cans or stubbies. Entering the extended little shack, I could hardly move for people chatting, singing, swearing, canoodling, or whatever. Pushing my way to the bar, I met the landlord again, and giving my obvious observation that he was quite correct at how different the atmosphere was now, as opposed to earlier on, I enquired why these folk risked getting caught drink-driving?

With him looking at me as if I was an alien from another planet, he said, "Ah, no worries mate. We only got one copper for this area, and one of

175

the pub's landlords in Augathella has just rung to say he's up there! What ya drinking?"

With that town being on the policeman's patch, you would think, well there is still a chance he could drive down quickly and get parked up near the pub to catch anyone that had had more than their legal driving-limit quota. But, I will try and put it into the perspective of the size of this country and the area this particular policeman had to patrol. Imagine you are in a pub in London and someone tells you the only copper in the area is up near the border of Scotland; are you going to risk it? (I'm not answering that one for you.)

The smell of the soil and the occasional sighting of a desert fox or the ubiquitous sightings of emu and kangaroo along with the vast feeling of emptiness and solitude gave me a feeling of complete relaxation. Out here you could hear yourself think at night while lying on the bonnet of the car and staring up at the millions of stars that had very little artificial light to disturb their gaze back to our planet. I had grown to love this vast inland isolation, despite being a boy born and bred on a coast.

Picking up Dan, who had written another order, we arrived back in Charleville at just before ten. It had been a thirteen-hour day and I had driven a distance of nearly eight hundred kilometres. Although that was a mammoth amount to drive in one day, especially on these roads, long journeys were to become not that uncommon, and once I reached the vastness of Western Australia the following year, it was pretty much the norm.

The next day I gave everyone the day off as the week had been a good one. Looking around the town we spied the visitor centre for "The Royal Flying Doctor Service" and we all decided to pay a visit. There are a number of these bases throughout Oz and they basically offer medical services for the people in these remote outback towns, homesteads or cattle stations. An accident or a sudden illness brings this service quickly to the needy, where taking a patient to hospital by air instead of by road over these great distances could mean the difference between life and death. A story that one of the guides told us was absolutely incredible, and to be honest, even to this day, I think he was having a laugh as the tale sounds too preposterous.

One afternoon, the service received a phone call from a farmer out in "Whoop Whoop" (Australian slang for some place out in the middle of nowhere). Apparently, he'd had an accident with some agricultural machinery out on his land and had cut his leg, which was now bleeding profusely.

Informing them that he was now back in his living room and was stemming the bleeding with some cloth, they flew out to his remote property. On reaching it, they entered his house and found him semi-conscious on his sofa, with a makeshift tourniquet and another piece of cloth attached to his leg. Well the top half of it anyway. The other half, which had been completely severed just above his knee, was lying on the floor some three metres away. The effort that must have took to get him back home is amazing isn't it? The humour in this little episode is that up until then he had not mentioned the fact that the rest of his leg was no longer attached to his body. Then again, I did say before that these Aussies were quite a tough bunch. The place is definitely worth a visit with its informative guides and their anecdotes.

The next day we headed down to Cunnamulla, where I paired the others up to work the town, while I headed to a tiny place called Eulo, just a stone's throw away. With only about twenty houses there and a pub, I drew a blank. Incidentally, it's here where the "World Lizard Racing Championships" are held each August, when the population is swelled by thousands. Driving back in what was now a quite wounded car with the exhaust blowing so bad that it sounded as if a V8 engine had now been put under its bonnet, it was time to think about heading to "Brissy"!

The next day was another lengthy drive as we set off just after seven. At first the weather was one of those particular cloudless skies that are endemic in the outback region. Reaching the town of Roma, big black clouds began to gather ahead of us, but I thought nothing of it. Half an hour later, and without warning, the wind and the rain began lashing down in what were almost storm-like conditions. The crack on the windscreen had now begun to spread like a lazy fork of lightning, and by the time we reached the very large town of Toowoomba, this menacing feature in the glass had travelled almost halfway down the length of the screen. My only thought was to silently will it into staying in one piece till we reached the city.

With the rain hammering down heavier than since Noah had set off in his ark, I didn't think it could get any worse, but it did! Heading ever eastwards in this appalling weather, the driver's side windscreen wiper suddenly vanished! Now, with a wall of water obstructing my view, I managed to pull over in this horrendous driving rain.

Getting out, we attempted to find the missing wiper blade back down the road, and then, realising we would have to find the nut that held it on, which by now would have been nigh on impossible in what had become terrible conditions, thought of another plan. This plan was to take the wiper blade off the passenger side and move it to the driver's. With no spanner, though, and the nut being on too tight, that idea ended. (With all those days travelling on those unsealed roads with the constant vibration of the vehicle travelling over those demonic tracks, time had worked the nut loose, until eventually letting the whole wiper blade come away after the frantic motion of it trying to do battle with the rain.)

Sitting in the car watching this deluge, something surprising happened. The rain stopped and we carried on our way.

Arriving at the large house in the West End of the city again, I was pleased to see my little Datsun patiently waiting for me. Unloading the bags, I suddenly jumped after hearing a shriek of such a magnitude of decibels that it could only have come from a female. In fact, if the pitch of this noise had been any louder it would have taken the severely injured windscreen out completely! Looking up at the doorway of the building, I could see the sales manager of the car we had just alighted from.

"What the fuck have you done to my car?" she screamed.

"We've been travelling on some rough roads," I replied nonchalantly.

"Where's the radiator grill gone? And what happened to the indicator light? And why is there a massive crack running across the windscreen?"

It was my turn to look at her as if she was the alien.

"We have been in the outback, love, and the roads out there aren't the best in the world," I informatively told her.

"What other damage is there?" she quizzed me again.

"Well, as you can see, you're gonna have to get a new windscreen wiper and wing mirror, and the exhaust is fucked as well!" I said, reeling off the battle damage.

As we walked up the steps to the house carrying our bags and pushing past her, I heard Dan's voice, "Oh Yeah! And you're going to need to get another spare tyre!"

As our ears were immersed in a wail of crying, I thought, oh yeah, I forgot about that one!

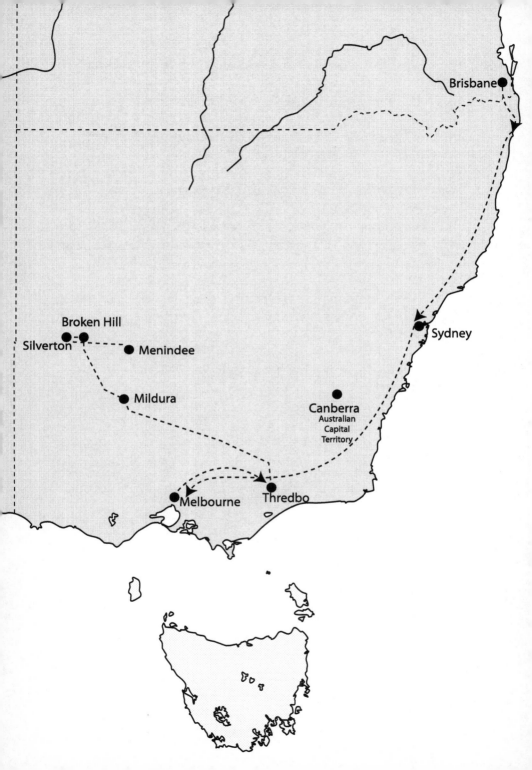

Chapter 9

I was once again reunited with Anna who had come down from Townsville via the coastal route. It was here that I found that my feelings for her were more powerful than I could really contemplate and that I was possibly falling in love with the girl. Images flashed through my mind of settling in this country with the girl of my dreams, but my world was soon about to come crashing down on me from out of the blue.

Opening my mail one morning, I was pleasantly surprised to see my passport with a visa stamp attached to one of the pages with the words.

ISSUED ON 06OCT92 WITH EFFECT UNTIL THE HOLDER'S APPLICATION FOR THE ENTRY PERMIT IS DECIDED AND THE HOLDER IS NOTIFIED IN ACCORDANCE WITH REGULATION 35.

This stamp had superseded my one-year working visa and was obviously an acknowledgement that they had received my application and were, in due course, considering it. Why this had taken eight months I had no idea. On there were two little conditions that highlighted the stamp; one of which concerned me to say the least.

NO RESIDENCE

NO WORK

The residence I could understand, as I was not asking to live in the country permanently, but the no work bit meant just that – I couldn't work. Without working how could I earn a crust, as the Aussies so often use the phrase. Speaking to the boss, he informed me that it was just a formality and that everything should go according to plan.

So, heading back down to Melbourne and doing several trips back and forth in time, again into South Oz, I began to feel like *Doctor Who*. Christmas was once again looming, but I was getting increasingly anxious to hear news from immigration. I didn't have to wait long to find out their decision.

I was asked to meet the boss in the city one morning; he had some bad news to tell me. My application for sponsorship had been rejected. I had to leave the country immediately. Taking a deep breath, I churned over in my head what I wanted to do now. The answer came back quickly. I was staying whether they liked it or not.

With this answer, he informed me that employment with the company was no longer possible as they would obviously see me still paying taxes from my wages, and the company would then be liable for a hefty fine. It was also his duty to inform the authorities of my intentions. That afternoon, I was asked to call immigration and speak to a Mr Kennedy.

With the current position I was in, a sort of paranoia hit me which led to my intention to keep the conversation as short as possible, just in case they were tracing the call and the next thing I would know was to see a police car pulling up outside the telephone kiosk.

I Informed him of my decision, and his broad Australian accent told me that from now on I was classed as an illegal immigrant and that when they caught me I would be deported, and would not be allowed to return to the country for five years. My response to this was, "By the time you catch me I will have seen so much of this country I wouldn't want to come back for at least five years anyway!"

There was silence, and then I heard him tell me that I could not go to America for five years either. My response to this was, "I don't want to go to America anyway."

Telling him to have a good day, I hung up. Standing in the kiosk, my mind raced and my legs started to feel like jelly. I didn't have a clue what to do, and I had now become the fugitive! My initial thoughts were to ask Anna to marry me, but I quashed that idea as I was in an awful situation with regard to who I could and could not trust. Also, I was not entirely sure about her emotions for me. If I moved to Sydney and somehow someone found out my status and reported me, I would soon be back on a plane to the United Kingdom.

Booking into a little campsite on the outskirts of the city, I realised I would have to sell the car to buy me more time and, if I couldn't think of a plan, a return ticket home. The boss informed me I would have to lie low and could no longer be in contact with the other employees in case one found out and informed the police. All alone and sitting in a caravan with the rain hammering down on its metal roof, I was thoroughly miserable and had an incredible urge to contact Anna.

Selling the car, I spent the next two weeks cut off from everyone I had worked with. Not even being able to bring myself to call home, I began to drink copious amounts of alcohol each day in my little caravan to try and forget the reality I now found myself in. My only thoughts were about returning home, but there was a huge conflict going on inside my head. I had grown to love this country, the culture and the people that occupied this great place and desperately wanted to see as much of it as possible before returning.

I thought of taking a bus up to Ayers Rock and then heading over to the north coast of Queensland again to see the Great Barrier Reef, which I still (despite being in the region for several months) had not seen. Knowing that as soon as I had given any prospective employer my tax file number that immigration would come knocking at my door, I thought of doing what thousands of people do not just in Oz but all over the world and that was to work for cash illegally. Whatever I ended up doing though, I would have to make my mind up quickly before my money dried up completely.

It was about this time the Irishman who I had met in Sydney had begun to get fed up travelling up and down the eastern seaboard of Oz, and having also overstayed his visa, he was contemplating returning home to the Emerald Isle. He had gone undetected by the authorities as Australia had thousands and thousands of illegal immigrants, and there was obviously not an effective system in place to trap them all, as he was still being paid his commissions and paying his taxes with no questions being asked.
With the boss inviting me to his home one afternoon, I once again met up with Terry. Talking over a few beers, a plan was hatched that would suit all three of us and this is what we came up with.

Buying a car between the two of us, we would head out into the wilds of this enormous country and work towns way off the beaten track, allowing us both to see sights and experience places that most travellers could not possibly dream of or experience themselves. Working together, we would split the commissions which would initially be paid into Terry's bank account. With the boss having two very experienced salesmen roaming the continent giving him no liabilities, he now offered to pay us four hundred dollars per order.

So, off we both trooped to see Helmut to find out once again what car would get us to Darwin and back. This time, though, we would definitely need a vehicle to carry out this task and further. Unbeknown to me at that time, once eleven more months had elapsed I would have covered another twenty thousand kilometres plus. And to put that into perspective once again, that would be greater than the distance from Oz back to my own little hometown in Wales. My real adventure was about to begin.

Finding a Mitsubishi Sigma station wagon, we parted with four thousand dollars. This wagon was to take us to places that only four-wheel drives or an insane Welshman and Irishman driving a two-wheel drive would fear to tread. Not being able to afford some of the newer gas conversion cars, we had opted for petrol.

The most difficult decision I had to make, though, was to cut all links with Anna, as it was impractical to carry on seeing one another when I would be thousands of kilometres away from her most of the time. This may seem an odd choice to make, bearing in mind my feelings for her, but this time I let my head rule my heart. Instructing the boss to tell her I had suddenly decided to return home for no particular reason, my links with her were severed ... for now.

Setting off in January of 1993, this year was to become one of my most memorable to date, where over the year I would see and experience stuff that would result in bringing stories back with me that would beggar belief! It was also uncanny as it was the first year since I had been a child that I had decided to buy and keep a diary. Most of my diaries during my childhood would last, at best, till March, after one mundane entry after another was written on each page. This one was to last the whole year. I guess deep down I knew that this year would be a lot different to the previous two ... I was not wrong!

The first few weeks of that year were pretty uneventful, travelling with my Irish companion to dozens of outback towns in Victoria and the south-east corner of New South Wales. One point of interest which I will mention, though, was climbing Australia's highest peak, which is called Mount Kosciuszko (pronounced cozzie-oz-co), and was named after a Polish explorer, Count Paul Edmund Strzelecki, who, being the first non-indigenous person to climb it, named it after a Polish national hero. Be careful if you ever get this question in a quiz, as it is not the tallest mountain in Oz if you include the Australian external territories, which is, in fact, Mount Mawson on Heard Island. I got caught out on that one once, and it's a bloody good job I wasn't on that television show at the time called Who Wants to be a Millionaire? It's not that high, as mountains go, either – just over two thousand metres.

Towards the end of January, and in the height of the Aussie summer, we decided to head into the semi-arid desert of far western New South Wales and the mining town of Broken Hill. It is the longest-lived mining town in the country and was discovered by the explorer Charles Sturt. He found a chain of hills, one of which, he noted, had a "break in it", and thus the name was born. This original hill was later to be found full of silver ore and no longer exists after being mined away. Being a prosperous place, we had to once again adopt the mindset that many door-to-door salespeople would have been constantly knocking their doors, and that we would have to persevere to find households that had no encyclopedias.

Leaving the town of Mildura near the border early one morning, we went that half-hour back in time again, despite not crossing the border into South Oz. (Broken Hill adopts Central Standard Time because of its remote position and close proximity to the border.) Heading into dry barren scrubland, this was what we had to expect for some three hundred kilometres before we reached this frontier town. I wondered what was ahead of us. Little did I know.

It was about nine o'clock when we switched on the radio to catch the morning local news, and from that day on, our bookselling locations were to dramatically change. Having travelled almost halfway to this desert mining town, we heard some dreadful news about one of the two mines at the town – it was closing down. The company, called Pasminco, at the time apparently owned both mines, but due to an economic downturn for certain metals, the north mine was to shut within three weeks with the loss of five hundred jobs out of a total workforce of eleven hundred. We couldn't believe it!

Stopping the car, we got out and sat on the bonnet. Staring out into the emptiness of the desert, we discussed our options while a dozen flies from Australia's army of billions buzzed us, triggering our Aussie salutes. We had reached our rubicon, as between the both of us, over the last twelve months, we had worked every town behind us for nearly a thousand kilometres. We now had no option but to carry on northwards and see what we could salvage out of this silver-mining outpost.

About fifty kilometres from the town, the desert started to change with little blades of green grass poking up through very healthy looking scrub and there was the occasional tree covered in leaves. Outside, it was just nudging a hundred degrees Fahrenheit in the shade, and the surroundings looked a bit out of place considering this oven-like desert heat.

It was about this time that I noticed a strange, large, erratic black cloud on the otherwise cloudless horizon. Watching it come closer and closer, it seemed to swirl from side to side and suddenly leap forwards and then retract almost as quickly, but still retain constant forward motion. Squinting our eyes, we tried to fathom out what this phenomena was in the glare of the sun. It reminded me of the scene from the film *Star Wars*, where Luke, Han and Obi-Wan Kenobi are in the *Millennium Falcon*, trying to work out what celestial object is in front them before realising too late that it's not a moon, but the space station the Death Star.

In almost an instant, our death star slammed into us. Hundreds of thousands and maybe millions of locusts began battering our cruiser like tiny meteorites. Activating our shields, well alright, our windscreen wipers, this only made matters worse as the screen got covered in a mush as the bugs that were nearly being atomised left their carcasses behind, and being spread across my viewpoint, they reduced my sight even more to what was becoming a rapidly dwindling vision of the road.

What with nearly half of the mining population of Broken Hill to vanish before our very eyes from the redundancies, and the knock-on effect that it would have on the town; with the flies and the locusts, I thought of the biblical plagues of Egypt and half-expected the town's reservoir to have been changed to blood; we drove through this maelstrom effect of never-ending insects.

Ploughing through locust alley and arriving in the town around mid-morning, the streets seemed eerily quiet, with very few people walking around. Fortunately, this was normal as with the heat now reaching forty degrees centigrade, most of the inhabitants in this town that were not underground mining sought refuge in the air-conditioned buildings.

Booking a twin room in a very rustic hotel, we decided to leave the air conditioning on as within minutes of it being switched off the room very quickly became a sauna. Heading out in the mid-afternoon furnace, we decided to split up to reconnoitre this quite large town of nearly twenty thousand people, to try and get a feel of how people were reacting to this very bad news for the community. With me now being the invisible man as far as the company was concerned, on any orders I wrote, I signed the customer copy, and on returning to base, Terry signed the copies that had to be forwarded to head office. I also had to change my name to Terry while knocking doors on my own in case a family mentioned my name to the head office in Sydney, when the company called them to verify the order and arrange a delivery date.

With us meeting back at the hotel at around nine, we both had the same news to tell each other, which was basically the fact that everyone was now worried with what was going to happen to their local economy, and that no one was intending on spending any money at all unless they had to.

The next day, after picking half a dozen locust corpses from the radiator grill, we worked another part of the town together. Writing one order from a family whose husband was employed by a telecoms company and not directly affected by this impending economic doom, we returned to our room to find it sweltering.

"Did you leave the air conditioning on?" I asked Terry.

"Yeah matey," Terry replied.

Matey was the word Terry would often use to address me, which I guess simplified things for him as half the time I didn't know whether I was Lance or Terry myself.

"Well it doesn't seem to be working now," I said.

The owner of the place came up and removed the front of the grill to our room cooling device and found a large block of ice inside it.

"Jesus Christ, boys, how long have you had this thing on for?" the guy said, sounding amazed.

"About two days," Terry replied.

"Well it's fucked till all this shit melts," he announced, trying to scrape some of the ice off the machine with his fingers.

That night it took ages to get to sleep in that sweltering room, as he refused to move us, and with hindsight we should have gone down to the bar and consumed enough alcohol to ease ourselves to sleep.

The next day we were back out in the giant oven again, and rapidly running out of doors to knock, we decided to pay a visit to the ghost town of nearby Silverton. It was here that they filmed *Mad Max 2*, and the pub there has dozens of pictures on its walls of Mel Gibson and the gang. Just thinking about this though, it's only in Oz that a ghost town would have its own pub!

Sinking a couple of iced sodas, we then drove out to Menindee, which is just over a hundred kilometres from "The Silver City", as Broken Hill is known. It is here where the school was that was built in a dip and hence was flooded that I told you about earlier on.

Driving through shallow flooded roads, we learned that this region had received a deluge not experienced for a couple of generations. Menindee, though well off the beaten track, is quite amazing. The air-conditioning units that sat strapped outside people's houses were almost the size of a small car, and bearing in mind temperatures here get close to fifty degrees centigrade, they needed them as well.

The other feature this town has is a huge irrigation system that feeds Broken Hill and South Australia with water. These large, quite shallow lakes, which are usually dry, help to catch the overflow waters from the mighty Darling River. Because of the recent sizeable rainfall, the desert had now been transformed into a sort of an oasis that was home to an abundance of pelicans, in numbers I had never seen before, nor since, and certainly must have included at least a thousand or more. The arrival of this rain also brought the locusts that thrive when conditions like these prevail in desert regions.

Without writing an order there (which we put down to bad luck), we headed back to the outback mini-desert city again. We now had to move on, as trying to sell books in this place was like trying to find rocking horse shit. Sitting at the bar in one of the pubs, I got out a detailed map of New South Wales, which on the reverse had a map of the whole of the country, albeit in obviously not so much detail. Poring over the map and shying away the occasional Aboriginal asking if we had a spare dollar or cigarette, we tried to work out where to go next.

The numbers of Aboriginal people had slowly increased as we headed further into the western outback of New South Wales. It was now common to have one or more of them ask if we had a spare dollar or spare cigarette. These two most common questions would sometimes be unintelligible, depending on what level of intoxication they were at, which ranged from a merry state to completely and utterly pissed. It was quite unnerving at first, as you could be in a street, in a shop or in a bar and one would quietly sidle or stagger up to you with the immortal words, "Have ya gotta dollar, brudder?" or, "Have you got a smoke, bloke?"

With me being a non-smoker, I could shake them off with the smoking question, and with the answer to the coinage question, I would merely ask if they could change a hundred-dollar bill; on each and every occasion the answer would be "No!" One clever fella, though, did offer to take it into a shop and break it down for me. You also had to be careful, especially in a pub, as later on when we really went off the tourist radar and worked places people would be advised not to tread, giving a dollar or a smoke to one and not the other could light the litmus paper of a very delicate tinderbox, which would be likened to a unknown amount of TNT getting ready to explode, as we were to experience on several occasions.

It was much easier to remain steadfast and not give into their persistence, which would have made any door-to-door salesman proud. Terry, after being pestered continually, would occasionally cave in, and would then be handing out cigarettes to every man and his dog in the pub, just to keep the peace.

Studying the map, we now had two options. Either head west and into South Oz or eastwards into the unknown territory of the outback of northern New South Wales. Having both worked South Australia, we decided to put that on hold for a few months, before venturing back into it and making plans to head north, through what they call the red centre, stopping to visit Ayers Rock on the way. So it was to the east we looked, and looking at the next town that lay some two hundred kilometres away, it was this town that I will probably remember more than any other to my dying days – Wilcannia.

The barman, who had previously been looking at the map with us and marvelling at all the places we had been to, walked back over to us.

"What's this town like?" I asked, pointing to Wilcannia.

His eyes suddenly widened and I could sense a sort of apprehension from him.

"Well, what's it like mate?" I asked again.

"That place is bad news, mate!" It was this reply that has been lodged into my brain ever since.

"You don't want to stop there," he very quickly added.

"Why's that?" Terry enquired.

The barman suddenly called out to three of his locals at the other end of the bar, all men in their fifties wearing their iconic Aussie headgear and garments that the outback folk wore.

"Hey Brian, Jeff, Bob. What's Wilcannia like?"

"Who wants to know?" one of the very sun-weathered faces replied.

The barman then explained who we were and what we did and told them we were thinking of stopping off at the town to sell books. Another statement then lodged into my grey matter.

"You fellas got a death wish or something?"

I looked at this very burly man and his friends, and wondered what could possibly be so dangerous about the place we were about to venture to?

"Is it rough or what?" I asked.

All three of them had a slight chuckle, and then the shortest of them spoke.

"Do yourself a favour, boys, and just drive through the town and onto Cobar. Or if you have to stop for gas, do so and then carry on. Don't stop!"

Cobar was the next town after Wilcannia, which was another two hundred and fifty-odd kilometres on top. It was then that Terry made one of his sarcastic and often funny comments.

"Should my matey here hold the shotgun while I fill up at the petrol station then, fellas?"

"Might be a good idea," one of them replied.

Looking back at South Oz, it was still too early to go there and head northwards as the top end of Australia was now in the middle of the wet season which would severely constrain our travelling. We contemplated heading to Western Australia, but both of us wanted to visit Ayers Rock. Besides the capital city of the state, Perth was getting on close to three thousand kilometres away – a big distance and a lot of petrol.

Listening to the inhabitants, I thought we would take this advice and just stop to refuel before heading onto Cobar. The crazy Irishman had other ideas though.

Heading off to another pub, we met some truck drivers and some old mining boys who had retired and decided to see their dwindling years away in the town. Terry probed them on what Wilcannia was like, and everyone's reply came back with negative vibes. Getting a clearer picture of what the town was like, it transpired that the vast majority of the town's population of less than a thousand people were Aboriginal. With most of them unemployed, the days were spent drinking heavily, and along with this pastime came the violence that this alcohol fuelled.

The people of this area had nothing but contempt for the indigenous population there, with the words "Blackfellas", "Bludgers", "Abos" and "Gins" (Aboriginal women) laced throughout their conversations with us. One of the eldest, who was in his seventies, who clearly had some deeply rooted racism within, suggested razing the town to the ground one night through military force while the black population slept. It was hard to understand the venom that came from what I would describe as "down-to-earth" and amicable chaps, and until I started to get under the skin of these indigenous people, I looked at them all in the same way as these men now viewed them.

The more I listened, the more I was hell bent on avoiding the place, while the more Terry listened, the more he wanted to go and visit what one trucker described as "hell on earth". Walking in the warm street lamped night back to the hotel, Terry's Irish accent travelled through the air as he tried to convince me to stop and work the town.

"Think of it matey. No one would have knocked that town because of its reputation. All we have to do is find some Aborigines that do work, and I bet they'll snap the books up, cos they've never had the chance to buy them before."

"But none of them work! And they probably can't read anyway!" I insisted.

With his sense of humour coming to the fore once again, his flashy smile lit the street as he said, "We'll find someone. And with regards to the reading, Mum and Dad can start with ELF and learn the alphabet themselves with the kids."

He had a point, as it was highly probable these Aboriginal people had never come across door-to-door salespeople and one of the comments that one of the truckers said rang in my ears.

"Hell! Even the Jehovah's Witnesses are too shit-scared to set foot in the place!"

As we headed across the Barrier Highway towards the town the next morning, another fact shot back into my head. The population was numbered at several hundred, and normally a town of that size would be lucky to have one policeman to patrol it. Wilcannia had sixteen!

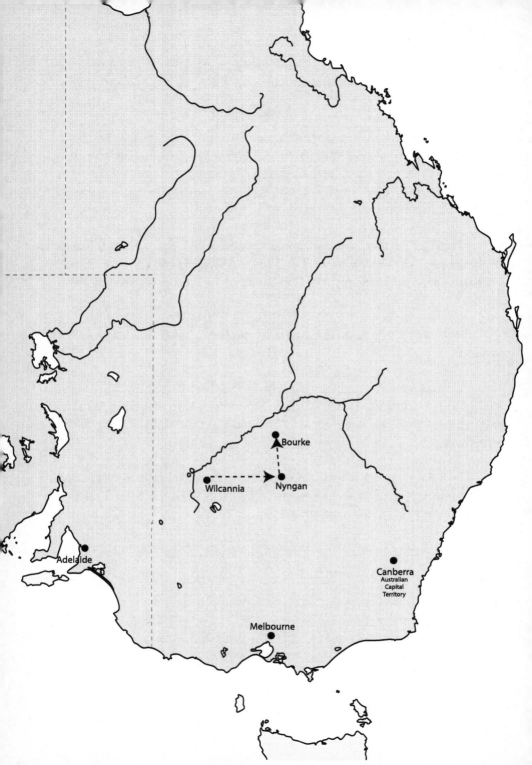

Chapter 10

Wilcannia came into our sights through the shimmering heat at eleven o'clock on Sunday the 31st of January 1993. The town was cooking in forty degree heat, and for the next seven days the mercury during the day was to live in the forties, with it hitting nearly forty-eight four days later in the town of Bourke (pronounced Burke).

As we entered the town, I noticed two Aboriginal men barefooted and dressed in what I can only describe as attire that looked like they had been transported in a time machine to the present day from the 1970s. Wearing colourful dusty-looking shirts and black trousers that were so flared that any Motown band would have been impressed, they looked towards us. With each clutching a large brown bottle, they occasionally swayed back and forth and side to side like blades of grass in an ever-changing breeze, with their levels of drunkenness up in the higher levels of intoxication. With Terry slowing the car down to a walking pace, I looked at them, giving a friendly half-wave from the open window. As we became adjacent to them, I made eye contact with their deep dark eyes as they stared back, and I wondered what they were thinking.

Opposite these two fellas were several single-storey houses ringed by a high fence topped with barbed wire and completely sealed in by a large closed gate. Initially thinking this was where the old folk lived for safety, I was quickly put right by a middle-aged white man as we parked up. It was the police accommodation. A slight breeze that felt as if it were being blown out by a hot hairdryer blew down a very dusty street that had welcomed the desert with open arms, and it depicted a scene from the Wild West of America but without the horses.

Doing a quick walkabout to gauge the size of the place, we crossed the road to avoid walking right past a pub that had half a dozen or so Aboriginal men and women outside its saloon-like doors, clearly all at the upper echelons of alcoholic merriment.

As we crossed, one of the men called out, "Hey, bro!"

Brother, bro, brudder, and bloke were all salutations that the Aboriginal people used when eye contact was first made with us. You could be halfway down a street and one such greeting would be shouted sometimes a hundred yards or so away. After turning around to acknowledge this greeting, you would then hear the "Have ya gotta dollar or a smoke?" line.

Looking back at the group, I could see the women wearing colourful, all be they faded, dresses against the backdrop of the interior of the pub, which was plunged into a pitch-black dark. Walking back into the town, we started to knock some doors, and although we failed to get into any homes, as people were either not interested or already had books, we quickly and obviously realised that the town had been knocked before by booksellers in the past.

From the general chit-chat from these white folk, we had already established that the Aboriginal part of the town was known as the "Mallee", and was located on the outskirts of the settlement. This was quickly followed by warnings for us not to enter this area, as the place was inhabited by drunken blackfellas and gins and that violence towards us was quite possible.

Again, derogatory remarks were made about them that made me think that perhaps the Aboriginal people in this town were nothing but a bunch of parasites that lived on state hand-outs, and that we should have just driven through and onto the town of Cobar.

Pretty soon we had knocked the whole white area of the town and had drawn a blank. It was then I heard Terry propose what we should do next and a sudden wave of trepidation hit me.

"Let's work this Mallee area of the town."

"What! Are you serious?" I replied.

"Why not?" My travelling Irish companion said with a smile of

196

devilment on his face.

"Well, because we might get our faces smashed in or perhaps both disappear and never be seen again?" I defended the question.

"No we won't" he said, trying to sound reassuring.

"But none of them work," I said, shaking my head and holding my hands up, still not quite believing what he was proposing for us to do.

"Ah come on, matey, we'll give it a go." And with him holding our little knapsack around his shoulder, and more importantly the car keys in his pocket, he began to walk up the street towards the perimeter of the town. Catching him up and leaving the tarmac roads of the main town, I wondered what the hell was going to happen to us as we turned into another street called Hood. I thought of that film *Boyz n the Hood* and thought, don't I know it?

Walking down Hood Street, we clocked, about a hundred yards ahead, about a dozen Aboriginal men and women, some clutching bottles, others carrying a box of wine. With them weaving from side to side, while others lolloped as if trying to find flat ground on what was already a completely flat sandy surface, they looked like a very strange choreographed dancing troupe from Michael Jackson's song "Thriller", but without the costumes and make-up.

With us skirting around them without incident, I noticed the houses had dramatically changed to structures that had been finished without the cosmetic touch-up of paint and other more personal touches such as house numbers and other intrinsic things that personalise a home. Furthermore, some of the metal window frames lacked that important feature that completes them, namely windows.

As we approached another building, a group of half a dozen Aboriginal children rounded the corner of it and froze in their tracks. Again barefooted and wearing T-shirts, dresses, shorts and skirts, and ranging from the ages of four to ten, they spied us with intrigue and wonder before they all suddenly turned around. Breaking into the best sprint each of them could manage, and in complete unison, they yelled out the words I would hear on countless occasions in the future.

"White fellas coming! White fellas coming!"

With them helter-skeltering back around the building, we followed them and came upon an open doorway. Terry, leaning through the aperture of the doorway, was confronted by the two youngest of the group.

"Is your Mummy or Daddy home?" he spoke, in his alien Gaelic tongue.

With their little mouths and eyes wide open and looking at Terry as if ET had actually landed on their doorstep, they stood rooted to the spot in complete silence.

"Can I help you?"

From behind the children came an Aboriginal woman who was as sober as a judge, and to be honest she completely threw me, as up until then in the town we had only seen female Aborigines as completely "out of it" as their fellow male counterparts.

"We're in the town selling educational books that will help the little ones do well in school."

At the stroke of a brush, Terry had just changed the door-knocking script for the both of us forever. Well at least for the Aboriginal folk.

"Well, come in," said she with a great big smile.

Entering the kitchen, we watched the children clamour around the table to receive their Sunday lunch. With pork chops sizzling in the frying pan, I watched with horror as the mother removed them from the pan and put them onto unwashed dirty plates. It was then that the smell inside the household suddenly hit me. It was as if my head had suddenly been plunged into the foulest dustbin full of rubbish that should have been thrown out weeks ago. With Terry standing next to me, I very quickly made an excuse and went back outside to throw up.

Wiping the sick from around my mouth, I reluctantly returned into the household. Terry, being Terry, hardly ate any food, and the stick insect that he was, it used to amaze me how he could survive on so little food each day. He had by now met the man of the house, and being aware of the smell but having very little if no contents in his stomach to regurgitate, turned to me and said, "Haven't Wayne and Julie got a great place here?"

Looking around at the unpainted bare breeze block walls, the filthy chairs and kitchen table where the children were now eagerly devouring their pork chops and mash, the stinking kitchen sink and the grime on the cooker that looked like it had never received a clean since it had been installed, I thought, what the hell are we doing in here?

With no trophies, no pictures on the walls and not a goldfish in sight, I wondered what our small talk would entail. Looking down at the floor and seeing many creatures from the insect world crawling around, I very quickly dismissed asking them the question of what sort of cockroach that was heading for a small plastic bowl full of water on the floor. I needn't have worried though, as Terry had it all in hand.

"Have you got a job? Is it permanent and forty hours or more a week? Have you got a phone? And can you afford seventy bucks a month?" That was Terry's new Aboriginal small talk, again created in one swift stroke. With a "Yes" to all four questions, we had been given a green light to proceed with the demo of our educational package.

Establishing that Wayne was employed by the shire council, I suddenly realised that this was the first Aboriginal man that I had come across that actually held down a full-time permanent job. Having been in dozens of these folk's homes over the last couple of years, not one of them had worked.

Without further ado, Terry walked into their living room and with the words of something along the lines of "Have a look at this", proceeded with the demonstration. With him laying the posters onto the dirty concrete floor, I marvelled at the kids eating their chops without them consuming a handful of flies at the same time.

Watching from the kitchen doorway, which, like the windowless window frames, lacked the key ingredient a doorway requires – a door – Wayne and Julie sat on a sofa that was torn on the arms and looked like it was infested with the all bugs that were not brave enough to walk along the floor. Looking around this airless room that was devoid of air conditioning and artificial light, it seemed surreal as I watched events unfold in this twilight setting, though the coolness of the walls had now lent some respite from the stifling heat outside.

As I was getting slowly accustomed to the smell, the children came in from the kitchen and began to participate with the camouflage scene in the prospectus. As I looked on, I realised that Terry had captivated the whole family, and with the family dog coming in to see what all the fuss was about, I wondered how we would get through the paperwork if they decided to buy the books.

When the closing questions came, Terry again adapted it to an Aboriginal close.

"Do you like the books?" he said, nodding his head up and down to prompt a positive reply.

"Yes," came the entire family's response.

"And do you want them?" he continued, with his head still bobbing and his eyes now wide open as if trying to hypnotise them.

The family all looked at one another and then, turning to Terry, unanimously announced with raised voices, "Yes!"

The paperwork was removed from our bag, and although we talked everyone through the contract word by word, I was pleasantly surprised that both parents could read. With the children jumping up and down with excitement and both parents telling us that such an opportunity had not arisen for their family before, I started to think that maybe we had possibly found a new market. I was not wrong!

Bidding farewell and telling them that the books would be with them within two weeks, I watched the children running around excitingly with their "Blue Heeler" dog barking, trying to drown their happy-sounding voices. I quietly hoped the order would pass the credit check and that they would soon be learning the alphabet or have their heads into Peter Pan, "Rapunzel" or "Rumpelstiltskin".

Leaving the house, we headed deeper into the Mallee area of the town, and with the children from the house we had just left now telling their friends what our purpose in town was, we very quickly gathered an entourage that would have made even the Pied Piper very happy!

"What's in the bag, mister?"

Now the new children that were following us questioned me, the bag holder, as Terry lit up a fag.

"See, matey," his cocky and justifiable voice sprang from his mouth. "We'll have orders all over this place by sundown."

This result so far was certainly encouraging, but it was not to last long. Going from house to house was an experience that will live with me for a very long time. Peering through windowless or broken windows, we could see people stumbling or lying around in semi or completely comatose states. Walking past one house, we saw half a dozen men and women fast asleep in the yard, cooking themselves in the blazing afternoon sun, with empty beer bottles scattered around. It was as if Pussy Galore and her pilots from the James Bond film Goldfinger had flown over and sprayed that knockout gas all over the place, as each passing dwelling and garden contained similar incapacitated human beings.

Knocking one door, we were met by a topless Aboriginal woman with a newborn suckling on one of her enormous breasts. Asking again, one of the few sober occupants of this crazy place, if her other half was in, she duly informed us that he was in the pub!

Walking through the Mallee, we came across a house where we were met by a burly young Aboriginal in his thirties dressed in just a pair of long burgundy shorts. Asking if he was the man of the house, his negative, yet sober, response was followed by him leaning indoors and calling out a name.

"George!"

From within the twilight interior came a tall Aboriginal man with shoulder-length hair, which was starting to grey in parts, and wearing a long white shirt and flared trousers. He introduced himself and enquired what the purpose of our visit was.

Shaking our hands, he invited us in, and walking into his spartan living room, we were followed by what seemed to be all the kids from the area. With adults who were clearly not affected by alcohol joining us, the room very quickly filled up with around twenty-five people.

With the burly Aboriginal now explaining to us that George was a tribal elder and known as "The Man of the Mallee", this quite elderly gentleman, for an Aboriginal, had a great influence over the people of this micro-environment of Wilcannia. Furthermore, he was employed by the New South Wales government as a liaison officer with the police force. This role was basically to mediate between the police and the Aboriginal population of the town, and to suppress any aggression that could suddenly turn into violence through any disputes or domestics or general trouble that was simmering or brewing. With these people having a great respect for George, they all listened intently and silently at what Terry was now telling them.

Studying George, I tried to guestimate his age, and putting him in his late fifties or early sixties, I realised he was one of the few older Aborigines I had met.

Now, this may sound strange, but the average life expectancy for the Aboriginal people of Oz, at the time, and yet again if my memory serves me well, was around fifty-five (but don't quote me on that). Many died far earlier due to the alcohol abuse that had ravaged their bodies, coupled with poor education on hygiene and health in general.

An Aboriginal man in his late twenties, and clearly drunk, joined our audience, but his sober neighbours asked him to leave. As he walked unsteadily around the room, we heard George call over to him.
"Dingle, you can stay and watch, but only if you remain quiet."

This voice of authority registered in the man's drunken grey matter, and Dingle stood at the edge of the crowd, nodding towards George while swaying back and forth.

With Terry starting the demonstration, I followed with the "Junior Classics", and looking at the small children sitting on the floor with their little legs crossed, with the older children and adults standing behind, I felt like a showman at a fairground, selling his wares to the crowds such men often attract.

Terry then began with the prospectus, and only just a few pages in, heard a slurred voice emanating from the group.

"Has it got any pyramids in it?"

With Terry now down on one knee and balancing the book on his other leg, he looked up, and realising the question had come from our drunken observer, he replied, "Yes, Dingle, the pyramids of Egypt are in the encyclopedia."

Dingle looked back at Terry with a sloshed smile.

Terry pressed on, and one by one he let each person look at the camouflage scene to see if they could find the rabbit. With several finding our fluffy animal, a few found the stick insect as well without being asked to find it. I guess it was true that the bush skills that they say these people have are second to none, and no smart stick insect was going to be able to hide itself from them – not even in a book!

As he reached the bowl of fruit and the primary colours question, Dingle asked the same question again.

"Are there any pyramids in it?"

Again, Terry looked up, and giving a half-smile, he replied, "Yes, Dingle, there are pyramids in the encyclopedia," emphasising the word "are".

Dingle once again looked back with a childish silly grin on his face.

Next came my turn with the explanation of how the reference service worked. Midway through this phase another question came from our pissed participant.

"Can you ask about pyramids?"

Replying a "Yes" to Dingle, I wondered what the hell the fascination was with "the pyramids?" With a couple of adults asking him to shut up, I ploughed on with the demo.

Letting Terry finish up with the Australia and New Zealand encyclopedia and the dictionaries, the bloody pyramid question was asked yet again, twice. Looking at Terry, I could see that his patience was wearing a little thin with this same question being fired at him, but again his humour overruled any temper building within him, and he came back with a "No, but we could put some in for you if you like" and a "Yes, it is under the letter 'P'."

By now, even the children were telling Dingle to shut up, and if the demo had lasted much longer, despite his generally good-natured temperament,

Terry would have battered him with the prospectus or money box.

With the demo coming to an end, the Aboriginal close arrived. With George agreeing to the question of whether he liked the books or not, followed by a multitude of voices echoing this, the question of whether he wanted them or not quickly followed.

There was suddenly a deathly silence as the whole room looked at George, and it seemed a lifetime before any body language was visible from the leader of their people. Shaking his head very slowly, I could almost feel a wave of disappointment hit me as he looked back at us and said.

"No."

This response even surprised Terry, and in the midst of his showmanship he had suddenly felt as if he had been shot down from a great height. Very quickly and unperturbed he came back with what we would call the "guilt" statement, and with a great big smile said, "But all the children will benefit from having a great education and will do really well at school!"

Again there was silence in the room, and as George dipped his head to look at the ground, I began to feel a little uncomfortable as this silence lasted for much longer than before. Looking back up, he looked straight at Terry, and momentarily pausing, he said, "I can't afford them."

The atmosphere in that room, on that day, at that moment in time, felt as if you could have cut the air with a knife.

"But it's only seventy dollars a month," insisted my Irish sales colleague.

"I know," replied George, "but it is still that little too much for me."

From the group, one of the mother's suddenly spoke. "I could give you five dollars a month to help you, George."

These words made the room burst into chatter, and with three other people offering five dollars each a month, things started to look hopeful and in turn generated excitement among what could have been a class full of kids.

George looked over at me, and fixing his eyes with mine I felt I saw a great sadness in his eyes. With his voice now barely audible he spoke again, "No, I don't want them."

Packing our posters up and placing them neatly in the bag with the prospectus and money box, we left the building with not a sound coming from within. Even Dingle had finally shut up!

Walking back down the red dusty road, we decided to call it a day and head off for Cobar where we would find somewhere to sleep overnight or sleep in the car if need be, though that rarely happened. As we headed back to the main part of town in the late afternoon sun, I felt a certain sense of relief at having survived Wilcannia unscathed. Discussing the afternoon's events with my Celtic brother, we began to hear a vehicle approach behind us at some speed.

A silver family saloon car turned right in front of our path, sending a cloud of red dust and sand towards us, and we heard the vehicle come to an abrupt halt. With the sound of the automobile's doors opening and the dust cloud clearing, we could see the Aborigine with the burgundy shorts and two other men with a similar build to him but with much larger muscular arms.

"Get in the car. George wants to see you."

This message from our shorts-wearing obstacle came in the form of a command rather than an invitation, and with us both looking at one another, Terry's humour attacked the little group in front of us.

"But we've just seen him."

With Terry producing a nice cheery smile, I wondered what was about to happen next.

"Get in the car." This instruction was conveyed to us once again, only from a different source who was now opening the rear door of the car wide open.

"Why? What have we done?" I asked inquisitively. "We have only just left him."

"He wants to speak to you." Again, a third and different voice this time.

By now my mind was racing and going into overdrive. What could he possibly want to speak to us about? He had already told us that he couldn't afford the books, and had made it plain that as a result of this, he clearly didn't want them. I tried to fathom the logic as to why he wanted us to return, and an awful thought came into my head.

Had we inadvertently embarrassed this very important man in front of his people, by him revealing that he didn't have the money to purchase what everyone could clearly see would have been beneficial for the Aboriginal folk of Wilcannia? And on that thought, were we about to be driven to the edge of town, beaten to a pulp, or shot and put into some unmarked grave? Was he going to take our car off us, only to sell it on one of the main streets at a bargain price of two thousand, one hundred and fifty dollars and say, "I'll have the books now, here's the cash," or put us into slave labour for the next thirty-eight months washing cars for locals, paying him seventy dollars a month until the books had been paid for?

All these things and crazier paranoia ran through my head, and although these guys were not going to let us pass, I was not getting into that car either.

Terry looked at me and I then made the decision.

"We'll walk back to George's house," I said firmly.

With both of us turning around and slowly making our way back towards this tribal elder's house, we quietly discussed what was going on in our minds as the car slowly followed behind us. Telling Terry I was hoping that we would come across one of the supposedly sixteen policemen that policed this town, none of whom had we seen thus far and had begun to wonder if they all took Sundays off, Terry was more concerned as to who would be put in the cooking pot first.

Arriving at the house again, we heard George's voice pleasantly beckon us in and the word "please" brought some reassurance to me. On entering, we could now see that George had moved to a table and chairs at the back of the room and also see that our exit had been well and truly blocked by the three Aboriginal men now standing in the doorway. We waited in anticipation of what he was about to say. Staring momentarily at us, he then spoke in a strong, firm tone of voice.

"I'll take the books."

With the tactfulness of a priest asking someone at confession, "Why are you telling me this?" Terry asked, "Why the change of heart, George?"

A little smile grew across this senior man's face, and asking us to join him at the table, we sat down next to him.

"When you left my house and the little ones realised they were not going to get any books, they all began to cry their little hearts out. And do you know what, boys?"

We both shook our heads and replied, "No?"

"They began to break my heart."

The burly Aborigine that we had first met at the door had now moved around, and standing behind George, he gently put his hand on his shoulder.

"But can you afford them, George?" I asked, making sure that this man was not going to get into any financial difficulty in the near future and then find he would have to return the books, making matters even worse. Now, this was a first for me as normally if someone wanted the books, they were having them and who cared what was around the corner in three, six, twelve months or whatever time. At the end of the day they were all grown adults and had decisions to make in their everyday lives, and if they came unstuck financially later on down the track I wouldn't care – I had been paid my commission.

This was different though, as I could see this man was going to shoulder a burden not just for his family but for others as well. Sitting there, we listened as to why George had changed his mind.

He had realised straight away, that the offers from the other families to contribute towards the books, although at first were quite genuine, were indeed empty promises as they would soon forget to make their contribution, and it would then be entirely up to him to find the money each month. He had calculated that if he could get the extra twenty dollars a month from the others for the first four months, it would be all he would need, as an outstanding loan he had taken out in the past would have by then come to an end and he would then have surplus cash.

Filling in the paperwork, he had already decided where the books would go in his home, which was an angle we would frequently ask families, as it sort of cemented the deal with them already visualising the books in their home. We would also ask them what sort of bookcase they were considering to buy, again to set the wheels in motion when they had committed to the purchase.

Informing us that his home would become a sort of library and that the children of the Mallee would not be able to take the books from the vicinity of the building, but could get access to the books any day they liked, I again hoped that the order would not fail the credit check.

Bidding farewell to us, he remarked at how bold we had been to venture into this area of town which was basically a no-go area for white fellas. Giving his blessing, he told us that if we came across any trouble in the town before we left, that we were to tell the troublemakers that we had been invited to the town by "George, the man of the Mallee". This would be sufficient to assure us a safe passage to the car.

With me not wasting an opportunity, I asked some of the adults and children that had returned to the house if they wouldn't mind having a photograph taken with me. Together with a kangaroo who had befriended the neighbourhood, Terry took a snap of me with nine members of the Mallee, including George.

Although we encountered no trouble that day, we were to find out that once you had received such a blessing from the tribal elders of a town or community, you were pretty much untouchable, and we were to find out on one occasion such a blessing probably saved our lives.

Filling up at the petrol station, we decided to miss Cobar and to drive onto Nyngan as we had formulated a plan to get up to Bourke where another large Aboriginal population were living.

Calling the boss, his response was that both orders would probably fail the credit check. He was wrong. Both orders were to "go up", as we used the phrase in the book business, and the Mallee was to receive its first set of encyclopedias.

Leaving Wilcannia just before sunset, our chatter was like two little children on Christmas Day, opening their presents with excitement and discussing what they had just received. If one of the flies from the Australian army of flies had been listening to us in the car that evening, he or she would have heard us tell one another that we were about to educate the entire population of this indigenous race and make a shedful of money in the meantime as well. We were euphoric!

Driving to Nyngan that evening, I thought about what we had experienced during the day. The warnings we had been given were justifiably right, as the community we had entered was indeed in an alcohol-fuelled environment that could generate violence in the blink of an eye. Although we had experienced none of the latter on the day, we were to see plenty of it in the future. What did surprise me, though, was that among those many drunken lost souls, there were people who just wanted to get on with their lives as best they could, and most importantly do the best for their offspring.

Arriving in Nyngan and working the town next day, we finished early to get up to Bourke, and passing the "Welcome to Bourke, Gateway to the Real Outback" sign, we wondered what we would come across here. Booking a chalet on the Paddlewheel Caravan Park, the elderly guy took our money, threw us a key and, telling us where he would be if we needed him, buggered off to the local RSL club. (RSL clubs, or Returned and Services League clubs, are social clubs all over the country, and although anyone can drink in them, they are predominantly meant for retired or serving men and women from the armed forces of Australia.)

Entering this accommodation, I initially thought we were back in Wayne and Julie's house back in Wilcannia. Stinking hot, with no air conditioning and with a stale musty smell, coupled with a floor and walls that looked like they'd not been washed for years, I sat on a single bed that looked as if it was about to collapse at any moment. Going over to the fridge, I opened it to find a layer of fat at its base so thick that my entire fingernail vanished in it as I initially attempted to start cleaning it myself. With no cooker, I thought enough was enough!

Telling Terry I was going over to the club to get our money back, and that if we had to, sleep in the car, I went to track this guy down. Finding him drinking a schooner of beer and shovelling money into one of the pokies, I demanded our money back.

"I can't do that, mate."

Looking at this man in his mid-sixties, with him pushing dollar after dollar into the slot and not taking his eyes off the spinning fruit machine reels, I enquired as to why this was not possible. Spinning around and jumping off the high stool he had been sitting on, he looked me squarely in the eyes and, pointing to the flashing lights of the metal friend he had just been donating money to, said, "Your money is in there!"

Crossing the road and into Mitchell street, I went into the "Royal Hotel" (now known as Port of Bourke Hotel) and found Terry in there. Deciding we would put up with the caravan park for one night, we booked into the Royal the following day, and it was to be our home for the next ten days.

With a slightly larger population than Wilcannia, with around two thousand people and again a significant number of Aboriginal people making up this number, the town needed more than sixteen policemen to police it. Bourke had thirty-six members of the law enforcement contingency, and the town needed it.

The drinking den of the Post Office pub would have a fight, or fights, either inside or outside of it, on a regular basis, day and night. These fights would involve fists, bottles, glasses, sticks and the innocent rock lying by the side of the road, or whatever. With men, and sometimes women, bleeding from the head, face, arms or legs, it was not exactly a family friendly pub. The Carriers Arms around the corner from this place was not that much better either. In all my time in these unsavoury places I only twice saw a white man fight an Aboriginal. The rest of the time it was black fella against black fella. (And on no accounts do I use those terms in a derogatory way.)

On one particular evening, after slowly getting to know the Aboriginal people of the town after being in their houses during the day trying to flog them some books, I decided to go for a drink on my own in The Carriers. Although Terry had instigated our venture into the Aboriginal area of the Mallee in Wilcannia, I had quickly got a grasp of how these people's minds worked, and though Terry would retreat to the relative safety of the Royal, I would occasionally venture out for a drink with an Aboriginal man who had just purchased a set of books for his family.

Entering a black bar as a white fella was suicidal, unless you knew someone. As a result, we would never venture into an Aboriginal bar till we had been in some of their homes and could identify a friend rather than a foe in these establishments. Walking into The Carriers on my own early one evening, I spied Cyril straight away, and approaching the bar, I had a barrage of "Have ya gotta dollar or smoke?" lines hurled at me. Turning and shouting

212

over to Cyril as to what he wanted to drink, the barrage turned to "I'll have a beer too bro!"

Ignoring the few cheeky ones asking for the extra alcohol, I sat down with Cyril and he introduced me to some of his brothers, cousins or just mates, some of whom were about to drop from the amount of alcohol they had consumed during the day.

And again, it is time to digress before we get on to the violence.

Each and every time I sat down among these people, I never ever had a problem with them. Sure, you occasionally had one looking for trouble, but you get that in society in any place around the world, and the vast majority of the time the troublemaker would have his steam taken out by his friends insisting I was no threat. The people I would sit and talk to were intrigued as to why I was in their town in the middle of nowhere in the first place, and wanted to know where the fuck the country of Wales was. I would usually buy a round first of maybe up to a dozen drinks or more and after drinking my beer enquire whose shout it was next, and it was never an issue. After several days, I could go into an Aboriginal bar and sink a few stubbies and leave without spending a cent. How many white fellas could say that?

Anyway, back to the reality of the story. At around nine (the days of working till ten had gone out the window, as we were now working in very unorthodox ways that the normal book business could never entertain), two Dutch or Belgian male backpackers walked into the pub. I could be wrong with this one but my limited vocabulary of French ruled out that they were from the land of garlic, wine, onions and snails.

Ordering a couple of stubbies at the bar, they were instantly bombarded with the "dollar" and "smoke" lines, which at first they ignored. With me being the only other white person in the bar, the taller of these two fair-haired quite athletic chaps nodded towards me as a sign of recognition that there was another non-Aboriginal person in the bar.

With me giving a nod back to him, I watched events unfold as these two chatted between one another, oblivious to the fact they were in a very, very volatile environment. With them ignoring the original opening lines from an Aboriginal, the indigenous person's small talk changed, and going on the back foot, he asked where these pale-skinned people had come from. The answer was a town further south, namely Dubbo, but I was still no wiser as to where in Europe these young men in their twenties were from.

Then came the question once again of, "Have ya gotta dollar brudder?"

With me listening to Cyril and the small crowd around our table, I watched as the foreigner reached into his pocket to give a coin to the enquirer. Only one thought entered my head – fatal!

Like bees to a honeypot, around half a dozen of his brothers swarmed around the two travellers asking for a similar amount of coinage. With both of them refusing to part with any further money, the scene began to change rapidly into one of aggression, with the question being, "Why have you given him a dollar and not me?"

Thinking that they should both drink up and leave, they then made a second mistake. They pushed one of the locals away. What happened next was a one-sided pub fight that happened so quickly I can only describe it as watching a pack of wolves tearing its prey apart.

The Aboriginals pummelling them with their fists, the outnumbered tourists were sent to the ground, and with blood starting to sink into the floorboards, I began to think Terry had the right idea of drinking in the Royal.

With this pack of animals kicking and stamping on them as they lay on the floor, I felt Cyril's hand grab hold of my forearm. Turning to look at him, I saw him shake his head slowly as a sign of not to get involved.

With them both semi-conscious, I watched as the mob rifled through their backpacks and then, dragging them both from the bar, together with their luggage, discarded them out onto the red dust road.

With myself and my new-found friends toasting to Australia and the Aboriginal people in general, I departed an hour later but found no one outside. Walking back to the hotel, I wondered if anyone back home in Tenby would ever believe this story, and thinking about the Kylie Minogue grandmother story as well, thought, no, they probably wouldn't.

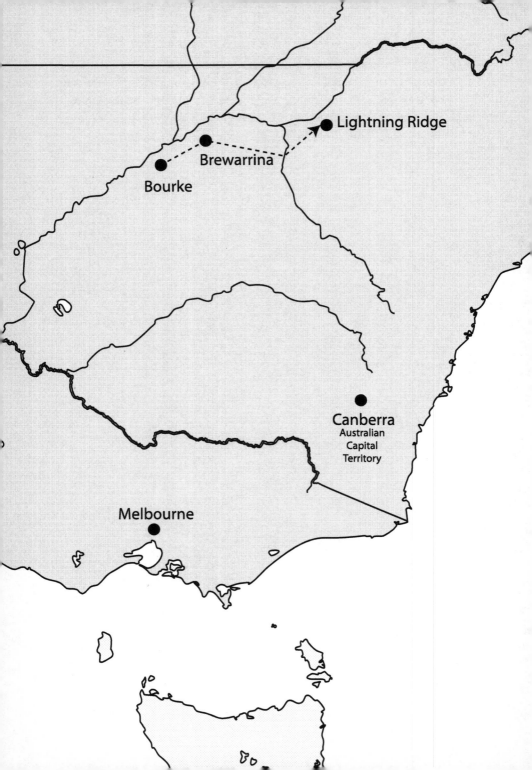

Chapter 11

Walking to the town's swimming pool one Thursday morning to cool off in the searing heat, I passed the courthouse with a line of Aboriginal men and women queuing up outside closed dark-green double doors, with similar coloured wrought iron gates open slightly ajar. Some of these people were attending the court to face charges which usually amounted to drunkenness in a public place or other minor misdemeanours. Now you're probably thinking "So what?" And that's exactly what those about to receive their sentences thought, as they staggered and swayed in the heat, with some of them possibly consuming their last drop of alcohol for some time to come.

Outside, it looked like they were all getting ready to go to a rave or rock festival as they sat on cases of lager or helped one another lift a box of wine above the other's head, while the recipient turned on the tap to allow the red or white stuff to flow down his or her throat. I will say this for them, though – they don't do anything by halves. From a bottle shop, a normal box of wine contained three litres. These monsters that they had acquired were normally sold to pubs and contained twenty. On that particular morning I saw no children and I guess they were all in school.

Arriving at the pool, I thought how sad it was that some of those little ones would return to their home to find that their father or mother had been taken away to some far-off location to be locked up in some prison to serve their sentence. This was unfortunately a trait in modern-age Aboriginal culture and many children were, and still are, taken into care.

The town of Bourke boasts a lovely asset in the Olympic-size swimming pool. With Terry being very fair-skinned, I only remember him once going for a dip as he would have to put layers of sun cream on before exposing his body to the very unforgiving sun that created a heat I had never experienced until now. Being darker than him, I had acquired a very deep, dark-brown tan, and knowing what I now know, I foolishly never applied suntan lotion to anywhere except my nose, which, if left unattended without cream, felt as if it were broken.

That afternoon, sitting in the shade of the little café by the pool, I glanced at the thermometer in the shade. Reading forty-eight point eight degrees centigrade, I thought, wow, now that is hot! Being a dry heat, I found it much more manageable than the stifling humid heat that, although maybe ten, fifteen or even twenty degrees cooler could knock you for six, zapping nearly all your energy. But that was generally experienced on or near the coast, and that was many hundreds of kilometres away.

This incredible desert-like heat, though, I found, took on its own characteristic. As the thermometer climbed through the thirties and entered the forty degree plus zone, you suddenly felt that the very warm winds that were blowing in from the interior had almost stopped. It now felt that this heat was prickling at your skin; you could taste and almost take a bite out of it. It was as if the wind itself had suddenly thought, I am exhausted and can't be bothered to blow, it's too hot!

Lifting my arms from the pool and resting them on the hot concrete, with the rest of my body still submerged up to my shoulders in an almost tepid water, the water on my exposed skin dried completely in a matter of no more than twenty seconds. Before another twenty had elapsed, I was plunging my arms, as well as any other part of my exposed body, from the sunlight back into the liquid to give it some respite from the intense burning feeling that had suddenly sprang upon me.

I enjoyed each day at the pool on my own, sinking an iced Coca-Cola or three, reading a book or the local newspaper, before heading back late afternoon to get ready to sell some more books. In the afternoon, the Aboriginal children would come to the pool after school, and this is where I found it quite odd. During the week I would only encounter these very dark-skinned youngsters, and not once did I see any white children at the pool. The only other white people I came across swimming in this man-made oasis would be off-duty policemen. Then again, I could not comment as to what the weekends were like as we bashed doors all day on the Saturday and Sunday.

Meeting these youngsters was very much like meeting their parents for the first time. A completely invisible barrier of mistrust prevailed. However, whereas the parents were suspicious of our motives until we actually revealed what we were doing, the children, on the other hand, had no confidence to approach you, which I guess in this day and age is a good thing to some extent. Once I had been in their homes, though, the barriers started to come down.

I found Aboriginal children initially to be much shyer than their white compatriots. They were never cheeky unless you started some banter up with them, and were always curious as to what you did, which I guess children generally are. Once the town's kids got to know me, the questions started coming thick and fast like, "Have you got a girlfriend?", "Have you seen snow?", "How long would it take to drive to where you live?" and "Why doesn't the man with the red hair come with you to the pool?" A dozen or more questions that children usually ask would be fired at me daily, which I would happily answer.

One afternoon I played a water-polo match with a dozen or more of them. Each time I got the ball, I heard the cry, "Get the white fella! Get the white fella!" while the off-duty policemen swimming by watched curiously as I was mobbed by a mass of little black bodies.

The main area of the town was clean and tidy, like all outback towns, but as I headed back to the Royal each day, in the distance you would see an unusual glare coming from the ground that was where a proportion of the Aboriginal people lived. This was "Glitter City".

Glitter City got its name from the large amount of broken glass that littered the ground from broken bottles and other glass objects. From the glare of the sun this would make the ground shine and sparkle like stars in the night sky or one of those glass glitter orbs you would see in the middle of a ceiling at a discotheque, hence the name.

Although we had sold some sets of books to Aboriginal families living in the main area of the town where they were in full-time permanent employment, our brief sojourn into Glitter City was a lost cause. Here the alcohol cloud hovered day and night, and because we could not locate any tribal elders we didn't stay that long.

With me still introducing myself as Terry, things started to get a little complicated when we were out having a drink in the evenings. It was then I decided to adopt my middle name as my first, so Lance Anthony Russell now became Tony. When a family mentioned to our head office back in Sydney that they had bought the books from a Tony and not a Terry, they at first became confused. Our boss informed them that Terry had met a guy in the outback who had turned out to be a great salesman. Although doing the demonstrations on his own, he was not that bothered at being employed properly by the company as he was thinking of moving on to pastures new in a very short length of time; this pile of rubbish was swallowed up at head office. Whether some of the directors "smelt a rat" with this story I don't know, but as long as all the orders had Terry's signature on and the business kept coming in, I don't think they were that bothered.

Sitting at the bar in the Royal one evening and talking to the locals, who were mainly white, I posed the question as to whether anyone knew what the little concrete trough at the foot of the bar on the customer side was for. Now, being me, I already knew the answer as, although not as knowledgeable as a lot of people, I am often found reading a book, newspaper or magazine somewhere, and had learned the reason why this concrete funnel had been created in the first place . Anyway, I thought several others would know too. Asking the dozen or so in the bar, only the barman knew the answer, but keeping his mouth shut while a huge smirk spread across his face, I quizzed some of the older chaps in their sixties, and I was genuinely surprised that they didn't know. Turning to the barman, who was only in his mid-thirties, I asked him to tell them.

"It's for pissing in," he said.

Yes, the trough was what most people would know today as a urinal, and if you think I am taking the piss with this story, read on!

Back in 1917, the Australian government introduced a law enforcing pubs to shut at six o'clock. This was done to try and increase the efficiency of the workforce, which in turn would increase the productivity of the country to provide Europe with supplies for what was then raging – World War One. It was basically to stop the men getting absolutely pissed out of their minds and then rolling home late and suffering the next day with hangovers. That was the theory anyway! "The six o'clock swill", as it became known, was the shut-off point for beer, and with the locals finishing work at usually five, with a lot of men that worked on the hot dry land being very, very thirsty, they had just an hour to get as much of the amber nectar down their throats in that time.

With the beer being served from a pistol-shaped tap attached to a long tube in what was a predominantly male environment, this saved time from carrying the empty glass from the drinker to refill it at maybe the other end of the bar. So, when the call of nature came, the last thing you wanted to do was waste time going to the toilet. Relieving yourself by urinating into the little gully, being careful not to spray your drinking mates next to you, the urine pissed off down the cement trough and into the drains below. This law in New South Wales was still in effect until 1955 and other states kept it going until well into the sixties.

It was abolished as the men would return to their homes drunk as skunks, and domestics in the family home had become rife between the hours of 6.30 and 8 p.m.

Knocking a door on a Saturday afternoon, we were met by a very large Aboriginal woman who, again in her late fifties or possibly even in her sixties, introduced herself as Elsie. Clarifying that she held a full-time permanent job at the local school as a cook, and with about half a dozen grandchildren surrounding this grey-haired lady, we asked the cementing question of where she would put the books. Now, this answer, even to this day, puzzled me, with her reply, which was, "We will put them in that empty corner over there and out of the way as no one reads in this house."

Right, here comes some more madness! On the contract, we would have to enter the customer's date of birth, which in normal cases would have been straightforward as everyone knows their date of birth, or should do. Not so in the Aboriginal world!

Asking the vast majority of the Aboriginal population that we had sold books to, what age they had reached – there was a complete blank. With no proper system in place at the time to record their date of birth, these forgotten people from the past had no proper recording of the time they had arrived on planet earth. In a nutshell, they didn't have a clue how old they were, let alone have a birth certificate. On their driving licences, their date of birth often showed up as 00/00/00.

Without a date of birth on the contract we had to make up a date as to when they were born. This was done by finding out the oldest child's age who was born after the Australian government had set up a system to issue birth certificates for these people. Once we had that, we would add eighteen, nineteen or twenty years on top to arrive at the parent's age, plus give an extra one, two or three years on to the father to make it more realistic. Writing it down and constantly repeating it to get into their heads the date of their birth we had just given them, this would hopefully help them remember when the company called to verify the order. In addition, we would instruct the children to remind their parents of this date during the week that followed, just to hammer it home to them until that important phone call came. We would also attach pieces of paper to their fridge, or somewhere clearly visible, with the names and dates of birth that we had given to each parent. On several occasions, though, as we left a home, we would still have the question of, "When was I born again?"

This tactic did not last long though, as after a week, those pieces of paper would have disappeared, and the kids would have forgotten the date of birth chant we had asked them to drum into their parents. It was not long after that we received news from the boss that head office was having trouble processing orders, as the potential buyers could not remember their date of birth, or, more worryingly, could not remember their date of birth they had been given by the salesman!

With an increase in orders flying in from Terry's outback bookselling business, the company was willing to overlook this requirement, and as long as the customers had full-time genuine employment, a telephone and had passed a credit check, all the orders would be processed. We were on a roll and now had to think up even more ingenious ways of getting around the employment and telephone criteria as we got into ever more inhospitable, isolated environments.

Leaving Bourke was quite a poignant moment for me, as it was here where I had attached myself to the Aboriginal culture and slowly started to get an insight into how these people reacted to the outsider. From the violence in the pubs or in the street, to the mistrust of the parents initially in their own homes and winning them around to purchase the books, to drinking with them as brothers in the pub, to playing with the Aboriginal children in the pool, I, at the time, felt fortunate that I had experienced something that most outsiders never would experience in a lifetime.

I could tell you more about this town, its history, the reason it got its name, about the eye specialist Fred Hollows, who did so much for this frontier town and the Aboriginal people and so on, but it is time to move on, as I have much to tell. Maybe, if this book sells well, I will write an extended version and then we will have a book of maybe the size of Lord of the Rings. That should then keep you all captivated through this entire continent, shouldn't it?

Our next port of call was a little town to the east of Bourke called Brewarrina (pronounced Bree-war-win-rah). And this is where the violence went really crazy!

On the final day in Bourke, we decided to take the day off as I wanted to spend another day at the pool, as I did not know when I would get to swim again in such a lovely tub of water. Also, we had decided to have a bit of a farewell drink with the locals at the Royal during the evening, who had turned out to be a great bunch that contained some right outback characters, albeit with a general aversion to the local Aboriginal population, especially from the Glitter City area, which was understandable.

After seeing those sad drunken folks venture into the town each day to cause a sort of mayhem in the town that, frankly, this quite hospitable town did not need, you had to look at it from the viewpoint of people who lived in the town itself.

Bourke had been kind to us, as over the past ten days we had written twelve orders, of which only two were to cancel. Again, we had found the Aboriginal folk keen to buy the books, and ironically enough, the two deals that we weren't to be paid on were orders from white families that had failed the credit check.

Now, this was another reason why we had decided to target the indigenous market. Very quickly, we realised that very, very few families had a credit history of sorts, as they had never had an opportunity to buy goods on credit. At the time, contrary to today's credit check, where a "no credit history" has an adverse effect on the applicant, a "no credit history" then meant they were squeaky clean, and as long as the other criteria was fulfilled the orders were processed easily. The only credit they would have possibly run up in the past would have perhaps been purchasing a television or sofa from the local store, but that would usually be an agreement between the storekeeper and themselves.

I was careful not to take too many beers on board so that I could see the road on my hundred kilometre drive to Brewarrina, and we arrived and booked into a hotel in the centre of town at around ten. Meeting a quite short but very stocky white lady, she introduced herself as the new landlady of the place. Showing us to our very basic but quite large room on the first floor and opening two glass doors that led out onto a lovely spacious balcony, we discovered the place was owned by an Australian brewery.

With her adopting a no-nonsense attitude to troublemakers, this apparently very tough lady had been drafted in from the suburb of Redfern in Sydney, where she'd had dealings with the indigenous population before. Having been told that she would have to bring this pub in this small outback town into order, after several landlords and landladies had given up on the place, she was just becoming accustomed to her new surroundings on what was her first night being there.

With the bar now strangely shut for that hour of the day, we sat in the back bar with half a dozen white locals and a businessman and his pilot who had flown in that afternoon to do business before flying out the next day to what would be much safer pastures.

Listening to the troubles that this town had recently been experiencing with the native folk, the main talk was generally hostile to these people, and then one of the elder gentlemen spoke up.

"My great grandfather once knew a good blackfella," he said, suddenly bringing the room to silence.

"Really?" the landlady replied, sounding astonished.

"Yeah sure," he paused to let his comment sink in, and then continued. "He worked for him for years, till my grandfather had to shoot him."

"He shot him?" I asked incredulously.

"Yeah mate. He caught him stealing from our land. He never did it again though."

"No?" I replied.

"No mate, a blackfella can't steal much after he's dead."

Again, like the story told at The Royal School of Doctors at Charleville, where that farmer had got himself back to his house carrying his severed leg, I don't know how much substance this tale had to it. At the time, I didn't pursue the story to find out what the police did to this man's grandfather, but on doing research for this book I have since learned that in the last century and before, an Aboriginal's life was not considered that important, and certainly at the turn of the last century the police would not have been that concerned providing there was no general outcry about the death of a native of this giant land. This guy also didn't make a joke about it, so I guess there is a ring of truth about it. The area has a long Aboriginal history attached to it, but once again, I am not going to dwell on this subject as there are history books for you to track down, with one particular very good one being Aboriginal Australians, a History since 1788, by Richard Broome.

After listening to the woman who was going to turn this pub around and not tolerate any shenanigans from the Aboriginals in the town, we retired and sat out on the balcony drinking beers and Mount Gay rum that Terry had recently taken a shine to. Sitting there on a lovely peaceful and incredibly warm night, we discussed where we would head to next, and with the combination of the tranquillity and alcohol, I found myself waking up in the same place the following morning.

Grabbing a newspaper, I returned to find Terry making his bed. "This town looks alright," I said with some hint of affection.

"Yeah matey, I get that feeling as well."

It was nine o'clock and the outback heat was beginning to rise very quickly. Walking out into the main street, we decided to work the town together to get a general feel for the place. The plan being that if we found a greater demand than we had anticipated for demonstrations, I would head back to the hotel and pick up my bag full of sales materials and we would then work individually. As always, we used the original door-knocking script in the main parts of a town unless an Aboriginal man or woman answered. The main reason for this was that we found the Aboriginal people to be far more receptive, and we would cut the bullshit and tell it to them straight as to what we were selling.

Working the main part of town, we only managed to write one order, with the general response being lukewarm due to the town having been worked by bookselling teams three times in the last three months. Looking to the outskirts of the town and seeing an escarpment rising up, with houses that looked half-finished on it, we realised that that was the Aboriginal part of the town. Heading towards it and watching smoke coming out from some of the buildings, I could smell meat cooking as the warm wind drifted down towards us. It was lunchtime and this town had a heavenly serene feeling to it as we headed further from the centre. By teatime, it would have been transformed into hell.

Reaching the first of these homes, I banged on a closed door only to see it leave the door frame and come crashing down at my feet onto the occupant's living room floor. There was a very hairy-faced Aboriginal man in his early to mid-thirties sitting in an armchair watching television; he looked up at us both, and frowning with a puzzled look, I delivered the "We're in the town selling educational books that will help the little ones do well in school," line.

"Come in," he said.

Walking over the door, we entered Donald and Itsy's home. Being introduced to their five children, ranging from the ages of five to fifteen, and discovering he worked on the Brewarrina shire council, we very soon had a very happy family asking us when the books would arrive. Asking Donald where we could locate a tribal elder or three to get permission to work in this area, we headed off to knock some more doors.

It was around three that we heard the first crack of gunfire coming from the other side of town. This rifle fire was to stop as soon as it had started, and this being the outback it didn't unsettle us in any way, as gunfire can sometimes be often heard in these places where perhaps a kangaroo or six are being killed for one reason or other, or perhaps folk are just fine-tuning their shooting skills through target practice.

On the point of these unusual furry, long-tailed beasts, a cull of kangaroos is sometimes given to licensed commercial hunters to bring the numbers down in certain areas of the continent, though, as a whole, the macropod family to which the kangaroo belongs is a protected species. Again, I could tell you more about these vast numbers of hopping marsupials, but we have to move on.

Meeting a couple of the elders and entering many homes, we found that a large amount of the neighbourhood was out of work. Writing another order in another home, an Aboriginal man came in to inform his neighbour that something big was going on down in the centre of town. With Desmond drinking his beer and leaving us to finish ours, he thanked us for visiting them, and saying that he may see us later, he hurriedly departed.

We left Desmond's house as dusk had begun to fall, and again sporadic rifle or pistol fire could be heard, this time coming much closer to us and almost sounding as if it were in the centre of town. As darkness descended, we noticed an unusual number of Aboriginal men leaving their homes to descend down into the heart of Brewarrina, some holding bottles of beer but others carrying, more worryingly, large wooden clubs and sticks. From where we were standing, we could also see several small fires ablaze which seemed to be coming from vehicles on the main road.

Wondering what the hell was going on down there, we decided to finish up and head back down into town. Turning into the main street, we were confronted by two policemen.

"Where you going, boys?" one of them enquired.

"Back to our hotel," Terry replied.

"You can't do that, fellas, we got some serious trouble going on," our uniformed officer informed us.

Looking down the main street, we could see three police cars parked horizontally across the road, with another half a dozen men of the law with their backs to us, peering further down the street to a quite sobering sight.

About one hundred and fifty metres further down the road from this police roadblock was a mob of Aborigines (and now I have to guess) of just over a hundred and fifty people, screaming and shouting and hurling the occasional piece of wood or rock at the barrier between them and us. At this point in time, we both suddenly realised that the hotel where we were staying was behind them and two blazing cars by the side of the road.

Now, if we'd run into this experience a few weeks before, we would have agreed with our law enforcement adviser that going any further would have been pure madness, and looking back at it now, what we did next was not a very sensible thing to do. Looking at Terry with my "deep in thought" look, I said, "Are you thinking what I'm thinking, Terry?"

"Yes matey, I think I am," he replied, nodding with a little smile.

Looking back at the police, I informed them of our next intentions. "We'll be okay, officers, we just want to get back to our hotel."

Both policemen looked at one another, and then the youngest spoke. "Are you guys nuts? There's a riot going on over there."

"Yes I know," I said smiling. "We probably know half those people in that crowd anyway."

"How the hell do you know that lot?" the older one asked.

"We've been in their houses all this afternoon," Terry said complacently. With the two men shaking their heads in disbelief as to what we proposed to do next, one gave us this warning. "Once you go past our barrier and head towards those blackfellas, you're on your own."

As we headed towards the line of police vehicles, one of the police officers that had initially met us shouted to his colleagues to let us through, and as we passed through them a couple of them questioned our sanity.

Walking towards this hostile crowd, I very quickly asked Terry if he could identify anyone. With him responding negatively, I scanned the angry faces to see if I could pick anyone out.

Digressing again, but I do have a very good memory at remembering names. Terry, though, having a very sharp brain when it came to numbers, had a dire one for remembering anything else.

"Do you recognise anyone?" I asked again anxiously.

"No," came his reply, as a large rock landed and rolled up to my feet.

"Come on," I said, ducking from a flying piece of wood. "You must see someone that you recognise."

"I don't matey, they all look the same."

With a small stone whizzing past my head, I turned to look at him and could see him fumbling around with a cigarette packet trying to open it with one hand, while retrieving his lighter from his pocket with the other. Fucking marvellous, I thought! Here we are about to be stoned to death and he's trying to light a fag. It was as if he knew he was a condemned man and was having his last wish.

Just then I spied a very bright yellow shirt in the crowd, and instantly recognising that I had seen it before that afternoon, I realised it belonged to an unemployed man who we had met at his house earlier. Searching my memory, his name popped into my head.

"Cedric," I shouted, pointing at him.

"Cedric, Cedric," I shouted at the top of my voice, waving my hands back and forth in the air.

Suddenly this saviour-to-be stopped shouting, and with his eyes wide open I could now see through his body language that he was explaining to the people around him that we were friend and not foe. At least that was what I had hoped for. As we got within fifty yards, Cedric left the crowd with four of his coloured mates, some clutching wooden clubs, and rushed towards us. I could suddenly picture myself as being Michael Caine in the film Zulu, shouting, "Front rank forward; front rank fire!" The only thing that was missing was our rifles.

Wondering whether being clubbed to death rather than being stoned was better, and perhaps quicker, this little squad of men surrounded us and started pulling us towards their main ranks. In a matter of moments we were swept along and swallowed by this very dark aggressive mob. What the police must have thought about our fate was anyone's guess.

Being pulled through the crowd, we emerged at the back of them, right in front of the doors of the hotel. Here, though we could still hear the yelling from the other side of the mob, it was bizarrely quiet as if we had entered an eye of a storm.

"You okay, fellas?" Cedric asked.

"Yeah, no worries," we replied.

"Go get yourselves a drink inside then. Everything's free tonight!"

We walked into the main bar to a sight that beggared belief. Scattered around the place was broken glass, pieces of wood, chairs missing legs and tables that had been overturned. Behind the bar were two Aboriginal men passing drinks to people on the other side while guzzling down bottles of beer and anything that came to hand. I say passing, as they certainly weren't serving as employees of the pub.

"Yo! Tony, Terry, what's going on, bros?"

Turning around from the bar, we saw another Aboriginal man whose house we had been in earlier sitting in the corner of the room with four of his fellow brothers and two white fellas that turned out to be tough stockmen that worked on cattle stations many miles from the town. This was the first time I had seen white folk directly mingling with these people but soon learned that some of the Aboriginals were workmates of these two guys.

"What ya drinking?" Moses asked us. "Everything is on the house!"

On hearing this little group roar out with laughter, I looked at the carnage around us with black men and women falling all over the place

231

from severe inebriation. Shaking my head and quietly laughing to myself, I thought, it doesn't get much madder than this.

With Terry already at the bar asking what they had and being as nonchalant as you could be, I decided on a double vodka and Coke. With the optics all missing bottles, a vessel of vodka was produced from a room behind. Now this was quite amazing, as everyone coming into the hotel who decided they weren't going to stay to drink left with bottles of spirits, boxes of wine or cases of lager, so that room must have been well-stocked. Grabbing a small glass and the bottle, and forgetting about the Coke, I sat down with the rest of them. Terry very quickly decided he didn't want to stay downstairs, and finding a bottle of Mount Gay rum hidden behind the optics, retreated upstairs to the relative safety of our room. Now again, this was another amazing fact. Although our bedroom door was locked, and despite the damage that had been created downstairs, our room, and more importantly our belongings, were intact. Pouring a large measure of vodka, I set to find out the story of how this madness had come about.

As most people will tell you, there are two sides to a story, but unfortunately I only have the Aboriginal one. Drinking with my new-found mates, I heard the story unfold.

At around two o'clock, a gin (once again, that is slang for an Aboriginal woman) had asked for a drink to be put on a tab after drinking it. When this hard landlady from Sydney refused this request and demanded payment, the Aboriginal woman took offence, and what then occurred was verbal insult after verbal insult until the licensee decided to ban this woman from entering her premises again until she had paid for her drink.

With no forthcoming grog, this female decided that the next best course of action was to go home and find a nice carving knife and to come back. Launching herself over the bar, she attempted to slash and stab the landlady (remember these were not family friendly pubs), but this woman was no pushover, and disarming her and giving her a few slaps at the same time, she sent her bloodied face back home to her husband. Now read into this any way you want as to what state the husband was in, but he returned with some friends of his and that is when the powder keg was lit.

A few local white fellas managed to get the landlady to a safe room in the hotel and then managed to whisk her to safety in the outskirts of town. By then, with the bar no longer having a manager, it was suddenly open all hours with no cash required. With news spreading fast that there was free grog in town, the Aboriginal wave from the escarpment overlooking the town descended like a tsunami, pushing anyone trying to bring law and order back to it aside.

With the police heavily outnumbered (though they would over the night receive many reinforcements from other outback towns), it was a free-for-all. With vodka after vodka going down my throat and meeting Desmond again, who had decided to pick up some free takeaway beers to celebrate buying his encyclopedias, the night became blurred until I woke up staring up at the barrel of a gun!

With my bare feet being kicked at the foot of my bed, my vision from suddenly being woken up cleared, and I could see an armed policeman in a flak jacket commanding me to get out of bed.

Doing as he said, I could see it was just about dawn, and from the light of the new day I could see Terry in just his underpants standing and staring at the wall, while another armed officer with his pistol pointed at his back fired question after question at him. With me still fully clothed, I was turned around and had my face pushed into the wall on my side of the bed, while being frisked by a third man of the law who had now entered the room.

"Which one of you has the gun?" I heard one of them say.

"Gun?" I said, wondering what the hell he was on about.

"One of you was seen to be wandering around on the balcony during the night waving a gun around," I heard another voice say.

"Well I've been downstairs most of the night," I replied, not having

233

much recollection of events after the story had been told.

"I was on the balcony for a while," Terry piped up.

"With a gun?" one of the officers asked.

"No," Terry insisted, with a silly grin spreading on his face, "only with a bottle of rum."

This infuriated the men of the law, and still being pissed I found it difficult not to laugh, despite the fact we could both possibly have been shot as they entered the room. Putting their guns back into their holsters, they then wanted to know what we were doing in the town, as it wasn't exactly on the tourist trail. I told them we had been working in the Aboriginal part of town, and that that was the reason we had remained unscathed. They then demanded we pack our stuff and leave the town immediately. When we questioned this, we were told that if we did not comply we would be arrested. On hearing this, Terry asked, "On what charge?"

The reply came, "We'll make something up."

It was time to leave.

It was strangely quiet in the town considering what had happened during the night, and I guess those that were not arrested (if any?) were sleeping the grog off back home.

Now, this rumpus is recorded in my diary as on Saturday 13th February 1993, yet strangely enough, while I have been trawling the archives to find this incident to see what happened to the landlady, there is no record of it at all. Not even in police records.

There had been other incidents, including a riot that took place in the town back in 1987, but nothing about the one we experienced. Whether it was not big enough to report, or due to its bad reputation for violence the police or other authorities put a blanket ban on reporting, or that it's just so common that it's just plain old news, I don't know. Anyway, I won't forget that night, that's for sure.

Next stop was the town of Lightning Ridge and that returned us to some normality, if you could call it that! This place is the land of the opal, a precious stone that we were to come across on a few occasions. (Not literally, but with towns that had links with the mineral.) On one of the postcards I sent back to my mother from the town is the fact that ninety per cent of all the world's opals are mined in Australia. Lightning Ridge also boasts that it is rich in black opals, which are a rare bunch and needless to say the most expensive.

As a result, people come from all over the world to seek their fortune fossicking and mining the ground in the hope of finding a nice pile of these gems. At the time, from chatting with the locals in the pub, we learned there were around thirty-eight millionaires in the town. A high proportion for a small place, as at the time the population was just over two thousand, I think.

With a decent number of orders rolling in at four hundred dollars a pop, I had acquired cash of over two thousand dollars that I kept around my person, and that was on top of the money I already had, which I had withdrawn from my Australian bank in case immigration froze the account. I was taking no chances now being on the run.

Going into a shop that sold opals one afternoon, I spied a beautiful watch with a face made out of opal with a gold surround of a carat I can't remember. The different green, blue, red, orange and yellow colours just mesmerised me, and so did the price. On leaving the shop, I had a lot less cash on my person, and it was (even to this day) the most expensive watch I have ever purchased.

As soon as our wages each week were paid into Terry's account, he took the lot out and gave me my half. He was taking no chances either.

Right, funny story time! Once, we were in a place called Port Augusta in South Australia. (Hang on, I'll tell you that story when we get there, which will be in a few pages time.)

Lightning Ridge uses bore water that is extracted from a huge artesian basin deep underneath the ground. There are two bore baths on the outskirts of the town that are like very warm baths. The two nights we stayed in the town, both of us took a box of wine up with us (not the Aboriginal size one, but the three litre one) to share while we soaked in these lovely waters into the early hours. This water gives off a smell of sulphur; you can drink the stuff, but it takes a bit of getting used to.

The first afternoon knocking doors in the furnace heat, I asked a white "old timer" if I could get a glass of water from him. On producing the glass, and my thirst being quite great, I proceeded to drink the clear water down till my brain registered the sulphur element in the liquid. Spitting out what water I still had in my mouth, and retching, the clearly retired man said, "You ain't tasted bore water before then, mate? Welcome to Lightning Ridge."

Here the Aboriginal population was not that great, and again, very few of them worked. Also, because the town was obviously wealthy, it had attracted many door-to-door salespeople over the years, and as a result many households already owned a set of books. The name of the town supposedly originates from the 1870s when some passers-by found the bodies of a farmer, his dog and six hundred sheep that had been struck by lightning. It is also the birthplace of Paul Hogan from the Crocodile Dundee films.

As the film actor Sir Michael Caine might say, "Not a lot of people know that!"

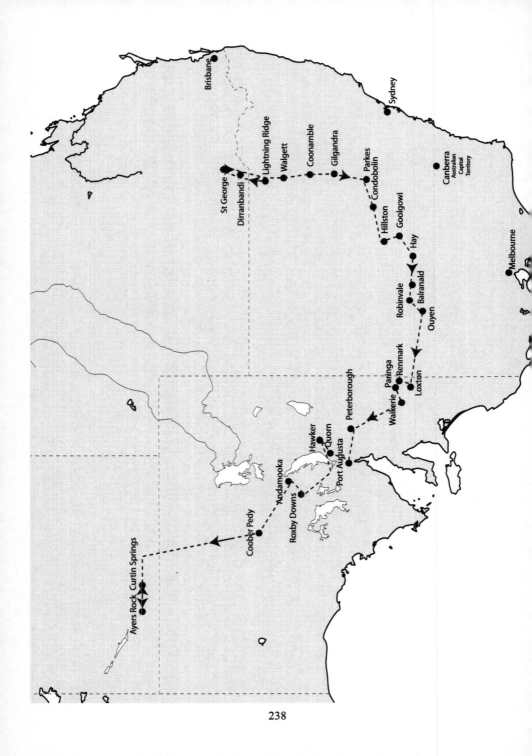

Brisbane

Sydney

Lightning Ridge
Walgett
Coonamble
Gilgandra
Parkes
Condobolin

St George
Dirranbandi

Canberra
Australian
Capital
Territory

Hillston
Goolgowi

Melbourne

Hay

Robinvale
Balranald

Ouyen

Peterborough
Paringa
Renmark
Walkerie
Loxton

Hawker
Quorn
Andamooka
Port Augusta
Roxby Downs

Coober Pedy

Ayers Rock Curtin Springs

Chapter 12

Lightning Ridge is just down the road from the Queensland border, and we knew we could only go so far before we entered the wet season in the tropics. At the time, the country had such severe flooding in the north-west that the government was considering making it a disaster zone so people could claim for damages. So, briefly crossing over the border to work in the towns of Dirranbandi and St George, we headed back down into New South Wales again and to the town of Walgett.

Here the town had more Aboriginal people than you could shake a stick at, and walking down the street it was like being in a race with spectators cheering you on from the side of the road, except instead of cheering, the voices said, "Have ya gotta dollar or a smoke?" It was constant and got to the stage where we would just ignore them as it was far easier to do so. Even Terry refused to hand any smokes away.

Going into a shop, I saw something for sale I had never seen before. Cigarettes sold individually. They were priced one for fifty cents or three for a dollar. Asking the shopkeeper if he had any postcards for sale he replied, "Not a chance mate, no tourist would be brave enough to come to this town!"

With half the population black and mostly unemployed, we began to think that the Aboriginal untapped market for books had remained untapped as no one could find a tap in the first place. Writing just one order in the town, we headed southwards again. After being in these indigenous peoples homes for nearly a month now, on practically a daily basis, it's amazing how the human body adapts. I had got used to the smell of rubbish in the air in these houses, and the smell of body odour secreting from their sweaty bodies that had perhaps not been washed for several days. I had also adapted to the immense heat, and I found I could get by with drinking a fraction of the water I used to require walking around in such temperatures. Even the flies did not bother us, and we had now got used to them crawling all over our arms, legs, or faces without bothering to swat them off. Acclimatising to all these new factors, we really were starting "to go bush", as the Aussie phrase goes.

Walgett, incidentally, is an Aboriginal word and means "the meeting of two rivers".

We now decided to inch our way across the map towards South Oz and to make plans to travel northwards up through the middle of this giant country. Leaving these towns, which had a high proportion of the indigenous race behind, we made our way down to Coonamble.

For the next two months we travelled westwards going through the towns of Gilgandra, Parkes, Condoblin, Hillston, Goolgowi, Hay, Balranald, Robinvale and Ouyen (pronounced Owe-yun), then over the border to Pinaroo and then up into South Australia to work the towns of Loxton, Renmark, Paringa and Waikerie. With the Aussie winter on our doorstep once again, we headed further northwards and into uncharted territory for the both of us.

Arriving in Peterborough, we calculated how much it would cost us to get us back up to the warmth of far North Queensland via Ayers Rock and Alice Springs and our next destination of Karumba on the shores of the Gulf of Carpentaria. With the distance being over three thousand kilometres, we also had to make allowances for the increase in the price of petrol as we got further and further away to ever more remote places. Setting aside a few hundred bucks to cover the fuel, we decided not to drive straight there, but to do some exploring by working some towns off the beaten track as we headed up there. This was decided despite the fact daytime temperatures were struggling to reach the high teens and the nights now being quite cold dropping down to zero or below.

At this point you're probably thinking "To hell with that, let's get back up in the sunshine", but the logic behind this decision was that we knew we would probably never have the opportunity to visit these places again, and remember, I wanted to see as much of Oz as possible before I went back home.

Arriving in Port Augusta, we quickly found out the locals affectionately called it "Port-A-Gutter". We were now three hundred kilometres north of Adelaide and this town certainly lived up to its nickname. With high unemployment and neighbourhoods with houses boarded up, it was fortunate that we had sold quite a few sets of books over the past few weeks, as the current place was dire. In my diary entry, I have written: Man what a place! Twenty per cent of the housing here has been condemned, so it gives you some idea of what the place was like. An idiosyncratic characteristic I also noticed was that the customary greeting of "G'day" had been dropped and replaced with "howdy". Whether the townsfolk were trying to take the piss trying to convince us that we were now in the United States of America, I don't know.

Our sales figures over the last few months, apart from the past few weeks where we had sold well over our average quota, had been up and down after we had left Bourke, but the good weeks cancelled out the bad ones, which is what sales is all about. We were more than keeping our heads above water and at the same time seeing plenty of different places and meeting characters galore, who often gave us their views on the economy, the culture, the politics, the weather, or whatever, of the country. We were on the whole achieving our objective, which was to travel the length and breadth of this great country.

Right, now to that funny story I promised you.

On the day we were to leave the town, our pay was due to be paid into Terry's bank account. It had been an excellent week just over a couple of weeks before, with loads of orders written. Obviously, waiting for the ten-day cooling-off period to expire and waiting for the books to be despatched, we were always two or three weeks behind before our commissions were paid. Arriving at the counter, the bank clerk informed him that he only had one dollar in the account, which was what was needed to keep the account open. Knowing that our pay would go in at around midday and not knowing if there were any banks where we were heading to next, he rejoined a very large queue to try again. Now, on this day it was also the day the unemployed received their dole money, which was paid directly into their bank accounts from the government. With quite a few Aboriginals, and I should say some undesirable white folk, who were clearly pissed, using very foul language and obviously waiting for their money to go in so that they could buy some more grog, fags and other essentials, it had become like an airport carousel with the bags going round and round as each person rejoined the queue to see if their money had gone in.

Each time Terry reached the counter, the teller would be quite offish as he was getting abuse from others in the mostly "unemployed" line, with them demanding why their money had not gone in to their accounts. On reaching the counter on his fourth turn, the teller hit the button and his eyes suddenly lit up.

"Wow," he said.

"I take it from that comment my money's gone in?" my Irish banker said.

The teller looked back at him and began to apologise.

"I am ever so sorry to have been rude to you earlier, but I thought you were with the rest of the scum in the queue! Yes, the money has gone into in your account. How much would you like to withdraw?'

With several thousand dollars now sitting in his account, Terry said, "All of it bar a dollar."

You see what I said earlier in the book, "Assumption is the mother of all evils".

After a brief sojourn to the towns of Quorn and the smaller Hawker, we headed up to the towns of Roxby Downs and Andamooka. Petrol had now gone from seventy cents a litre to eighty-two cents, and once we got to places that were so far away from civilisation that even the wildlife asked you for directions, it was then to reach over a dollar.

Roxby and Andamooka are just over thirty kilometres from one another, but one might as well be in the lush pastures of New England in America, with the other being on planet Mars. Arriving in Roxby first to gauge the size of the place, we were amazed at what we saw. The climate in this region is arid with very little rainfall, and with the red desert of rock and sand, the last thing we expected to see were green manicured lawns outside people's homes with healthy trees growing everywhere.

This is because Roxby Downs is a mining town. It is a purpose-built town that was constructed with money from the South Australian government and, at the time, the Olympic Mining Dam Company. Like the mining towns I worked up in Central Queensland, money was not short by far, and the money that had been pumped into this town was phenomenal. To attract the best brains, engineers and skilled workers in the country, and indeed the planet, Roxby Downs was transformed into a lush oasis on the fringes of a harsh desert to accommodate their workers and families. Providing state-of-the-art facilities that included schools, swimming pools, shops and comfortable social facilities where the men and women could relax after a hard day's work, this green and pleasant land looked well out of place. All the houses were identical and the whole place looked like it had been created as a model in some workshop, blown-up in size a thousand times and plonked onto the ground in this harsh, unforgiving and inhospitable environment. The mine extracts copper, gold, silver and uranium, where the largest single deposit in the world has been found. Walking around this surreal landscape, we checked out the motel rates, and realising they had mining town prices, we decided to set up base in Andamooka.

With the tarmac road vanishing, we arrived at the little opal mining town. It was like going back in time fifty years or so. With piles of rock scattered all over the place from excavations, signs warning people not to stray off the main roads due to hidden old mineshafts, houses dug into the ground, caravans of different sizes, and houses that looked like they had been knocked up overnight made out of brick and rusty old corrugated iron, it was again surreal, if this time for a different reason.

Finding a tiny campsite that hired out small touring-size caravans, Terry took the car to find a shop to buy some food and his daily newspaper, *The Australian*. Leaving me with the task of finding a map of this desert outpost, I went to find the campsite owner again to see if he could help.

"Go back to the caravan, and I'll be over with one in a minute mate," he said.

Five minutes later, he was at the door with just a long stick in his hand.

"Right, you want a map then?" he asked.

"Yes please," I replied.

"Right, here we go."

He then began to draw a map of the town in the red Martian-like soil by our caravan, giving a running commentary as he went.

"This is where you are, and from this street you turn right and head down to the main street. Have you got a torch?" he asked.

"Yeah," I said frowning. "What do you want a torch for?"

"I don't want a torch, but you're gonna need one when it gets dark, cos there's fuck all street lighting here, and you don't want to fall down a mineshaft now, do ya?" Sounding like my mother scolding me when I was a child, I listened to him intently.

"You got the shop here, the post office here, petrol station here, pub here ..." As he mentioned each business, he embedded the stick deep into the soil to somehow make it stand out from the road network that was expanding about our feet, outside our little temporary home.

Watching the earth map get larger and larger, I was slowly forgetting which business was which and began to focus on the areas he had pointed out where hidden mineshafts would be. Thinking that he would suddenly stop and then erase the map with one of his boots, then hand me the stick and say, "Right, now you draw it," as if in some sort of memory game, he finished up.

"Right, you got that?" he said, shaking the stick in the air like an old schoolmaster.

"Yeah, I think so," I said uncertainly.

"Right, well I'll be off." As he turned to leave, my curiosity got the better of me and I had to ask this guy in his fifties the question.

"Do many people fall down these mineshafts?"

"Sometimes," he replied.

"And what happens?"

"Nothing much, as you usually can't find them."

I looked at our first ever soil map, and going back inside the caravan to unpack my stuff, I heard Terry return, pulling up outside our home and sending dust everywhere.

Getting out and entering our shelter, he asked, "Did you get a map, matey?"

"Well I did have one," I replied.

"So where is it?" he said with a big smile.

"Underneath the car!"

"Underneath the car?" he said, flummoxed.

"Yep, and you have just gone and destroyed it!" I then told him about the map-maker.

Travelling back to Roxby, we split up and wrote an order each after knocking about two hundred doors between us. Both orders were paid in full with cheques. Like the hours of business we kept, the days of keeping door-knocking sheets were long gone, as we could both remember where we had been and where to return to if we had made a mental appointment with someone at a later time. Also, we were now answerable to no one.

The next day we decided to knock Andamooka and finish early to meet the locals at the pub. Flicking through the television channels waiting for Terry to get ready, I came across the Imparja television channel again. This is the Aboriginal channel, which has all sorts of stuff on it from their culture. You also know you are out in "Whoop Whoop" as the channel is only accessible in the remote places where a large proportion of these people live.

Entering the bar, my eyes slowly adjusted to the dark ambience of the place that this semi-subterranean pub presented to us. Because of the tremendous summer heat that sends temperatures into the meltdown region, many homes are partly or completely underground, to escape or, should I say, alleviate this furnace that burns in and around the town during those months on a daily basis. The place reminded me of the "cantina bar" from the film *Star Wars*, without the beings from all over the universe in it.

With only a few people in the place, I challenged Terry to a few frames of pool at the table, which, judging by the condition of it, was the first pool table ever made. As the night wore on, the "winner stays on" challenge was adopted, and as I mentioned before, although I was no pool shark, I could usually hold my own at the table.

Playing several players that had settled in the town to seek and find a fortune from the opal fields around, I began to realise that this mining game was a lottery of sorts. Yes, there were millionaires in this town, like there were in Lightning Ridge, but for every lucky millionaire there were probably hundreds, if not thousands, that were eking out a living on small to very small finds every now and then. To find a rich seam of opals you had to be very lucky indeed!

Getting beat a couple of times, I returned to the table as the challenger at around eleven o'clock, with the pub now quite busy. Beating another challenger, I then faced a slight and indeed quite a small grey-haired and stubble-faced man in his early to mid-seventies; an Italian, who had come to the town many, many moons ago in the 1950s to find his fortune. This chap we found both interesting and intriguing, with his stories about the town and its characters over the years. Once again, I have no idea how much substance was behind these stories, but they kept us amused for a couple of hours before we decided to leave. Needless to say, he had still not found that rich elusive opal seam.

Staggering back in the pitch-black to our little caravan, I was grateful for the advice of having a torch, and as we both walked, I tried to build a mental picture in my head of the soil map trying to remember where the mineshafts were.

Just deviating from the story again; we were well-equipped on board our vehicle, even though a two-wheel drive was not suitable on some of the roads we took our Japanese chariot on. Apart from the torch, we had sleeping bags, batteries, always had crisps or other snacks on board, beer and most importantly a twenty-litre container holding not wine, but water, which would allow us to stay alive for a few days if we broke down in a remote part of the desert. On top of that, we had now acquired an optional extra that every vehicle should have – a spider!

At first, we noticed a spider's web appearing on the dashboard every now and then, and despite clearing it away, a new one was quickly built by the following morning. Sitting in the car one night discussing the day's business, it suddenly appeared from a crack between the dash and windscreen in the far corner of the passenger side. As it scurried across towards the driver's side in the moonlight, I switched the interior light on. With our little arachnid coming to a sudden halt as if a spotlight had been put on him, we tried to identify the species to determine whether it was dangerous or not. With its body length being around three centimetres and identifying it as not being the poisonous redback, we were not that sure whether it was the deadlier funnel-web. Taking no chances, I decided to kill it with the prospectus that was close to hand. Bringing the book down hard, the little bastard was too fast for me and in next to no time was back down the crack. He or she had learned his or her lesson, though, as for the next few nights we could see him or her peeping from the crack as we took it in turns to drive. Over the weeks we decided it was no threat to us and actually let him or her build a little web to trap little flies and other insects. The spider in turn got bolder over time and would come out in the daytime to drag its prey back to its lair. It became a sort of in-car entertainment system that killed the boredom on these long journeys of ours.

It was 23rd of July and Coober Pedy (another opal mining town) was to be our next stop. Arriving in the town later than expected, we decided to get a bite to eat before finding some accommodation. The town was currently in the national news due to a German girl backpacker who had gone missing nine days ago. It was the third disappearance in as many years for the town and speculation was rife of whether it was a local or someone from out of the area responsible for all three missing persons. Sitting in a roadhouse, we struck up a conversation with a policeman, some truckers and some locals. Informing them that we had come to town to sell books, we were told the reception we would get from the townsfolk would be frosty at best. The last thing they were going to do, informed the officer of the law, was to let one or two strange men into their home due to the current circumstances. Thinking about it for a minute or two, we quashed the idea of staying and decided to drive through the night to the Northern Territory border.

With us telling a few stories about some of the Aboriginal areas we had worked, the law enforcement man gave us this advice.

"Boys, you're heading back into deep Aboriginal land again. You will see them by the side of the road trying to flag you down, but you don't stop. Not even in the daytime. If one steps out onto the road and you hit him or her, drive on and report it at the next town's police station. You don't stop whatsoever."

There was a pause and then one of the truckers spoke up.

"That is unless you get a strike!"

"A strike?" I said, not knowing what he was on about.

"Yeah, a strike. Where you knock them all down!"

Laughter filled the room and it was time to go.

The backpacker's body was found a year later down a twenty-metre mineshaft and a local man was charged and convicted. The other two people (both young females) at the time of writing this were yet to be discovered and the search still goes on. No one else has been charged with these disappearances at present, and this sad story should send out a message to always be on your guard no matter what country you are in. These incidents should, however, not deter you from visiting the town, as again it is quite a unique place due to the number of houses built underground to escape the fierce summer heat. You can even stay in an underground motel there.

Arriving over the border at five thirty in the morning, we decided to pull over into a lay-by, put the chairs back and grab a few hours' sleep. Waking at just after eight thirty and climbing out of the car to stretch my legs, I could once again feel the warmth of the Aussie winter sun. Today was Ayers Rock day.

Uluru, as the Aboriginal people call it, is not on the doorstep of Alice Springs, but four hundred and fifty kilometres down the road from this town in Central Australia. Now I don't know why I am telling you this as we were to turn off the Stuart Highway well before "Alice", as we were coming up from the south. Anyway, we still had over three hundred k's to go ourselves before we were to be rewarded with a sight that really is breathtaking.

Turning left onto Lasseter Highway and hurtling onwards, I began to feel like a little child again on a daytrip out with Mum and Dad, and as I counted down the kilometres in my head, I looked from the passenger side in anticipation and an air of excitement. I wanted to see it before the red-haired Irishman saw it!

Now, the next thing I am about to write will trigger a mass of brains reading this book that have driven on this road and they will scream out, "Yes I thought that as well" as Mount Conner comes into sight. Mount Conner, also known as Atilla or Artilla, comes into view well before Uluru/Ayers Rock, and waving my hands in the air pointing with a raised voice saying, "There's Ayers Rock, I saw it first," I then felt a bit of a fool when Terry pointed out we still had just over a hundred kilometres to travel before reaching it. It is a sort of taster of what is to come and nevertheless is just as impressive. If there are any rock tappers reading this, then like me you will know that this inselberg consists of all sorts of stuff from the rock world, but I am not going into the subject anymore as the only time I tap a rock is when I tap one with my foot.

Driving ever closer to our goal for the day, we passed several Aboriginal men standing by the side of the road trying to flag us down. The policeman's words rang in my ears, and looking at Terry, he said, "Don't worry matey, I ain't stopping."

Before long, Terry had won the "I saw the rock first" game, as he spied the huge object in the distance. It's a long and monotonous journey, and apart from seeing a few camels, several cattle and more Aboriginal folk trying to hitch a lift, it is wise to rest at the roadhouses every now and then as this stretch of bitumen has claimed many lives from weary drivers in the past.

Parking near the office, we each purchased a ten-dollar ticket to allow us to enter this national park. Being eager to get to the top of this monolith to grab an eagle's-eye shot of the surrounding desert, I bounded up to the top ignoring all the signs and literature boards that I normally immerse myself in when visiting somewhere new. Now, whether you believe me or not, I missed the fact that Uluru is considered sacred to the Anangu Aboriginal people. They do not climb it themselves as it is considered spiritual and that a path that runs along the rock crosses a "Dreamtime" track, where an event in the ancient Aboriginal history occurred thousands and thousands of years ago, almost back to the start of time. I will come back to the sacred bit after I have descended.

Taking steps as big as possible up this giant rock, occasionally using the hand-held chain that lies about a metre from the ground to pull me up ever quicker, I reached the summit after experiencing a more difficult climb than anticipated. Unrolling my very detailed maps of the Northern Territory and South Australia while taking in the awesome view, I could just about make out Mount Woodroffe, the tallest mountain in South Australia some hundred and fifty kilometres away in the Musgrave Ranges. Looking straight down, the desert below bounced its shades of green, brown, orange and red back up to me. I was now almost three hundred and fifty metres above the ground and had people from all over the world walking past me, jibber-jabbering in all sorts of international languages as I took in this magnificent scenery. Turning to my right, I could clearly see Kata Tjuta or The Olgas (the English language equivalent) twenty-five kilometres away. To the right of them in the vast distance lay another line of mountains known as the Petermann Ranges that stretched to the border of Western Australia. Turning Northwards, I tried to see the giant dried-up body of salt water known as Lake Amadeus, but with the heat making the ground shimmer slightly, it was all but impossible to see this length of crusty white powder that is one hundred and eighty kilometres long and ten kilometres wide. Turning almost full circle, Mount Conner looked back at me from the east. With the cloudless light-blue sky and a warm northerly breeze blowing, surrounded by these extraordinary geographical features, I appreciated afterwards the reason why these indigenous people felt this place spiritual, though as far as spirits go and as far as I am concerned, they are only found on the top shelf at the back of a bar.

With us descending after a half hour or so, I began to read the literature spattered over the boards outside and inside the tourist information centre. Apart from the deaths that had resulted from the unfit, elderly or plain foolish climbing the rock in sometimes blistering temperatures over the years, I came across the "We will take your money but would prefer you didn't climb our rock" bit.

Actually, that's not fair to say, as I understand that any national park around the world needs income to maintain and keep these parks in tip-top conditions, and I am happy to contribute to their upkeep whenever I visit such a park. However I will say this, and I am not being funny as this debate could probably go on for umpteen dreamtimes. If something is sacred, spiritual or has something of great significance that means a lot to someone, or to many people, then a barrier of sorts needs to be put into place to protect that object and to stop unwanted people intruding. Such measures are apparently in place to stop people from climbing Mount Conner where the tracks approaching it have been littered with tyre-busting spikes. Kata Tjuta is out of bounds for climbing as it's considered being in the same league as Conner and Uluru, though having said that you would have to be "the human fly" to climb those huge round objects, which are higher than Ayers. The argument goes that if the Aboriginal people stopped tourists from climbing the rock then no one would bother to travel there to see it, meaning their income from tourism would dry up. This I think would not be the case.

The whole experience of being in the desert and seeing these different formations of basalt, granite, sandstone and whatever from ground level is still something to take home in your memory for a long time, if not until the day you die. Perhaps not so many people would venture there at first, but tourism is expanding across the globe every year and I am sure numbers would soon start to creep up again, and if not, then the region could be remarketed for different reasons to visit.

Now you may be wondering whether I would have climbed it had I read the signs first. The answer is probably yes. You should have few if no regrets in life, and seeing all those people climbing to the top, then hearing from them what they had seen from being up there, I know I would have been thinking I should have climbed it for myself. For the Aboriginal people of the area it is a difficult decision to make, but maybe I have given them food for their thoughts. Incidentally, Uluru has no translation into English whereas Kata Tjuta means "many heads".

Walking around Yulara, the purpose-built tourist town that has accommodation for both staff and tourists, along with shops and an airport on the doorstep of Uluru, I marvelled at the Aboriginal art and woodcarvings that were for sale there. This indigenous art world creates some of the most magical and colourful paintings that have a story behind them from the "Dreamtime" that I have ever seen. Over the next few month's I was to be offered gifts from these people ranging from their musical instrument – the didgeridoo – to a giant turtle shell, though each and every time I declined as it was impractical to transport them in our already cramped car without damaging them. The one exception was from a family in the Aboriginal community of Hopevale in the far north of Queensland where I accepted the offer of a boomerang adorned with its colourful artwork, but we will come to that later.

Heading back to the rock to watch the sunset project a theatrical vision of light onto its surface, I stood among an international body of people of around two hundred, most clutching cameras that would have picked up the Sea of Tranquility on the moon judging from the lenses attached. Holding my little Halina 110 camera, I watched as the rock transformed from a bright orange to a deep-red as the sun descended towards the horizon, triggering a multitude of camera flashes as the light of the day diminished. Stopping for an overnight stay at a campsite at Curtin Springs approximately one hundred kilometres from Uluru, I decided to write a letter ... to Anna.

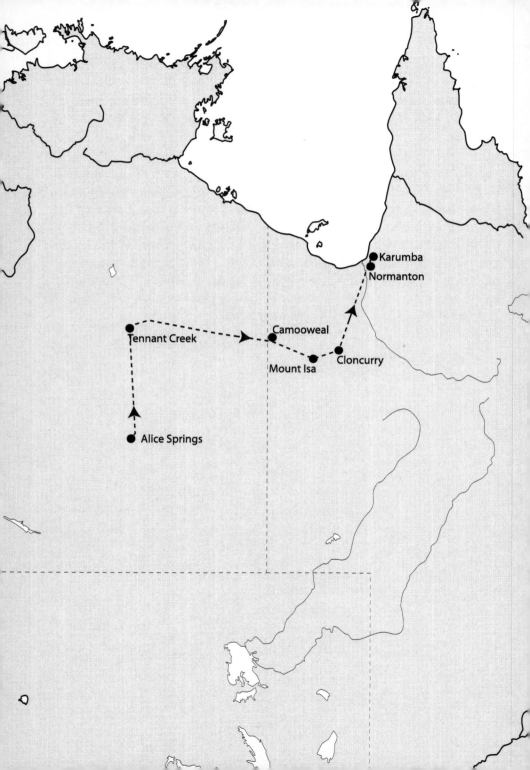

Chapter 13

Arriving in Alice Springs, I posted my letter to Anna. It had not been an easy one to write, and I must have written it three or four times before deciding to pop it in the envelope and seal it. Advising her that I was still in the country, I told her that I had made the decision to leave her, due to the fact that I wanted to visit parts of this country that would have taken us into very inhospitable territory and did not think it fair to put her under that pressure to come with me. Now, at this point, you're probably thinking "Well she sold books as well so why not?" The truth is that I would have had to reveal the fact that I was now an illegal immigrant, and call me paranoid or what, I was terrified we would somehow split up and she would spill the beans, sending me back home long before my time was due. I know all this sounds a little crazy, but at the time my world was upside down (literally) and I was not thinking straight. Asking her if she wanted to write back, I said I could pick her letter up from the post office at Mount Isa in Queensland in about ten days. I quietly hoped that some correspondence from her would be waiting there for me upon my arrival.

The first thing you notice when you head into central Oz is how dark the Aboriginal people are. The folk I had met previously in the outbacks of Victoria, New South Wales and indeed some parts of Queensland had a very deep colour themselves, but I had not seen the Aboriginal race as dark as this since being in Townsville on the far north coast of Queensland. These people were jet black.

We were to stay in Alice Springs, or "The Alice" as it is sometimes known, for the next ten days, though we should have left much sooner as business was terrible, writing just three orders, two of which were later cancelled. Not a day went by during which we would come upon drunken indigenous folk lying in the street, or by steps outside flats in the rougher areas of the town where we were working. This town of just over twenty thousand was a bit on the wild side to say the least. Occasionally, you would see an Aboriginal man or woman with a head wound from either falling down or having been involved in a fight. Police would be putting them into their wagons after fights that would break out in one of the pubs or on the street. Just for their own safety, they would be helped into a wagon, as they could sometimes fall down in the middle of the road from severe inebriation. One night (and I should point out that this is totally unadvisable), I took a walk down the middle of the dried-up Todd River, and looking over to the river banks on either side, could see homeless or transient indigenous folk asleep or talking around fires. Their calls to me were mostly incoherent, but occasionally you would recognise the words "brudder" or "bro" beckoning me to come over to them. The dark indecipherable phantoms that littered these banks painted a sad picture, and I did not stay long. As I say, it is not something I would recommend for anyone to do, so do not be tempted to walk on this alluvial plain at night.

On the subject of the Todd River, a very unusual boat race takes place every September called the Henley-on-Todd Regatta. You may ask yourself what's unusual about that?

The boats are assembled at the starting line, and waiting for the starter's pistol, only one thing is missing – the river! It is the only boat race held in the world on dry land. Competitors with their washtub metal frames around them, sporting flags, banners and whatever else that makes this crazy, colourful race so eventful, run a part of the Todd River to the finish line, pummelling the deep, soft sand with their feet, spraying their fellow challengers and onlookers with water as they go. This iconic race was actually cancelled the month after we left the town due to – wait for it – flooding! It is the only time in its history that it has not been held. The river is obviously in full flood in the wet season when it arrives around November/December time.

Sadly, like the capital city of Canberra, Alice Springs did not make much of an impression on me and I was quite glad to leave. Maybe it is much different today and maybe they will now allow you into Lasseters Casino wearing jeans, not like then, when they refused me entry.

Some of the pubs we drank in were indeed very rough, and during one evening my Irish drinking partner was approached by two different drunken indigenous men who attempted to wrestle a cigarette out of his packet.

By now, we had developed a sort of sixth sense for detecting forthcoming trouble. Terry and I could quickly reduce tensions in what could become a very precarious episode with these people, or get the hell out before things really kicked off. Anyone naïve or foolish enough to attempt to do what we did should do so at their peril. Remember, we had worked and been in these people's homes, so mentioning a Christian name, surname or even a nickname of an Aboriginal person could very quickly defuse what could suddenly become quite a confrontational episode. Cast your mind back to the foreign backpackers that were badly beaten in the pub before; they did not have that same advantage to fall back onto.

So leaving "The Alice", we headed further north up towards the town of Tennant Creek, and at this stage I must say I am glad I kept a diary, as I would have never remembered this day in a month of Mondays (yes I did say Mondays), or at all – "Picnic Day"!

Writing two orders in this town of nearly three thousand, with a large proportion of the population being of an Aboriginal descent, we almost got through the day with no violence. Walking back to the car, we witnessed a domestic of sorts erupting in one of the houses that we had failed to gain entry to earlier, due to the fact the children had failed to wake their two parents who were fast asleep from a heavy drinking session. With both of them now awake, we watched them through their living room window, shouting and screaming at one another until the woman suddenly rushed outside, with her partner following close behind her. With more shouting and screaming, the customary exchange of bodily blows started, punching and pulling one another's hair outside their home, luckily with no sight of the children. With the town now engulfed in darkness and only the moon lighting up this spectacle, we carried on walking as usual as if nothing was happening.

Oh yeah, what is "Picnic Day"? It's a bank holiday held on the first Monday in August for the Northern Territory, but you will have to look up what the celebration is all about, as I now have to cross the border back into Queensland and do not have the time to tell you. What is the hurry you ask? Well, I have to get to Mount Isa to see if there is a letter from Anna waiting for me.

Arriving at a little town called Camooweal, just over the Northern Territory/Queensland border, we found a little campsite that had small caravans to rent on the bulldust ground that they sat on.

"You ain't got a tent have you, boys?" the camp owner enquired.

"No," we replied.

"You sure?" he enquired again.

Wondering whether this was one of those memory games again, like the owner of the park in Andamooka would spring on me as he erased the soil map and I would have to recall all the items we had in our car, I replied, "No, we don't have a tent."

Questioning my ability to remember what we had on board our motor vehicle, he asked once again. "You sure now? Cos you don't want to be putting a tent down here, I can tell you." Giving him a definite affirmative, he wrote down our car number plate, and booking us into a small touring caravan, he said sternly, "Just make sure you don't put a tent down, boys."

Wondering why he was so worried that we had a piece of canvas for our shelter, we headed into this tiny settlement of just a couple of hundred people. Going door to door, we came across typical Australian families who had been introduced to encyclopedias before and had either bought them in the past, were not interested or could not afford them. Finally, finding an Aboriginal family whose husband worked for another council, Scott and Andrea's five children danced around with delight as we left their home that, unlike other Aboriginal homes, had paintings and photos on the walls, a coffee table and yes, a goldfish!

Deciding not to go to the pub, we headed back to the campsite with some well-deserved cold beers, ready to cook our staple diet primarily consisting of either pasta with beef sauce, fish fingers, sausages, burgers, mashed potatoes or whatever tasty nutritious delights we had decided to munch on that night. By now, I was again carrying surplus cash on me, and it was at this point that I decided to start sending money home. I could now see a little light at the end of my Australian adventure tunnel, and although this light was a tiny pinprick, I thought I might as well plan for my financial future for when I returned.

After washing up, I checked the car was locked, and cracking open a beer, I lay on the bonnet staring up at the starry sky, with the very warm, still, quiet evening only interrupted by the occasional sound of insects playing on my eardrums. On the subject of insects, our spider in the car was now doing exceedingly well with his food supply. Reaching a warmer climate, his web was catching more flies and other little exotic morsels from the insect world, and he was now dining "à la carte" on a daily basis.

Finishing the beer, I called out to Terry who was inside the caravan reading one of the many novels he would purchase now and then.

"Do you want another beating at Trivial Pursuit?"

"You mean do you want a beating?" the reply came.

Setting out the Trivial Pursuit for the umpteenth time to do battle again, I had forgotten who was in the lead in this mammoth competition. Was it Wales or Ireland?

Sitting around the little table throwing the dice and moving our counters around, slowly collecting the little pieces that eventually make up the pie, the only other noise was that of our questions and answers, not forgetting the sound of ring-pulls from our cans of beer. About half an hour later, we could hear a distant and constant rumble slowly getting louder outside our tiny tin home. At first thinking that it was thunder, I quickly dismissed it as the incessant noise got louder and louder.

"What the hell is that, matey?"

"I'm not sure," I replied.

Very slowly, the caravan started to vibrate, and as the little loose pieces of pie on the board started to do a merry little dance, the touring caravan began to shake ever so violently.

"Is it an earthquake?"

"I'm not sure," I replied again.

Suddenly, we heard the sound of cattle with their distinctive noises emanating loudly as if they were almost outside our door.

By now the caravan was rocking back and forth, and the little pieces of pie were break-dancing, doing the moonwalk and whatever other dance styles they could muster, before they fell off the table. Terry opened the door and looked outside. Peering around the corner of the doorway, I was confronted with a scene similar to one you may see in Africa, like watching the great wildebeest migration across the Serengeti. This time, though, it was beef cattle stampeding. Buffeting other people's temporary accommodation and motor vehicles, a large beast came rushing past, kicking up dust between our car and the doorway where we were both now standing.

"No wonder he made sure we didn't have a tent," my opponent said.

He was right! If we had been camping in a tent that night we would have been trampled to death.

The next day we drove the short distance to Mount Isa. Changing some Aussie dollars into sterling, I called home and told my mother that I was about to send some cash home and for her to put it into my bank account for me. Once she had received that envelope, I would then send another, and then another, until this flow of cash built up enough for me to buy a car and other things I may need when returning home.

Walking over to the post office, I knew that there was mail possibly waiting for me from home, as I had instructed the folks to send it two weeks' previously. With the clerk handing me four envelopes, I recognised the handwriting of my mother, my brother, my great aunt and … Anna.

Opening the mail from my family, I received an update on the gossip from back home. The dogs were slowing down and taking them for a walk had become a slow and protracted affair. My great aunt's hearing and eyesight had got worse, and my little brother's letter contained stuff which involved lots of drinking, fighting and waking up in places that he couldn't remember going to the night before. Then I opened "The Letter". Now, again you are probably thinking "What the hell is he playing at? He's hurried to get to Mount Isa to see if he's received a letter from her and he opens it last?" The reason I was reluctant to open it first was that I was afraid that I would read words along the lines of, "I never want anything more to do with you".

In it, Anna expressed her disappointment at the way I had left her, which was understandable. Still single, she still held strong feelings for me and knew I had not returned home, as she had called my parent's back home in Wales, only to find I was still in Oz, which caused her some confusion. This I knew to be true, as my mother had told me a few months ago that a girl with an Australian accent had called enquiring about my whereabouts. At the foot of the letter, she had put her telephone number and the words "Please ring". Thinking about calling her immediately, I then thought it best to gather my thoughts and call her when we reached Karumba.

Deciding I would drive first, we headed eastwards to the town of Cloncurry before turning northwards for the four hundred and fifty kilometre drive to the coast. This particular part of the journey was to see the landscape transform dramatically from the hot dusty desert surrounds to the rich savannah grasslands that took us deep into tropical Queensland. Getting out of the driver's seat mid-journey and jumping into the passenger side, I reached onto the back seat to retrieve a box of wine and a couple of plastic glasses. I was to be barman, and my only customer, my driver, would soon be joining me for a drink once he had finished his cigarette.

As dusk descended, we entered the town of Normanton. We had left the Aussie winter far behind us once again, and this town was to become memorable for not only the violence on one particular day, but for other reasons as well. Entering the "Purple Pub", we struck up a conversation with both white and blackfellas who seemed to get on well with one another. The talk revolved around what we were doing in town, what they did for a living, to betting whether they would ever see one of the locals that drank there ever again. A young Aboriginal man had apparently got completely pissed the night before and then decided to go for a swim in the river. They found his shirt, jeans and sandals by the riverbank the next morning; he had completely disappeared.

"Drowned?" I enquired.

"Or a croc has had him," my fellow drinker replied.

Now, in this part of Queensland called the "Gulf Country", the rivers here are infested with crocodiles. Loading the car up with a slab of VB, we headed into the night to Karumba. With the headlights picking up the adjacent wetlands, the road was a highway for dozens of leaping toads that were at the mercy of the car's tyres. At first, I thought they were tiny kangaroos, but by then I was just finishing the dregs from the box of wine sitting on my lap, and all sense, reasoning and dimensions had long gone out the window. Arriving at a campsite on the banks of the Norman River, we booked into a cabin with two rooms. One room contained two single beds; the other was a basic kitchen with a small dining table. This was to be our home for nearly three weeks, in which time we would sell a huge pile of books and instigate the sort of job creation not seen since President Roosevelt had introduced his "New Deal", which was implemented to lift America out of the terrible Great Depression in the 1930s.

The next morning was an early rise. Not because we had to, but quite simply because the cabin was slowly baking us oven-like under the powerful early morning sun, with the old air-conditioning unit fighting to keep the heat down, gasping like an old man struggling to blow out tiny puffs of cool air. Opening the door at just past seven o'clock, I was greeted with a clear blue sky.

Walking around the camp, I gave a little yawn as my eyes settled on the Norman River glistening in the bright sunlight. With the river's backdrop lined with mangroves, I half-expected Humphrey Bogart and Katharine Hepburn to turn a bend in the river aboard the *African Queen*.

After a quick shower and a wash of the smalls, hanging them together with my towel on the communal washing line, I headed for the shops in this special little place. Passing the "Animal Bar" (more of that later), the temperature had risen into the mid-twenties and nine o'clock was still a good half hour away. Here the temperature in what they call the "Top End" of Australia would be a balmy dry heat of twenty-nine to thirty-three degrees every day. These clear blue daily skies were only to be interrupted by a rare natural phenomena called "Morning Glory" (and again, more of that later).

Walking along, I came across a sign that announced the end of the Matilda Highway. The origins of this start at the New South Wales border just over eighteen hundred kilometres away, and it took you through the outback heartland of this second largest state of Oz. Even after two and a half years of being in this country, the distances would still sometimes make me think in wonder at the size of this island continent. Walking further along, I came across a second sign, which revealed that Karumba had a rich history in aviation. The town served as a port for the great flying boats travelling en route from Sydney to the United Kingdom during the British Empire days. It was also a base for the Catalina flying craft during World War Two, where they were hauled out of the river and up the boat ramp for servicing by the RAAF (Royal Australian Air Force). Now, enough of the military stuff, I hear some of you say. Get on and tell us more about this place.

Okay! Reaching Karumba Point, where the mouth of the Norman River meets the enormous body of water that is the Gulf of Carpentaria, the sea was sparkling in the early morning sunshine and it looked extremely inviting as an opportunity for a quick dip. With the sea temperature at that time of year being in the mid-twenties, you would think, well hell, why not? Apart from this large expanse of water being warm enough to match a lukewarm bath, it is probably (in my eyes at least) the most dangerous body of water in the world. When nature created this, it must have thought, what the hell can I put in this gulf to stop humans swimming in it? The Gulf of Carpentaria's defences are formidable. Firstly, before you even enter the water you have to slip and slide across the mud flats, through the minefield of stonefish buried just slightly underneath, with their poisonous dorsal fin spines, which can kill in a very short space of time, sticking through the surface. That is, unless medical attention is quickly administered. (There are no bleached white beaches up here!)

On entering these shark-infested waters, you would also have to contend with poisonous sea snakes and box jellyfish, or sea wasps as they're sometimes called. These almost transparent marine stingers can kill within minutes. After achieving a safe successful swim and heading back to dry land, you would then have to tread the stonefish minefield once again, and if you thought that was easy, think again! The entire coastline has its ultimate defence – the saltwater crocodile. Having this knowledge already logged, I decided not to dip a single toe in the water and headed back to the campsite.

Knocking the campsite owner's door, I asked her if she was an early riser, and on finding out that she was, I expressed my interest in watching the "Morning Glory" phenomena. Knowing it occurred shortly after daybreak, I asked her if she would wake me by banging on the door so that I could witness this unique display of cloud activity that happens in very few parts of the world. Telling me that this oddity only happened in the months of August, September and October, she warned that there was still no guarantee that it would happen while we were staying. So, what exactly is it, I hear you ask?

Just after dawn has broken, the clear skies over the gulf seem to bring a reassurance that the day is going to be a grand one indeed. However, on the horizon far out to sea appears a cloud. Not just any normal cloud you see leisurely floating around with not a care in the world. No, this great barrel of a cloud, that is so wide it fills the entire horizon, comes at you like an aerial juggernaut and gives you the impression that the world is about to come to an end in a very strange and peculiar way. It's as if a giant rolling pin is rolling towards you, pulverising anything that gets in its way. Of course, the cloud is way up in the sky causing no damage whatsoever. But the size and speed that it comes in makes it truly amazing. That's not all either. Sometimes these clouds come in multiples, each one after the other in waves like the oceans of the world sending waves towards the coastline. After they disappear inland, the clear sky remains for the rest of the day. This strange weather pattern has flummoxed meteorologists from around the world. There are some theories but they are not entirely sure.

After cooking some burgers and sausages on the campsite communal barbecue, I decided to make the call to Anna. As the ringtone burred away, I heard someone pick it up at the other end.

"Hello," I said.

From the other end of the line came a "Hello, who is speaking please?" The non-Australian female accent penetrated my eardrums, and recognising the Russian accent, I realised it was her mother.

"Hi, this is Lance speaking. Is Anna there please?"

"One moment, please," she replied.

What seemed like an eternity passed and then I heard her voice. Chatting about all sorts of things, I kept my status as an illegal immigrant from her, but silently thought I would reveal this fact when she mentioned we should meet up again. This was going to be no easy task though, as I was now over two thousand seven hundred kilometres from her.

After hanging up the phone and promising to keep in touch with her, I headed back to the cabin feeling as pleased as punch at having made the call. I would now have to work out a plan on how we could meet up. Deciding to work Karumba on another day, we chose to make the seventy kilometre drive back to Normanton to see what we could pull out of the hat there. On reaching the town, we decided to work together, but after knocking doors for several hours, we only managed to sell two sets of books. Establishing that the town had been visited before by booksellers just over two years ago, we hit a brick wall. Finding that many of the houses we knocked on had

Aboriginal families within but with no proper employment, we thought our journey to this remote town was going to turn out to be a complete waste of time.

With every family receiving welfare benefits from the government, which incidentally is known as "sit-down money", we were at a loss as to how we could sign these people up. All across the country these indigenous folk received this money. It was common to come across this situation whenever I entered an Aboriginal person's home in the cities or towns up and down this huge geographical mass, and who could blame them. They received this money each week to do "fuck all!"

Normanton was different though. Here they had implemented a scheme where, although they received their "sit-down" coins, they also did work of sorts to help the community as a whole. For example, if someone was good at mechanics, then that person fixed the motor vehicles in the town. If he or she was handy with carpentry, then they fixed broken tables and chairs, made wooden bowls or whatever. In other words, the community kept everyone busy or as busy as possible with these odd jobs to try and keep them off the grog. (At least in the daytime anyway!)

The frustration we had was that these people could afford the seventy bucks a month but had no proper employment that we could link them to, so enabling them to qualify for the books. To compound matters we had inadvertently shown families the prospectus so to satisfy their curiosity as to what we were selling, and this in turn brought a little sort of resentment towards us, as the parents were unable to buy these educational materials for their children.

It was about this time, while talking to an Aboriginal father called Ronald, that a plan began to hatch in our heads almost simultaneously. Ronald explained he was a labourer for the community, and his brother, Neville, told Ronald each day what to do. Neville was his supervisor – his boss! Now, if we could put his occupation down as labourer for some made-up business of Neville's, like "Crocodile Creek Builders", for example. Then put Neville's telephone number down and for Neville to say that he was indeed the owner of such a firm and that Ronald did indeed work for him and had done so for the last "x" amount of years, then that would fit the criteria that Crowell International required to be able to process the application successfully. (The company never actually checked to see if businesses were legitimate.) Bingo! Ronnie's books would be winging their way to him within a fortnight's time. Sounds confusing? Not to us!

Over the next few days, we created all sorts of businesses and rehearsed with the families on a daily basis what to say when the company called to clarify an order. If they didn't have a phone (which if you remember was another essential ingredient to be able to receive the books), we would use a public telephone kiosk number, which were scattered around town. Contacting our boss and informing him of our intentions, this clandestine conversation, he informed us, would cost him a few slabs of beer at least. At the head office in Sydney, he had a mole (undercover agent). The mole would sometimes let slip through the net certain orders that did not conform to Crowell's strict criteria so that our boss could meet his monthly sales targets and, in turn, get his bonus. The mole's job was now to tell us when the company would be ringing a certain family who did not have a phone. Well, as far as the company was concerned they did, but they wouldn't realise it was a telephone kiosk that they were calling. We could then arrange for the husband or wife to stand in the kiosk to receive the important call. This elaborate and intricate scam was to benefit all, and soon the numbers of books sold in this unorthodox way very quickly crept into double figures.

We quickly realised we would have to stay in the town for at least two weeks to make sure these orders were as watertight as possible. At four hundred dollars each in commission, this had to be done properly. Keeping in regular contact with the families, we would play the game each day of
"What's my trade?"

Drinking in the "Purple Pub" during each day or evening, blackfellas would come up to us and say, "Hey! Tony, Terry. I'm a plumber, or carpenter, or gardener. Right?"

When the calls started to come, we had a couple of incidents where the people who did not have a phone did not have the confidence to use a public phone box (seriously!).

On one occasion, a very highly confused and technophobic man who had to remember that he worked for a fictitious company and had to remember his type of employment and for how long he had worked there, turned to Terry while he was on the phone to the head office in Sydney and said, "Hey Terry! What's my name?"

The look on Terry's face, with him waving his hands in front of him and voicing a silent "I'm not here", was a picture, I can tell you.

One afternoon, we noticed a brightly coloured small beetle trapped in the spider's web. Bright colours in the natural world tend to send messages to predators to beware. While driving back to Karumba, our in-car spider entertainment appeared and we watched it drag its prey down to its lair. Obviously, being a stranger to this part of the world, mister or missus spider may have failed to spot a dangerous piece of food as we never saw him or her again.

A few days after arriving in Karumba, there was an early morning hammering on the door with a female voice shouting, "Morning glory is coming!"

I leapt out of bed and tried to wake Terry. His mumbled expletive reply signalled to leave him in his bed. It was 7.30 a.m.
Rushing out and looking into the blue skies of the gulf, I could see a long, thin, dark cloud, the whole length of the horizon, coming towards me at speed. This was despite there not being a breeze in the air. As it passed over me, I could feel tiny droplets of water landing on my face, and then I heard a cry.

"There's another one coming!"

Looking back towards the horizon, I could make out a similar looking beast heading towards us, and again there was not a wisp of wind. It was like a Roman army sending legion after legion in to attack us, as these uniformed, coordinated cloud formations marched towards us. There are some fantastic pictures on the internet, so tap into it and have a look at "Morning Glory".

The barbecue each evening was used to its full potential, and although the Gulf of Carpentaria is full of nastys that will kill you, it is also a larder full of delicious seafood. The prawn fishing industry is massive in this part of the world and the barramundi is one of the tastiest species of fish on the planet (in my mind anyway). It was here that I first tasted crocodile, and although a protected species, they are reared specially at crocodile farms for human consumption. Tastes a bit like chicken, though nicer. It is one of my favourite meats.

One afternoon, we were in an Aboriginal family's home and I asked the children what they had been doing that morning.
"Fishing!" all four boys shouted.

Turning to the youngest who was about six, I thought I would have a little bit of banter with him. "Did you catch any crocodiles?" I asked.
The little boy nodded and replied, "Yeah, my dad caught one this morning and we all skinned it so we can eat it later."

Suddenly one of the older brothers ran towards this little chap, and placing a well-aimed punch into his belly, sending him doubling up, he said, "No we didn't."

The youngster, who was now groaning from the impact, looked back up towards me and spluttered, "No, no, we didn't."
His mother looked over to me and smiling said, "He's always joking, that one."

Obviously, as I said before, the crocodile is a protected species, but I guess in remote parts they are covertly hunted, and the authorities are not aware. Besides, if the occasional local is taken by a croc now and again, then there's no harm in a little payback every now and again, is there?

During our time in Karumba, I spoke to Anna on several occasions and with her birthday just a few months away agreed to meet up with her. We just had to agree on a location.

"The Animal Bar" was a favourite haunt for the more adventurous backpacker who made it to Karumba. With a pool table and a good supply of grog, it had people from all over the world turning up there. The band The Red Hot Chilli Peppers' song "Animal Bar", from their 2006 album *Stadium Arcadium*, is about Karumba.

Karumba supposedly also has a dark secret that will give the willies to those superstitious readers reading this. No Aboriginal lived in the town, and once dusk arrived, every indigenous person left the town before nightfall. The reason for this was that many moons ago during the Aboriginal "Dreamtime", a fierce battle took place between two tribes. Many warriors were killed and now the spirits wander the town at night. I didn't see any, but then again we were both pissed every night, which brings me onto the subject of the devil drink.

My diary entry for 15th August 1993 reads as follows: Drink rest of wine and generally try and waste some time – man – no wonder the Aborigines are always on the piss with fuck all to do in places like this – reminds me of home.

The fact was we had sold all the books we could, but couldn't leave until we had let everyone clarify their orders and get a date from head office for when their books would arrive. With so much time on our hands, it was a daily trip to the "Purple Pub" and other drinking dens in Normanton. We preferred drinking here rather than at "The Animal Bar" as we could have a laugh with the locals, telling jokes, stories and playing "What's my trade?"

They say the Aboriginal people are just a bunch of pissheads, and maybe they are. Unlike the other Aboriginal parts of towns we had worked in previously, Normanton, as I said before, had some sort of structure in place that gave these indigenous people a sort of purpose in life. Instead of waking up and thinking "What the hell do we do today?" and once again heading for the pub or bottle shop with their "sit-down money", these people could go off and do certain chores and then perhaps indulge in some pastime like fishing or hunting (no crocodiles though). There was some heavy drinking in the evening, though the violence we experienced in the town was quite mild. Apart from the fight breaking out at Henry and Lucinda's house told about earlier in these chronicles, we witnessed only minor scuffles. Maybe we were lucky? I don't know.

Another reason people drink so much up here is the hot sticky heat. Here, in the months that build up to the "wet season", the humidity is uncomfortable to say the least. With no air conditioning, it is almost impossible to sleep at night. Some sleep outside during this time, but many have a drop or two of grog each evening to help them reach "The Land of Nod". Now, I know it was now the dry season and nights were quite mild and it was relatively comfortable to fall asleep, but our excuse was that we were now in training to prepare for those intolerable conditions that lay ahead.

Normanton had been a huge success for us, and selling only one set in Karumba, we certainly made the numbers up with twenty-two sets in the town. In some ways it was to be a blueprint for what we were about to do next. Poring over our very detailed map of Queensland, we decided to start working the Aboriginal communities proper. Calling the boss and telling him of our intentions, his main concern was that we did not have permits to enter these settlements, and should we apply for them, they could, if successful, take months to arrange. The permit system is in place to stop tourists traipsing through these communities that have a completely different culture to that of the Westerner. We'd already found a way around this, and this was to meet the tribal elders of each community to gain their permission to work in them before knocking doors.

Deciding to head to Cairns, we found an Aboriginal community just over three hundred kilometres north up on Cape York – Hopevale.

Leaving Karumba and passing through Normanton to head eastwards to another coast and Cairns, I was, in a way, quite sad to leave this part of Australia, a place that very few people experience. It's a world apart from the resorts of The Great Barrier Reef and The Gold Coast. Here was the real Oz. Again, because of the nature of our work, it allowed us to get a sense of the underbelly of Oz and make a sort of (albeit) loose bond with the Aboriginal people. This fascination was slowly growing on us, and I think we both now realised that we were doing something very special in our lives that most people could only dream of. We would have a couple of days of relaxation in Cairns before getting back under the belly that is the true part of Australia. And then more madness!

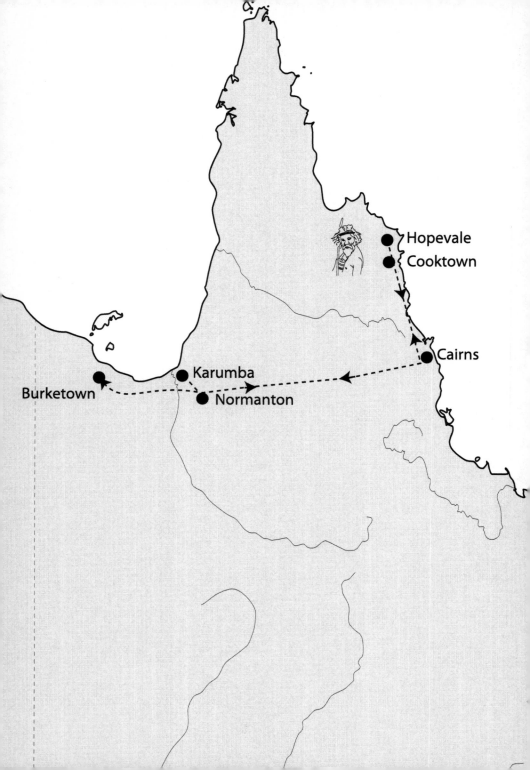

Chapter 14

The seven hundred kilometre journey to Cairns gave me time to dwell on things. I was now beginning to see the Aboriginal people in a different light. At this stage, you're probably thinking, "Of course he would, he is making a small fortune from them." And yes, you would be right. We were now making money that we could never have dreamt of earning in other towns or cities, but only because we had found an untapped market and by using our ingenuity to get over certain obstacles, were achieving goals that would suit all parties.

These people had never had the opportunity to buy educational materials for their children before, and as one Aboriginal woman said, "It was the best thing since bread was sliced.' (Her words not mine.) Just like any parents, they wanted to give their children the best step-up onto the education ladder as possible. It had also started to become quite exciting, and in a way felt rewarding to see these youngsters jumping up and down, running around the place with their excitable chatter at the thought that they were going to receive these books in the very near future. The general level of appreciation, not only from the children but the parents as well, surpassed that of the non-Aboriginal families that we had sold to in the past. I am not saying that those families were not as grateful for us calling at their homes with this educational package, but in Western society, children can be spoilt rotten with easy access to toys, games, games consoles etc. (Remember the boy that could not remember he had been given an expensive organ for Christmas, all those chapters ago?)

About two hundred kilometres from Cairns, we saw a hitch-hiker and decided to stop for him. Getting into the car with his bag, we very quickly learned that this man in his fifties was from what was then the war-torn country of Yugoslavia and was looking for a lift to where we were heading. He also had a medical condition, which most people would know as "verbal diarrhoea". With him hardly coming up for air, despite giving him a couple of beers, most of the conversation consisted of him talking complete and utter bollocks. I decided against telling him to shut up and quietly wished that the rear seat had an ejector system attached to it. Seeing Terry had increased his average speed to well over a hundred kilometres an hour to get us to our destination as quickly as possible now that motormouth was aboard, I sat and gritted my teeth until finally I'd had enough.

"Will you shut the fuck up!" I said.

With him now being silent, we carried on and Terry reduced his speed. This silence was to last for about two minutes and then the drivel started again.

"Stop the car, Terry," I said.

When the car stopped, I turned around and told him to get out. His face suddenly froze, and I could see the blood draining from it.

"I'm sorry," he said in his European accent. "I won't say another word." And he didn't. Not even a "Thank you" when he got out of the car. Maybe he was lonely and just wanted to chat, but on that day that fella drove us to the brink. We vowed from that day onwards we would never pick up another hitch-hiker again. Little did we know that later the car would become a local free taxi for the Aboriginal people, but you will have to wait quite a few pages till we get to that story.

In Cairns we decided to spoil ourselves and book into a nice hotel near the seafront. Though I could have been travelling with someone that I found hard to get on with, this was not the case as we both shared the same sense of humour, and that was half the battle. Booking into separate rooms and agreeing to go our separate ways for a couple of days, I took the car into town to book it in for a well-deserved service. Again, like Canberra and Alice Springs, Cairns did nothing for me. The flash bars and clubs I skirted round and ended up in some of the more rustic bars chatting to locals and backpackers from all over the world. On the second night, walking back to the hotel, I heard a voice shout my name.

Looking across the road, I could see a group of Aboriginal men. Crossing the road, I came across Benny who had bought the books from us in Normanton.

"What the hell are you doing here?" I asked. Bear in mind he was nearly seven hundred kilometres away from home.

"I'm visiting my brother who lives here," he said.

He asked where his books were, and I told him that they were on their way. Introducing me to his brother and his mates, the customary handshakes were made. With the whole group being in quite a sober state, they asked me where I was heading.

"Off to bed," I replied, and then we parted.

In hindsight, and even to this day I think what if I had brought them back to the hotel bar as guests. Imagine it. I walk into the hotel with five Aborigines dressed in grubby T-shirts, jeans and thongs (sandals), and then buy them drinks all night with the other clientele thinking "How the fuck does he know them?" The only thing that stopped me doing that at the time was knowing we had to drive to Cooktown the next day and I needed to get a good night's sleep.

The next morning I had a brainwave regarding where I could meet Anna – Perth. I would fly her the three thousand, three hundred kilometres across the entire continent to Western Australia for her birthday. All I needed to know was whether she would agree to it or not. I called her and she was thrilled that we would meet up again, even though it was almost three months away. Calling into a travel agents, I purchased a return flight for her and popped the ticket in the post.

The drive to Cooktown, although a fair bit of it on an unsealed road (it's all tarmac these days), was a pleasant enough journey. This mainly inland route presented us with sugar cane fields that soon turned into lush tropical rainforest, which lay on either side of the road. Looking into it made me think how hard it must have been for the pioneers of this country to hack through such impenetrable jungle to get to where they wanted to go. Stopping the car to switch drivers, the sound of the birdlife calling back and forth made it feel like a paradise that only had the iridescent turquoise waters of the sea missing.

Arriving at Cooktown, we booked into one of four cabins on a small campsite that also had caravans and offered facilities for people with tents. Unpacking quickly, we jumped back into the car and headed for the town's post office to pick up a package from head office. Inside the package were two new prospectuses to replace our old ones, a pile of fresh posters and half a dozen or so money boxes, which would be a little beer money for us if a family wanted to buy an extra box or two. These were sold for between twenty and ten bucks depending on how much haggling was done.

Heading off for Hopevale, this short journey, mostly on unsealed roads, brought us to the "Welcome to Hopevale Aboriginal Community" sign. The sign basically told us that we had now entered lands that were held in trust for the benefit of the Aboriginal community of Hopevale. These traditional lands belonged to the "Guugu Yimithirr" people (and I'm afraid I have forgotten how to pronounce that one). These people hold quite a significant place in the modern history of Australia, as their ancestors were the first Aboriginal folk that Lieutenant James Cook met when he brought his ship, the HMS Endeavour, to the shores to get it repaired after running aground on the Great Barrier Reef. The year was 1770 and he was here from 17th June till 4th August. Oh, and he was made a Captain later, just in case you are thinking "Hang on, he's got that wrong!"

The history, not just of these people but the other dozens and dozens of Aboriginal people throughout the continent, is fascinating, and here's just one little interesting fact. The word "Kangaroo" comes from the "Guugu Yimithirr" language: the language recorded by Cook and his crew while the ship was being repaired revealed the hopping marsupial's name and was written down as "Kanguru", which is how it would sound if these folk spoke to you in their native tongue, "Ganjuru". It has since been refined to the modern-day spelling of the word.

Anyway, I could go on for ages about these people, but I have to get on and sell some more books. With the noticeboard informing us that we had to report to the council offices, we parked up on the perimeter of this little settlement and walked in to try and find them. Before long, the early warning Aboriginal signal sounded, as two young boys spied us coming down the dusty road.

"White fellas coming! White fellas coming!"

Turning on their heels, they ran back into town repeating the same words until their voices diminished into silence. Finding the offices, we entered what was a very clean, well set out little building. Explaining the purpose of our visit and understanding that we needed to speak to tribal elders before we could carry on, we were pointed to a house where a certain elder by the name of Solomon lived. Walking over to his house, we were again surrounded by young children who were curious as to what we were doing.

"What's in the bag mister?" The usual question was fired at us.

"Crocodiles," I replied.

This led to an enormous amount of laughter from them, and they ran and skipped around us as we walked to Solomon's open doorway.

Looking into what was obviously the living room, I shouted a "Hello" into what looked like an empty household. Waiting for what must have been half a minute or so, I again called out a few salutations, before a tall, slim Aboriginal man of about fifty years old walked in from another room. Looking us up and down, he squinted slightly before saying.

"What can I do for you, fellas?"

Explaining our purpose, he then asked us to show him what we were selling. Asking if his other half was in, he was curious as to why his wife would need to be present. Informing this very important man that this was our company's policy, he shook his head and said, "She is not here."

Now, we could have just shown him the books, and his blessing or permission to move on would have been sufficient. However, we stuck to our guns and insisted that his wife was present before we revealed the product that we were selling. In hindsight, I think that maybe they thought our intentions were genuine, insisting that both parties were present, as often the spouse was not around and she would have to be found. On the other hand, it may have been offensive questioning these elders, insinuating that their word alone was not enough for us to carry on. It never became an issue, so I guess how we went about this process was, as a whole, acceptable to them.

Instructing one of the many children behind us to go and find his mother, a little boy ran off, and very soon a large busty woman with a very colourful dress appeared. Solomon introduced us to his wife and we began showing them the books without the script we normally used. This casual approach we adopted was usually for the elders, and we soon returned to the script when we were in action in the rest of the community. Why we did this I am not too sure, but I think this initial very casual approach worked, as we soon gained the vital "blessing". Showing them the books, we waited for Solomon's response.

"You will have to go and see Joshua Harold, Thomas Mitchell, Ishmael Robins and Frazer Jacks before you can sell these books to the people in our town," he said.

Explaining that we had his blessing to carry on with what we were doing, he instructed the older children to show us where these people lived. Picking up our posters from a very clean tiled floor and packing them into our little knapsack, we turned to follow the children to our next destination.

"Where are you going?" he asked.

"To go and see the other elders," I replied.

"Not yet," Solomon said.

We stood at the doorway wondering what was next.

"How much are they?"

"Seventy dollars a month," I replied.

"I will have them," came his reply.

Here at Hopevale, everything was structured and we did not have to carry out the job creation scheme like we had to in Normanton. Here, all the men were employed by the shire council and head office only needed to contact the council offices to confirm that they were employed.

A tribal elder's blessing to work in their town was one of the most powerful tools a man could have without raising a fist or weapon.

One afternoon, and in fact it was on Saturday 4th September 1993, we turned up at what was a very quiet settlement. With no children to greet us, we wandered around empty streets. It was like being on that ship, the Marie Celeste. Walking around the town with all the houses doors open and not a soul to be seen, we shrugged our shoulders and turned around to head back to the car and back to Cooktown. Then, from around a building in front of us appeared a drunken Aboriginal man holding a shotgun.

"What are you doing on our land?" he bellowed, staggering.

"We are selling educational books for the little ones to do well at school," Terry replied.

With our inebriated obstacle waving the gun around as if Harry Potter was about to cast a spell with his magic wand, he frowned and said in a slurred form of speech.

"Who said you could come here?"

Now if you remember me telling you earlier, I am very good at remembering names but something suddenly and dangerously happened – my mind went blank!

With my mathematical genius of a colleague a complete waste of time at remembering names, I half-expected him to say we couldn't remember, but if this helps you, the square root of a hundred and forty-four is twelve.

With my memory working at a million miles an hour, the names suddenly started popping into that grey matter of mine. "We have been invited here by Ishmael, Thomas, Frazer, Solomon and Joshua."

The man looked hard at us, and giving a little squint, his deep, dark eyes almost felt as if they were penetrating our very own. Nodding his head several times, he turned and staggered off. Now, even to this day, I wonder what the hell would have happened if I had not been able to pull those aces out of our "happy family" Aboriginal playing cards pack?

As I said to you before, once you received a blessing from the tribal elders, you were pretty much untouchable. These leaders commanded great respect and were not only men to turn to if a person had problems or certain matters at hand, they could also act as judge and jury if someone carried out a wrongful act in the eyes of their own rules and laws. Obviously, if a murder or a very serious crime was committed, then the might of the Australian law enforcement agency would be required to bring the accused to court. On other matters, however, these elders could dish out justice that ranged from the spearing of bodies to banishment from their community for the rest of one's life. This was the worst punishment a person could receive because Aboriginal people were intrinsically linked to the land on which they were born. To ostracise a person from their homelands and told never to return is the height of shame, leaving them with the feeling of being an outcast for the rest of their life.

If that man had pulled the trigger killing the both of us, it would have been very unlikely that he would have been able to return to Hopevale if he was ever released from prison.

Returning to the car, we heard a shout from behind us.

"Hey, fellas."

Turning around, we saw an Aboriginal man standing in the doorway of his house.

"Are you the encyclopedia men?" he asked.

"Yes," we both said simultaneously.

"Well come over here. I want to buy your books."

Walking back over, we entered Sammy and Rhonda's home. With the household spick and span, this community had also been well educated about the importance of hygiene. The smell of rubbish that had been prevalent in those indigenous people's homes back in New South Wales and the centre of the Northern Territory was absent.

With Sammy explaining the reason for the town being empty – every Saturday, most of the adults and children went off fishing and hunting – we started the demonstration. Finishing up and finding that they could afford the books, Terry began to set the paperwork out.

"This is a gift for you."

Sammy thrust a boomerang adorned with colourful markings into my hand, and then one into Terry's.

"Thank you," we both replied.

"No! Thank you," Sammy said warmly, shaking our hands. "I now have something to teach my children with that will hopefully give them opportunities that I never had when I was younger."

Now, MacMillan Publishers, the parent of Crowell International, published thousands of books worldwide, covering all sorts of topics. Although we had our standard package, we would occasionally give extra books away to try and close a deal – The Science Library, which consisted of ten volumes, which I mentioned earlier, would be an example. With

Terry sorting the paperwork out, I plunged my hand into our little knapsack and pulled out several posters. Making up a story that his family were the hundredth family in Queensland this year to purchase the books and had just won a prize that entitled them to extra books, I began to unroll posters that normally never saw the light of day. With my Irish colleague looking at me incredulously as I rolled out poster after poster, he suddenly realised the madness that had gripped me and joined in pulling out more unseen posters from the bag. We both, at one stage, wondered if the company would ever process the order, but we had earned the company tens of thousands of dollars over the last few months, without giving any free books away to clinch a deal.

Ending with *The Complete Works of Shakespeare*, we had now inadvertently turned Sammy and Rhonda's home into a potential library. The sale agreement had books from gardening, to an eighteen-volume set of English classic literature, a thesaurus, a giant atlas and a six-volume set of recipes from around the world. When we left Hopevale for the very last time, I quietly wished to be a fly on the wall in their home when the delivery truck arrived. The delivery would have filled a huge amount of space in their home, with over a hundred books being delivered.

The person responsible for processing the order did enquire about such a large order of books and questioned the fact that that particular order probably meant a loss for the company. Again, "The Mole" stepped in and got the order processed. I sometimes wonder if Sammy returns from a fishing or hunting trip and cries out to his wife, who is holding a recipe book, "To be, or not to be, what dish from what part of the world are we eating tonight, Rhonda?"

I have fond memories of Hopevale, and apart from receiving the boomerang as a gift, it was here that we were offered a giant turtle shell each, which as I told you earlier we had to decline due to the impracticalities of carrying them around for fear of breaking them. I don't think customs would have been too chuffed either. Here was a very well set up little community, and it was the first time that I saw a women's shelter where spouses could seek refuge from their violent drunken partners. Fellow members of the community guarded this building day and night, while the elders tried to sort out these domestics.

Right! What is spearing of bodies all about, I still hear you ask? I mentioned earlier that it was a punishment that the tribal elders can dish out, but have yet to tell you what it is. The customary laws of the Aboriginal people vary enormously over the continent and are so complex that I cannot even begin to go into detail about them, as it would take up too much space in what is supposed to be an easy reading piece of work. Very, very briefly, I will explain.

Aboriginal law and order was around long before Cook and his men landed on Terra Australis (Australia). If someone did something wrong, depending on the severity of the crime, the punishment could range from the perpetrator giving something tangible to the victim as compensation (i.e. kangaroo furs, crocodile skins, or whatever), to the offender being put to death. "Spearing" is just that: where an incision is made into the convicted criminal's body by a spear. Depending on the nature of the crime, it could be anything from "a thigh spearing" to an infliction somewhere on the torso, maybe multiple times.

It may sound barbaric to some readers, but this is very important to the Aboriginal culture, and as a result, the Australian eyes of the law often look the other way, unless of course, this corporal form of punishment becomes a capital form, or the recipient receives a torture from which the government cannot avert their eyes. "Spearing" is also involved in initiation ceremonies – where a boy crosses the threshold to become a man, for instance. Many times, you will see scars on these people's bodies, but they don't necessarily mean that they are all criminals. It just means that they are tough enough to endure pain and that it gives the person a certain status among his people. There is much more to explain, and initiation ceremonies are held for females as well, but I simply do not have the space to go into what is a very complex subject.

Incidentally, apart from the shotgun episode, we experienced no violence. Mind you, we were always safely in Cooktown by around eight, so who knows what went on after then.

Taking a day off before we decided where to go next, we wandered around the town that is named after our great explorer. Cooktown is a lovely little place, and if you ever get to Cairns, try and hire a car or take an excursion, even for just a couple of days. It is well worth it.

Trying out a few of the bars, we found a good restaurant and booked a table. Killing time while we waited for the table to become available, we took a walk along the jetty. Peering down at a boat alongside it, I could see about a dozen fish on the deck, some almost a metre long. From out of the wheelhouse came a bronze-coloured man with bleached blond hair.

"That's a good catch you got there," I shouted down. "You'll eat well tonight."

Looking back up and rubbing his chin, he replied.

"Catch, mate? That's the bait!"

Terry looked at me with the expression that said, "You idiot!"

With Terry finishing off his oysters and me polishing off my barramundi, we got the map out. The waitress poured Terry a large rum. I had recently acquired a taste for the fortified wine of port and placed a large glassful of the deep-red colour liquid onto our outstretched map. Realising that we could go no further north than Hopevale without a four-wheel drive, Cape York was definitely out. We needed to find another Aboriginal community, and the nearest one by sticking to the sealed roads was back in the Northern Territory. Borroloola was a distance of nearly two thousand, five hundred kilometres. Yes that's right – 2,500.

There was an alternative route, which led across the top of the country from Normanton to another tiny town called Burketown, which then led on to the Aboriginal community of Doomadgee, and that took you up to the border of the territory and a place called Hell's Gate. From there it was a hop, skip and a jump to Borroloola, a total of just over sixteen hundred k's. Not only would we knock nine hundred kilometres off our trip, but we could also work Burketown and Doomadgee on the way. To give you an idea on another scale of the distance we were about to travel, it would be the equivalent of driving from London, through the countries of the Netherlands and France and onto Warsaw, the capital city of Poland in the far east of the country.

Pointing to the very thin black line that indicated there was some sort of track from Normanton to Borroloola, Terry made a comment that would ring in my ears constantly as we journeyed to these two very remote settlements.

"They said the road was pretty hard going and could only be done in a four-wheel-drive."

"Yeah, all the white folk said that, Terry, but if you remember, quite a few of the blackfellas in Normanton said they had done it in their two-wheel drives before, visiting relatives."

It was settled; we would go across the continent on the most northerly route possible, though my eyes became fixated with the tiny place near the border. I wonder why it's called Hell's Gate? I thought. I was soon to find out.

The next day the plan was to drive to Normanton, rest up and travel to Burketown the following day. The car had other ideas. Travelling on what was a relatively well-maintained unsealed road, one of the little sharp stones put a tiny hole into the radiator. On top of that, the automatic transmission started slipping out of gear every now and then, and so we were held up in Cairns while the car got fixed.

Two days later, we were off again, on what was to be a mammoth trip of over one thousand kilometres that would nearly see us finishing the car off for good. The drive back to Normanton was straightforward, and arriving at just past six o'clock, we should have stopped there for the night, but in our wisdom decided to push on. Refuelling, we headed off into the dusk and the unknown.

At first, the road was just like all normal unsealed roads that we had driven on over the years, and with the headlights picking up natural hazards like potholes and deep sand, the car was carefully manoeuvred around them. As Terry had driven the first part of the journey, I was now at the helm. Fortunately, we both decided to leave the alcohol alone till we got to our destination, which for what we unknowingly had in front of us was probably a good idea. Slowly the road worsened, with the thin layer of bulldust in the middle of the road turning into deep, red sand. With the engine beginning to whine now and then as it propelled us through this tough treadmill of a road, another hazard, this time from the natural world, was thrown at us – Echidnas!

"What are these," I hear some of you ask? Giant hedgehogs, with spines that would take out the tyres of our vehicle without a problem if we ran over these small boulder-like creatures. Swerving around the little walking hazards that shuffled through the night, the car would every now and then want to leave the road and head into the bush, due to the sand slewing the vehicle back and forth.

Just when we thought it could not get any worse, we came across the first dried-up creek bed. Traversing across a very rocky surface, I quietly hoped that we would escape any punctures. Reaching the other side unscathed, we met the sand again, and that is when we first became stuck. Digging the sand from around the tyres with our hands, I reversed and then floored the throttle to see if I could drive it onto a clear patch in front of us.

Moving a little further ahead, the car halted once again. With the engine heaving and groaning and the front tyres trying to get a grip on this soft, gritty surface, I depressed the throttle. In the darkness, our hands became makeshift shovels again, and completing the task, I reversed and threw the car into the sandpit, only for it to come to a stop. We were now one hundred kilometres from Normanton with over another hundred to go before we arrived at our destination. With nothing but wilderness around us, we dug the car free and once again reversed to try again. It was now almost nine o'clock.

Taking a swig of water, I looked up at the starry night, and listening to the little creatures in the bush chattering away to one another, I suddenly thought they were probably saying, "Look at those idiots without the four-wheel drive!"

Deciding to dig two channels in the sand for the tyres to get us to the clear patch, it was not long before we were both sweating profusely from the still-warm air. Soldiering on, I wondered how many times we would be carrying out this task on our route. I didn't have to worry. There was worse to come!

Eventually reaching firm ground, we managed to drive for about an hour at no more than thirty kilometres an hour. Occasionally stopping to scoop sand out of the way of our tyres, we again crossed another dried-up creek bed. Having the pleasure of driving without any obstacles for about twenty minutes, we came across the dried-up Leichardt riverbed. This was no ordinary creek but a river, albeit during the dry season – dry as a bone.

Crossing the rocky bed, I had to be extremely careful not to steer the car into one of the deep gullies that only a robust four-wheel drive could handle. Time and time again, we came to impassable troughs. This meant Terry getting out of the car and crossing to the other side of these obstacles to try and find a safe passage further up or down the dry waterway so that I could cross without us losing the car. All the time while I drove trying to find a safe spot to cross, I had to be careful that I didn't bottom out the car, and with Terry shouting out where particular hazards were, I concentrated my eyesight ahead and into the car's headlight beam. Reaching the other side, we came up against the sand again, and that was when we thought, fuck it, it's now definitely time for a beer!

Pouring the warm amber nectar down our throats, we laughed at what all the people we had worked with in the past might now think if they could see us and how crazy we were at finding places to sell books. Breaking the back of the journey, we eventually arrived at Burketown at two in the morning.

With the town in complete darkness except for the moonlight, we drank some more beers on the bonnet of the car, marvelling at our achievement at getting so far in our two-wheel drive automatic transmission station wagon. We still had to get through Hell's Gate and into the Northern Territory, but we didn't care. We were in one of the most remote frontier outposts on this entire continent.

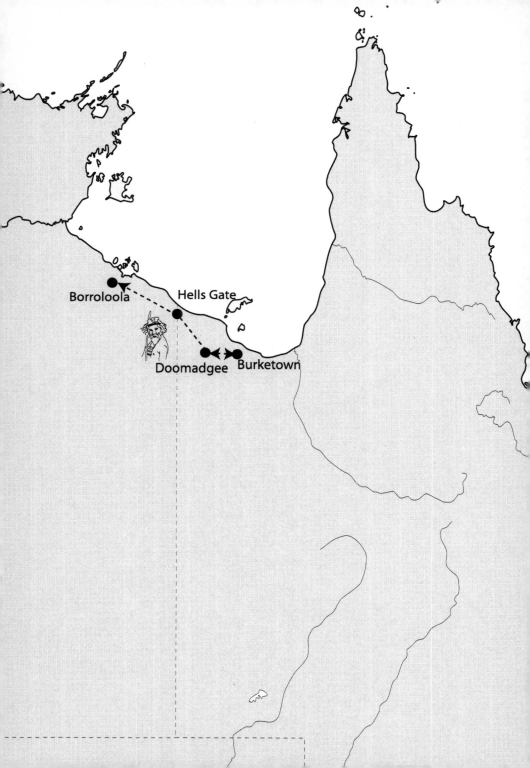

Borroloola

Hells Gate

Doomadgee

Burketown

Chapter 15

Burketown is a tiny outpost that makes Normanton (pop. 1,000) and Karumba (pop. 500) look like large populated areas in comparison. Here the population at the time was around one hundred and fifty, and when I say this place is remote, only the Aboriginal communities in the deserts can surpass it. Waking up in the driver's seat, the bright early morning sunshine filled the car, and with the seat down, I pulled myself up to look out the open window. Coming towards me on the dusty road were two very odd birds. At about a metre in height, with a grey plumage, their stilt-like legs carried these big beaked, red-headed avians gracefully towards me. Like a husband and wife taking an early morning stroll, they walked past the car. As the nearest drew level with me it peered towards me as if to say "Good Morning". These were Brolgas.

These birds were a main feature of this town, and over the few days we stayed here, I would be intrigued at how relaxed they were with human beings in their close proximity. Sometimes there would be half a dozen wandering down the street as if in a gang, and if there had been a pet shop in town, I am sure they would have sauntered in to get their daily birdseed. This country never ceased to amaze me!

The wetlands that border the Gulf of Carpentaria are a paradise for any twitcher, and coupled with the birds that nest in the savannah as well as the squawkers in the more densely vegetated areas of the Northern Territory, they could run as a cast from a film. From Lorikeets to Parakeets, from Cockatoos to Bustards, Lemon-bellied flycatcher to the Great Billed Heron, they are all on the star billing up here in Gulf Country.

Booking into the Burketown pub (there is a new one there now as the original ninety-two-year-old building burnt down last year), we were to stay there for the next four nights and sample some fantastic food. From crocodile to barramundi, camel to buffalo, prawns to emu; this was real bush tucker (Aussie slang for food).

Driving out to Doomadgee Aboriginal community, we met up with the tribal elders, and after securing a few orders on the first day, we headed back to Burketown.

Again, here I noticed a different level of cleanliness and hygiene from the one at Hopevale, and although it was not terrible, it would have been horrific and totally unacceptable to the average person who liked to keep their household in some shape and form. Here and later on, it was not unusual to also find two families sharing one household, with mattresses spread out on the floor in the corner of their living room and perhaps a curtain hanging from the ceiling to protect people's privacy. You could find ten or more people living under the same roof that only had maybe three or four rooms. Again, the interior of these bare breeze block places were devoid of paintings on walls, ornaments, and only had very basic furniture.

One afternoon, I was doing a demo and came to the camouflage scene in the prospectus. Asking the family if they could see where the rabbit was hiding, the daughter began to giggle and I thought nothing of it. With the youngest trying to look behind me after his older sister had whispered something to him, I turned around and could see that a mid-sized mongrel of a dog had now entered the building. Having crossed the bare concrete floor, it had momentarily stopped over the ELF poster to deposit a big pile of steaming excrement onto the ELF character's happy smiling face.

"That's our dog," the girl happily announced.

With the parent's looking around me as well, the mother quickly shooed the dog away while her husband said in a blasé tone of voice, "I'll clean the shit off your poster afterwards, bro."

This was door-to-door sales, Aboriginal style, and when I signed that family up, I duly informed them that anyone buying a set of books got to keep the posters as well!

On the business side of things, although the community had a population of close to a thousand, many were out of work or out of their minds on the devil grog. The ones we could sell books to were employed by the shire council, but it was impossible to set up a job creation scheme as a lot were too pissed to remember what we had said, and also the lack of telephones in the community did not justify us staying around for that long. Driving back to Burketown just outside Doomadgee one evening, we saw a lone male Aboriginal trying to flag us down. Although not exactly pissed, he wasn't exactly sober either. With a strong smell of alcohol reeking from his breath as it wafted into the car, he asked for a lift to Burketown. Recognising him from the day before, we duly agreed. What happened next made me realise why it is not wise to stop for Aborigines by the roadside.

Turning around he shouted back into the bush, "Come on fellas."

Six Aboriginal men came running from behind a dense bush.

"You can't all get in here," I said.

"Yes we can," he replied.

With the rear doors being opened and the sound of the tailgate going up, four of them climbed into the back seats while the other three squeezed into the back, with one having his face pushed up to the glass as I closed the tailgate on them. Driving back the almost one hundred kilometre journey at a snail's pace with the rear tyres rubbing against the wheel arches, we limped back to Burketown. The next day, three of them wanted a lift back to Doomadgee, and on finishing our shift another eight wanted a lift back into town. Deciding that we would only take six, we contemplated putting a sign on the roof saying "Indigenous Cabs". Now remember, this is not normally a wise thing to do, but again we had been in these people's homes and had received their tribal elder's blessing, so don't consider doing this if you are out in these regions travelling by yourself as things could turn pretty nasty.

In the build-up to the wet season, the humidity was becoming very noticeable. With no air conditioning in our room, we would stay down in the bar and sleep outside in the beer garden. Talking to a pilot who had brought an aircraft in on a chartered flight one evening, he informed us that he was taking off at seven the next morning to take his passengers to Darwin. This trip was not cheap, as each passenger had paid five thousand dollars to do this specialised tour.

"How do you manage to get a decent night's sleep in this heat?" Terry asked.

"Same as you guys," he replied. "I get totally pissed!"

The morning before we were due to leave for the Northern Territory and the town of Borroloola, I wondered how bad the road was going to be and whether we would make it there or not. Standing in the post office, about to send some postcards back home, a policeman came in behind me.

"What's the road like from here to Borroloola going through Hell's Gate?" I asked.

"What are you driving?" he enquired.

Walking back towards the glass door, I pointed at our chariot covered in red dust.

"That!" I said

"Two-wheel drive. You got no chance, mate. You'll have to go back down the sealed highway the way you came and go around the long way."

"We didn't come up on the sealed highway," I duly informed him.

"What! You came along the top in that thing?" he said, incredulously pointing at our Japanese road warrior.

"Yes," I replied.

"Strewth, you'll piss the rest!" he said, shaking his head and not quite believing what I had just told him.

The next morning was an early start. Although the law enforcement officer had given me encouraging advice that the rest of the journey was going to be relatively easy, we still had three more rivers on our map that we had to cross, and we still didn't know if they had water, and if they did, how deep they would be! This length of the journey was almost five hundred kilometres, and we would need all day to get to our destination with a quick stop at Hell's Gate roadhouse to refuel. Setting off at nine, with myself at the wheel, we soon met the sand again, and the motion of the car sliding back and forth gave you the feeling of being on a fairground ride.

For a while the sand disappeared and the light smattering of bulldust on the surface returned, making the drive a lot easier. Thinking that the rest of the journey was now going to be a doddle, I was quickly proven wrong when the sand returned once again. With the car struggling to pull us forwards, we were now barely doing twenty kilometres an hour. With the tyres throwing sand and fine red dust into the air, we soon had a film of the stuff on our bodies and clothes. Stopping to dig the wheels out a couple of times, it was hard to believe that this parched landscape was sometimes under deep water for months on end during the wet season, trapping the people in Burketown and other outlying stations, who then relied on supplies being brought in by air.

Six hours later, we met a Land Cruiser coming the other way on what was now almost a single sandy track. This was the only vehicle we were to see during our whole journey to Borroloola, which gives you some idea how isolated we were. Half an hour later we arrived at Hell's Gate. This is a real frontier outpost, and as we got out of the car by the petrol pump, we were met by a young white girl no older than sixteen.

"How's it going?" she said, in that typical Australian accent.

"Great!" I replied. "Can you fill her up please?" I asked.

"No worries mate, but you'll have to move her over to that pump over there."

Looking across to where she was pointing, I could see another pump with the label reading "Diesel" on it.

"We need petrol, not diesel," I said.

"We ain't got no petrol," she replied.

"What do you mean, you ain't got no petrol? This is a roadhouse isn't it?" my co-driver enquired.

"Sure is!" our young non-petrol attendant replied.

Looking at the two solitary fuel pumps standing not twenty metres from the tiny building that she had just emerged from, I tried to get my head around what she was saying.

"So you got no petrol?" I stupidly asked her the second time.

"Yep," her nonchalant answer came.

"So when are you gonna get some more petrol then?" Terry asked.

"Tomorrow maybe."

"Tomorrow?" my Irish inquisitor asked, turning his head to one side.

"Yeah! Or the day after, or the day after that, or the day after that even! Do you want some diesel?"

Trying to fathom out whether this girl was for real or that maybe diesel up in this neck of the woods was like Foster's or VB, and we could have a few glasses of the stuff to drink while we waited for the petrol to arrive, I now began to realise why it was called Hell's Gate. We had inadvertently been sent to hell, but to actually get in there, we had to find our own means to land in the place. It was as if the devil had set this elaborate cruel puzzle himself! (The place actually got its name from the fact this was as far you could go, with a police escort, in the times of the pioneers searching for new land to settle on. From here on, you were on your own – to fight the elements, the flora and fauna, and any aggressive Aboriginal people that may come your way.)

With my mathematician friend turning all sorts of arithmetic, algorithmic, and algebraic formulas and whatever else around in his head, I asked him a simple question. "Terry, have we got enough fuel to get to Borroloola?"

With his eyelids blinking as his brain computed the question, his response came back to me loud and clear. "No."

"About how short are we?" I asked.

Terry rubbed his chin, and combing back his red mop of hair with his hand said, "About ten k's."

We had to make a decision. Stay at Hell's Gate for however many days it took for a petrol tanker to turn up, and sleep in the car and drink ourselves senseless in the daily rising heat and humidity, or risk it and try and see if our Japanese metal friend could get us to our destination on the fuel it had left in its belly, hoping Albert Einstein travelling with me had got his sums wrong in our favour.

Looking at one another, we both nodded and said, "Fuck it! Let's go for it!"

Leaving Hell's Gate in the mid-afternoon heat and travelling into unknown territory without enough fuel to get to our destination, I sometimes, to this day, wonder what the hell was going on in our crazy heads. With the sand getting deeper as we drove to the Northern Territory border, we were forever stopping to dig the wheels out.

Seeing a very lonely sign announcing that we had just crossed the border and were now back into the Northern Territory, something strange happened.

The road changed. Gone went the sand, bulldust and narrow tracks we had been driving on. Now we were on a two-lane red, orangey-coloured, well-maintained surface. Thinking we had got over the worst of the journey and quietly thanking the Northern Territory government for using their budget to look after their roads better, we cracked open some beers and toasted to being back in "The Territory" again. Hurtling onwards, stubby after stubby was consumed on this Martian dust road. With it being corrugated in parts, making the car rattle and shake our bones to pieces, I didn't really care, as I was just glad to leave all that sand behind. As dusk descended, I asked my colleague to break open a box of wine.

Being so close to the equator, the sunset was rapid, and before long we were in darkness, and that was when we got a puncture. Stopping the car, we got the jack out and began to change the wheel. With the headlamps still on, I watched as a snake nearly three metres in length crossed the road in front of us. With the markings of a "King Brown", I was grateful that this highly venomous and deadly reptile had chosen not to cross this track under our car. Now, this may sound amazing, but after almost three years of being in this country, and bearing in mind the remote jungle and desert tracks I had driven on and the places I had been to, this was just the third snake I had seen.

Throwing the punctured tyre into the boot, we had to make sure we didn't have another one, or we would be well and truly stuffed. Crossing a trickle of a river called the Calvert, we likewise met the same volume of water at the Robinson waterway. With the wine flowing at more than a trickle, we were soon quite merry and now, unperturbed by the fact that we would not quite make it to our destination, laughed at all the scrapes and stories that we had picked up on our travels.

Everything was going fine, but then we came up to the Foelsche River. Stopping the car, we could see the other side of the riverbank approximately fifty metres away through the headlamps. With the river flowing at a walking pace, we had no idea how deep it was, though in the next few minutes, two crazy acts were to happen, and this was obviously down to the amount of alcohol we had consumed.

Act 1: Opening the passenger door, Terry took his shoes and socks off and began to roll up his trousers.

"Where are you going?" I asked.

"To test the depth of the water," his drunken Gaelic voice said.

"Alright," I said, thinking that he was having a laugh.

Standing on the sharp riverbed stones, he walked towards the river, and with me still thinking he was having me on and that this was his idea of doing an Irish clown act, he headed towards those dangerous waters. Half-expecting him to turn around any minute, I watched with amazement as he entered the water. Thinking that maybe he knew something that I didn't, he reached a level just below his knees. Watching him standing there motionless only a few metres from the car, I watched as he suddenly turned around and headed back towards me.

"Well," I asked, "how deep is it then?"

"I don't fucking know, and I don't intend to find out."

"Why's that?" I said, trying not to giggle.

"Why?" he said, his eyes now wide open and giving me a deranged look. "Because that fucking water could be full of crocs!"

Bursting out with laughter, I turned to him and said, "I was wondering when that fact would have lodged into your head."

With him then referring to me with the choice phrase of the "C" word, I wondered what to do next, which leads us onto the second crazy act.

"Well, you walked a fair way in and it didn't seem to get any deeper," I said, half-kidding myself. "Let's have a go."

Pushing the accelerator slowly down, we inched into the water and began to cross. Very slowly, the river got deeper, and as it approached about half a metre, I could feel the weight of the water wanting to carry us downstream. I was now committed and needed to make a decision. I couldn't go back because if I stopped the car there was a very real danger that we could be pushed downstream or the wheels get bogged down on the riverbed, and we would be stuck in what indeed was a crocodile-infested habitat. With the weight of the water increasing and still thirty metres to go, I realised that if I maintained this pace there was still a chance the car could be swept down by the increasing force of the water. It was at this stage that I decided to push the throttle towards the floor to gain forward momentum. Willing the vehicle to get us to the other side, I half-expected to hit a gully of some sorts and then find us both semi-submerged and heading out for the Gulf of Carpentaria with a crocodile in the back seat asking "Are we there yet?"

Our semi-amphibious vehicle ploughed through the dangerous waters, and in next to no time we were on dry land once again. Back on "terra firma", I drove until, in the distance and with us now on high ground, I could make out the lights of a settlement below. It was Borroloola. Driving into the town on a steep downward escarpment, the car suddenly ran out of petrol. Freewheeling the vehicle the rest of the way, we found a pub with accommodation and turned into the car park. We had made it, and thankfully Einstein had made a mistake with his petrol consumption sums! It was now ten o'clock.

Seeing that the main bar was full of Aborigines and a few redneck stockmen (white men that worked with cattle), we entered a quiet little bar adjacent, from where we could look across to what was the life and soul of drinking in outback Australia.

"What can I do for you, fellas?"

"Two VBs and we need somewhere to stay for a few days," Terry said.

The barman, who was a tall, lean, young and very black Aboriginal man, nodded at us and turned to grab us some beers. The first thing I noticed about Edwin was his white teeth, which told me that this man looked after himself. (Many Aboriginal people did not look after their teeth, and as a result, by their mid to late twenties, many of their teeth had long gone to the tooth graveyard.)

"Where did ya come from?" our purveyor of fine ales asked.

"Burketown," I replied.

"Burketown," Edwin said, frowning. "Not many travellers arrive this late in Borroloola from Burketown."

"No, it took us a while. My name is Tony, and this is Terry." Holding out our hands, Edwin introduced himself and gave us both very firm handshakes.

"Is that the local's bar next door?" I asked.

"Sure is, but you don't want to go in there," our barman said, shaking his head.

"And why not?" my Irish connection asked.

Edwin, looking at us, and then throwing a glance over his shoulder and back to us again, said, "You might not come out of there alive."

Now the next thing I said to him was probably a bit unfair, as he didn't realise that I would be holding a different pack of cards the following evening. Looking at this clean-shaven man dressed in a smart black shirt and jeans, I decided to make a bet with him.

"Edwin, I bet you fifty bucks I will be drinking next door tomorrow and will have no trouble at all."

Squaring this Welsh alien traveller up, he asked how I could do that.

"Do we have the bet?" I asked.

Curious, he replied with an uncertain "Yes" and then said, "But don't say I didn't warn you if you get beat up in that bar tomorrow night!"

The next day I went down to the petrol station and bought a petrol can, filled it up, and returned to put it into our starving motor vehicle. (Although we had most stuff on board, we never got round to buying a petrol can as we always filled up at every opportunity.) Deciding to drive our automobile down to the garage later to fill up, we set about bashing doors. Here, there were no Aboriginal parts of town as such, as the indigenous folk far outnumbered the white folk, and as a result, we found several fairer skinned families living next door to their darker neighbours in a town that numbered around six hundred. Also, after meeting some elders, we found that the attitude was, "You do what you want bro." Soon we had seven orders under our belts.

Heading back to the hotel early that evening, we went straight into the local's bar. Scanning the crowd, I picked out Saul and Samuel, two Aboriginal brothers (by blood) we had sold to earlier in the day.

"Saul, Samuel, what you guys drinking?" I shouted over what was quite a loud talkative bar.

With the brothers' request for two beers, there was suddenly a lot of chatter among the crowd. How did these two white fellas carrying a knapsack know the "Savo" brothers? I could hear them saying, spying us with suspicion. Looking around, I saw Alfred, another Aboriginal we had sold to earlier, and Eric, a white truck driver. Calling over to them, I enquired what they were drinking too. Reaching the bar and putting our bag down, a large, tall, muscular, scruffy, heavily facial-haired Aboriginal man sidled up to us.

"I'll have a drink too, bro."

Looking straight into this stranger's eyes, as dark as the deepest pool you could imagine, I said, "Well you get this shout and I'll get the next."

For a moment there was no reaction, and then slowly a half-smile appeared on his face.

"How do you know my people?" he asked.

Telling him the nature of our work and name-dropping a couple of tribal elders into the conversation, I called Edwin over, who was finishing serving some white middle-aged travellers who were in the bar that we'd been in the previous night. Looking across to us, his eyes widened and he rushed over to me. Without him knowing what we had been doing earlier that day, he asked us if we would go to the other bar before he would serve us. Before I could answer though, our new friend spoke up.

"Edwin, they are drinking in here with me."

Going over and sitting with the Savo brothers, it transpired that our scruffy fellow drinker had just come out of prison and was a right handful, as we were to find out the next night when a fight broke out spilling blood all over the tables and chairs. Within two minutes, Terry had given away his first fag and it was not long before he was reaching for another packet as indigenous smoker after indigenous smoker approached him. It was like watching someone going into battle when Terry was preparing to go out, except instead of loading up with ammunition and attaching grenades to himself, he would be positioning packets of cigarettes around his body. Two packets in each back pocket of his jeans and one in a front pocket. One placed in the breast pocket of his shirt and one to start him off in his hand. He would sometimes get through a hundred fags in a night and only smoke twenty!

On the subject of the prison population here in Australia, here is a very interesting fact. The Aboriginal population make up just three per cent of the population of Australia, yet their numbers in the prisons around the country, as a percentage, far outstrip the non-Aboriginal people that are incarcerated. I am not going to get drawn into the subject as it is too controversial, and as I said before, this book was meant for a little medium light reading at best. All I will say is this. Being jobless with no purpose in life, coupled with the boredom that is presented to someone every day who live in places like this, it certainly doesn't help.

Going over to the bar later, Edwin handed me fifty dollars.

"Here you go brudder, here's the fifty I owe you for the bet!"

"Thanks," I replied, and stuffed the note into my pocket.

Calling Anna, we both talked excitedly about our forthcoming little holiday in Perth, and that night I fell asleep a very happy man. The next morning I awoke at just after daybreak, and doing a quick calculation on what the time was back home, decided to call and see if anyone was home. With my mother answering and me finding out that both my brother and father were out tasting the amber nectar, I informed her that I would send more money home when I got to the town of Katherine and then again when I reached Darwin, the Northern Territory's principal city.

The question, again, was inevitably asked, "When are you coming home?"

I thought for a moment and then replied, "Next year."

"When?" I heard an anxious raised voice come down the phone line to me.

"Not quite sure yet Mum, but I'll keep you informed."

Telling me that she missed me terribly, I couldn't realise the emotional turmoil she was going through after not having seen her eldest son for over two and a half years. With my parents not being able to afford to fly out to see me, they just had to sit and wait until I returned. Not being a parent myself, I can't see the emotional link that parents can have with their children, though in this day and age, with technologies like "Skype", it must make it a little easier to have facial interaction rather than just a faceless voice.

Drinking in the local's bar each night, Terry would sometimes leave early, and this would annoy our fellow drinkers, thinking that he didn't enjoy their company. Getting back to our shared room, I brought this issue up and it very quickly escalated into a tense argument. Although we got on well with each other, we were in fact two different types of people. I was always out mingling with people, whereas Terry was a bit more reserved. With us shouting at one another about our differences, he then threatened to abandon this little adventure, which would leave me without an income. It was then that I punched him in the head.

Rolling around in the room and exchanging blows, we got up, and pushing each other off, he picked up his holdall full of his clothes and walked out the door telling me I could find my own way to Katherine. Standing at the doorway and shouting expletive after expletive after him, I watched as he started the engine and then sped off into the night.

Sitting by the swimming pool, thinking if I would ever see my Irish colleague again and wondering how I would leave this place, I heard a voice.

"Hey Tony, it's Eric. Are you okay?"

Eric, who was an Aboriginal lad not much older than fifteen or sixteen, had seen the bust up I had just had with my travelling companion. Standing in his thongs, dusty dark shirt and jeans, he cocked his head to one side.

"Yeah, I'm okay!" I replied.

"Do you want a drink?" Eric asked.

"Yeah, I do Eric," I said. "Where you at?'

"Over there." He pointed to a small fire burning on some scrubland about five hundred metres away.

"I'll get some beers," I replied.

Grabbing two six-packs of stubbies from our fridge, I wandered over to the fire. Meeting a dozen Aboriginal men in their twenties and thirties, some of whom I had met before over the previous days, we chatted in a semi-drunken language. Exchanging our thoughts on the world that we lived in and the vast differences between our cultures, our topic turned to food and Australian bush tucker.

"Have you tasted snake before, bro?" I heard a voice from the darkness say.

"No," I replied.

"Someone go and find a snake," I heard another voice say.

After some time, a fellow brother came wandering out of the darkness and up to the fire. Holding a snake that was about two metres long and motionless, he threw it onto the fire.

"Now that's good tucker," I heard one of the dark faces flickering in the light of the fire say. Looking at the serpent cooking in the fire, Eric again appeared from nowhere with a petrol can in one of his hands. Sitting down next to me, I offered him a drink from my stubby, which he gratefully received. Returning the bottle to me, I took another swig and it was then he said something that will stick in my head for a very long time.

"You're not like the rest of the white fellas Tony."

"And why is that?" I asked.

He looked at me with his young man's face and said, "Because no white fella would share his bottle with an Abo!"

Eric, lifting up the petrol can and unscrewing the top, said, "Do you want to try?"

Smelling the strong pungent petroleum vapour coming from the opening of the can, I wondered what he was proposing I do with it. Placing

308

his nose over the can, he took a very deep sniff inhaling the fumes from the liquid inside and down into his body.

"It's good," he said, holding the can towards me.

Looking into the fire and seeing "Slippery Sid" cooking in front of me, and my fellow dark-skinned brothers sitting opposite me with their faces aglow, with a teenager holding a can of petrol by my side as if it were some sort of bong, I thought it was surreal.

It was then that I heard the sound of a car, and looking over to where the highway was, I could see a vehicle's headlamps heading towards the town. It was Terry! In his drunken state, he'd eventually calculated that he didn't have enough fuel to get to the next roadhouse, as all that was in the fuel tank was the petrol I had put in earlier from the can. He would have run out of petrol and still been over a hundred kilometres from the nearest roadhouse. Watching him park the vehicle up outside our room, I made my excuses. Telling my fireside friends that I would return, I walked back over to see if we could patch things up. On reaching the door, I changed my mind, and finishing off a couple of stubbies and finding one of the back doors unlocked, I decided to sleep in the car in case he decided to leave without me in the morning. The next morning not much was said, and we treated each other as if nothing had happened. The cracks in our partnership, though, had started.

If you think about it, we had done very well. It was now mid-September and we had been living in one another's pockets for over nine months, sometimes in very basic and cramped accommodation. With the now harsh everyday climatic conditions, the flies, the mosquitos and the dust, it all had a bearing on our general mental attitude towards one another. The build-up to the wet season is incidentally known as the silly season, where people who can no longer cope with the heat and humidity commit suicide, or even homicide. I guess you have to live in these conditions without the trappings of modern technology like air conditioning, to get an idea of what drives people to do such things.

Laying out the map, we decided to head next to the Aboriginal community of Ngukurr (pronounced Nooker). Discussing briefly what we would do over the next couple of months, I expressed an interest in the termination of our partnership once we had returned to Melbourne after crossing the vast Nullabor plain of Western Australia and into South Oz and then Victoria. At the time I mentioned nothing about the forthcoming meeting with Anna in Perth, only that I would be briefly staying with fictitious long-lost relatives in the city. I was in fact to book an apartment in the northern suburbs of the city for the both of us for the duration.

Before leaving Borroloola, I made a point of making sure Edwin was working the morning we were leaving. Thanking our extremely accommodating barman, who over the few days shared stories, jokes, and gave us advice on who would probably buy books from us, I passed fifty dollars into his hand as we made our farewell handshake.

"What's that for?" he asked.

"Here is your fifty dollars back from the bet I made with you," I said.

"No bro, you won that fair and square."

"No I didn't," I said, shaking my head. "I cheated."

"No brudder, you didn't. I lost!"

Looking into his eyes and still holding the fifty dollar note tight in his hand, I said, "Well, please take it as a tip!"

Another chapter had closed in the Aboriginal world of Australia, and another was about to open. A chapter that will make many, many readers gasp at how isolated this island continent has been.

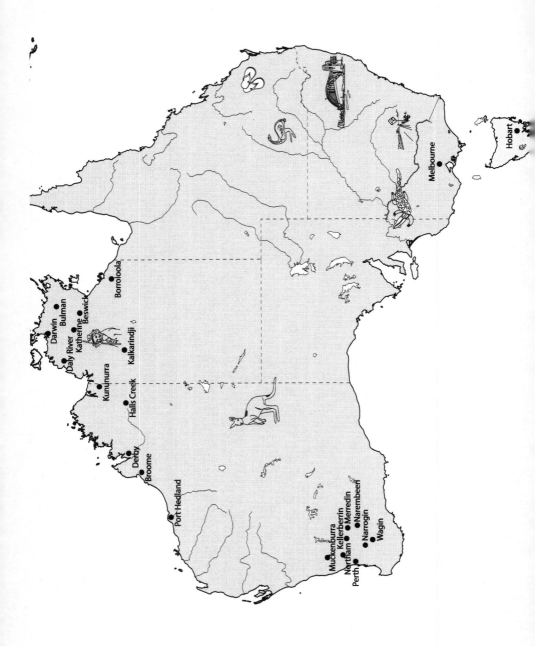

Darwin
Bulman
Katherine
Beswick
Daly River
Kalkarindji
Borroloola
Kununurra
Halls Creek
Derby
Broome
Port Hedland
Muckenburra
Kellerberrin
Merredin
Narembeen
Northam
Narrogin
Perth
Wagin
Melbourne
Hobart

Chapter 16

Arriving at Roper Bar, which is on the Roper River, we were now in a place that had a population of eight, along with two Blue Heelers (two dogs) and a cockatoo. This was to be our base from where we would work the Ngukurr Aboriginal community, which was a twenty-five minute and thirty kilometre drive away. We were in a very remote part of Australia that very few outsiders saw.

Booking into a very cramped non air-conditioned cabin with just two single beds, a table with two chairs and a gas stove, we found the toilet and shower block twenty metres away. During the time here, I began to realise that what myself and my Irish companion had been doing over the last few months, no one had done before (well not to our knowledge anyway). We were pioneers in the bookselling world of encyclopedias, in lands that had never been explored before by hawkers, peddlers, salesmen or whatever you would like to call them. Here, these people had previously had no opportunities to buy books, vacuum cleaners, insurance policies or even acquire bibles that are handed out by the various religious groups that go door to door. Indeed, these communities were not on the Western world radar for selling stuff door to door at all.

We were now bringing the written word properly to the Aboriginal people. (Well that is a load of bullshit, but we were now bringing educational books to people who previously could not get access to them before.) Even our boss had now decided to send a team of three salespeople up to Thursday Island where the "Torres Strait Islanders" lived at the far northern tip of Australia.

Heading off to see what we would experience at yet another Aboriginal community, we crossed the concrete causeway that traverses the river with a few inches of water trickling over it to give the tyres a well-deserved wash. Ngukurr is a dry community, which means it is, in theory, impractical and against tribal law to consume alcohol within the settlement. The place (at the time and I hope still is) was so well run that it took us both by surprise.

The tribal elders did not tolerate the fact that their people could drink alcohol in the vicinity. Having safe shelters to protect spouses from their violent partners, these people, like Hopevale, had a well-structured community. The first couple of times we entered this very remote settlement, that had a population of just under a thousand people, we heard the children sounding the "White fellas coming" alarm, though after a day or so almost everyone had got used to us walking the streets.

One afternoon, a teenage Aboriginal girl said to me, while walking back to the car to get another moneybox, "Are you the encyclopedia man?" Replying yes, she then enquired when I was going to knock on her parent's door.

Within a matter of days, we sold dozens of sets of books, and as the community had everyone employed by their shire council, these orders were processed with no trouble at all. With our cancellation rate practically zero, we were now making big money. The downside was the humidity and the mozzies. It was now impossible to sleep at night without guzzling down a dozen beers, a cask of wine, a cask of port or a bottle of rum. One night I decided to sleep under the stars, and the mosquitos had a feast on the parts of my body that were not covered in insect repellent. Even going to the toilet and washing your hands you had to make sure you reapplied the repellent back onto your washed skin or they would have you.

Leaving Ngukurr for the last time, the children gathered around us and either shook our hands or asked us to do "high fives". We also found that five Aboriginal men required the services of "Indigenous Cabs". So, for the five hours and three hundred and fifty kilometre drive to the large town of Katherine, seven black and white sweaty bodies traded stories with one another as we all finished the beers we had left in the car.
At Katherine, we booked into a nice motel called the Paraway where we were to stay for several days; swimming in the pool in the day and propping up the bar at night.

Venturing into the town's pubs on several occasions, it reminded me of Alice Springs where the large number of drunken Aborigines kept the police

314

on the go for most of the time. Despite meeting some Aboriginals in the town from Ngukurr, and having a beer or two in these drinking establishments, the intensity of friction within was much greater than the other pubs we had drunk in over the past few months. The town acted like a hub where people came from the north, south, east and west. You had Aboriginal people from many distant, different lands, and this simmering powder keg often ignited with violence. For once, we stuck to the motel.

With the wet season almost on top of us, we knew we would soon have to make plans to head south before the floods began to block the roads. Terry had been to Darwin before, and although he didn't much rate the city, I wanted to go and visit Australia's most northern metropolis.

Studying our map in detail, we then decided to go completely the other way and off the radar entirely. The logic being that if we could sell a pile of books in a remote jungle settlement like Ngukurr, we could do the same in remote communities in the desert. How wrong we were. Finding a remote Aboriginal community on the fringes of the Tanami Desert called Kalkarindji, we decided to head there, and from there go deeper and eventually reach Balgo, which was deep in the desert itself, sleeping in the car if we had to.

Driving away from the lush green foliage, the journey of three hundred kilometres turned into semi-desert surroundings when we arrived at Top Springs. Here there is no town, just one building – the pub! Staying there overnight, we headed off to Kalkarinji, another two hundred kilometres further inland. This narrow sealed road was to take us to an environment we had not yet experienced.

Arriving at this community was like going back to the Stone Age. Here, the women huddled around in dusty, grubby dresses, and the men stood back and eyed us with great suspicion, while the children either hid behind their mothers or peered from around the doorways or window frames devoid of glass. Gone was the interaction we'd had with the Aboriginal folk we'd met in the past, as each salutation we gave to these people was met with a silence or a reply we could not understand. We realised we had come up against a barrier not even our ingenuity could get around, and that was the barrier of language.

Going door to door was like being on an alien planet, as each and every person we met could not converse with us due to their inability to speak English.

Just about to give up, we found an Aboriginal man who did speak English. Inviting us into his home, he introduced his non-English speaking wife and his three children, who, although quite young, from the ages of four to eleven, could understand and speak the same lingo as us. Finding that they had a telephone and that this man was employed as a tracker by the police force of the Northern Territory, Terry decided to do a demonstration. (A tracker was, and still is, a vocation that involves tracking and hunting down not so much animals, but humans: people who had escaped prison, or criminals that had recently carried out a felony and were now on the run. These professional trackers were in a league of their own with regards to studying tracks that felons had left behind. Knowing how long ago a person had been at a certain place, and where the fugitive on the run was possibly heading, the chances of these naughty people running away from the law were greatly reduced.)

Sitting in a spartan living room on a filthy sofa, I looked on as the children watched a brand new television that had been delivered the day before and was now sat on a large black oil drum. Looking around the room, I could see the remote control lying on the floor. Getting up to retrieve it, I pressed a few buttons, and finding it not working, I removed the battery cover to find them missing. With Terry proceeding with his sales technique, I scanned the room to see if I could see any batteries. Looking in the cardboard box that it had arrived in, which was now discarded outside, I rummaged around the polystyrene and plastic bubble wrap, but with no luck returned and sat back down again. Determined to find the batteries, I bravely began to probe the sides of the cushions with my fingers, and that is when I found them. Removing them from their plastic packet, I inserted them into the remote control. With Terry midway through the demonstration and the three children watching the television, I pressed the remote and changed to a different channel.

What happened next was amazing. With the mother not being able to understand English, she had quickly got bored with my Irish colleague's script and had begun to watch the television with the kids. When the channel flicked over, and with no one near the television to change the channels manually, she suddenly got up and shrieked. The children appeared perplexed but not as startled as their mother, as they turned around to see what possibly could have made the TV change in such a strange and sudden way. With the eldest looking at me holding the little black plastic box, he asked if I had been responsible for the action. Pressing a button again, I raised the volume and this made the mother look at me wide-eyed as if I had some strange telekinetic powers. Handing him the remote, all interest was suddenly lost with buying the books, and when Terry asked the Aboriginal man to sign the sale agreement, only to hear that he couldn't write, I said, "It's time to go."

Now this is going to amaze most of you as it did me at the time. Staying in the pub in Top Springs for a second night and chatting to the locals that lived on cattle stations in the vicinity, we told them the problems we'd had with communicating with the people of Kalkarinji.

"You should have got down to Balgo," a well-weathered face said.

"That was the plan initially," I replied.

"Well it's a good job you turned back when you had the chance or you might not be here now telling your story, isn't that right, Bruce?"

Another much older chap joined in the conversation, and Bruce began to describe what it was like at that settlement.

"It's like going back in time to when time actually began. Only a few weeks ago the supply plane was attacked by some people from the place and the pilot had a spear thrust through his legs while they robbed the aircraft of the provisions."

"Really!" we both replied simultaneously.

"Yep!" Bruce said as he continued. "They are a bunch of savages down there in Balgo. Do you know the first time they clasped eyes on a white fella was in 1976?"

Now bearing in mind Cook had sailed his ship to the shores of this continent in 1770, it had taken over another two hundred years before white people stumbled across Balgo. If you find this story hard to believe, I have another one in a few pages time at which point you can actually check the authenticity yourselves on the internet.

Checking into the Paraway once again in Katherine, the next day we headed for Darwin and Terry was right, as the city that had a population of around seventy thousand (at the time) did not have that profound an effect on me either. Staying in the Northern Territory's principal city for three days, I found out that it had been bombed by the Japanese during World War Two in 1942 and was almost taken off the face of the earth by Cyclone Tracy in 1974. We soon made our journey southwards again via a slight detour to the Aboriginal community of Nauiyu Nambiyu, or Daly River. There, we were to sell another pile of books.

Arriving back in Katherine, we delighted the owners of the Paraway when we booked into them for a third and final time, sending their bar takings back up again. Deciding to head back into the jungle, we headed for the Aboriginal community of Beswick just a hundred kilometres away. It was here that we were noticed by more than the Aboriginal folk.

Shopping in a store a few days later back in Katherine one afternoon, I was approached by a small white-bearded man who accused me of ripping the Aboriginal people off with the price of the books we were selling. On informing him that everyone in the entire country, whether they be black, white, yellow or whatever colour, paid the same price for the books, he stormed out of the store. I was told soon after by the checkout girl that he owned a shop that had lots of custom from the Beswick community and that his credit charges were astronomical; his customers would end up paying five times the amount for televisions and sofas than if they had purchased them in a store in Darwin. I thought afterwards that this hypocrite probably

318

considered us as a threat, taking those indigenous people's disposable incomes away from him when they could have been going into his greedy pocket.

After Beswick, we attempted to get up to Bulman in Arnhem Land, but not even our road warrior of a vehicle could get us through the sand on the tiny track that led to this remote place and we had to turn back.

All Aboriginal communities that we had worked in up until now had one common factor. The same film star was an idol to adult and child alike. Now, can you guess who? This was now the mid-nineties so you could have the likes of Mel Gibson, Kevin Costner, Harrison Ford, Tom Cruise, Sylvester Stallone, or whoever was walking on the tinseltown parade in Hollywood at the time.

No, none of them got a look-in! In what was the film world of the indigenous people at the time, you could guarantee that every household that had a video recorder also had at least one copy of a Bruce Lee film. You would see the youngsters in these communities nigh on a daily basis practising karate chops or kung fu kicks on their brothers and sisters, and occasionally running around re-enacting a scene from Enter the Dragon or the Australian version they had made up, "Enter the Wombat" (that was a joke by the way). It was fascinating to watch the youngsters trying to launch their karate chops at our little knapsack after we had jokingly told them that we had snakes and crocodiles inside.

The heat and humidity were now accompanied by heavy showers akin to stepping under a shower in your home with the water pressure on full blast. These warm showers were a precursor to the wet season starting properly, and it was now time to head for Western Australia and down to Perth. Sending more money home from Katherine and then Darwin, I was now eager to meet up with Anna and to see from there where my path would eventually lead me.

The day we left Katherine for WA (the term commonly used for the state of Western Australia), I had a huge hangover from drinking in the motel bar till the early hours. Now this is very unusual for me, but on that day the last thing I wanted to do was drive. With Terry taking the wheel, we started off on our five hundred kilometre journey to Kununurra, which was just over the border.

With the temperature hovering around a hundred degrees Fahrenheit in the shade, I asked Terry to keep an eye on the engine's temperature gauge and to reduce speed if need be so not to cook the engine. Falling asleep, I awoke a few hours later to see him hurtling along at well over a hundred kilometres an hour with the temperature gauge needle now living in the red zone.

"What the fuck do you think you're doing?" I said. "You're going to blow the engine!"

"Aw, don't worry matey," he replied. "Everything is fine."

As those words left his lips the oil light lit up on the dashboard and then we heard a loud bang.

Slowly the vehicle ground to a halt. Shaking my head, I looked at him and said, "How long has the gauge been on the red for?"

"I'm not sure. Anyway it's been driving fine up until now!"

"Of course it fucking has," I replied, "because up until now it has had water in the radiator keeping it cool."

We were now twenty kilometres from the border and another thirty from the nearest civilisation, which was the town of Kununurra. Trying to flag down passing motorists, an Australian family from a small town in WA called Fitzroy Crossing, who were returning from Darwin, finally stopped. Informing the man that we were members of the Australian road recovery service, he said he would go to the first garage he found in the town and ask them to come out and get us. As their Land Cruiser headed off, I sat on the bonnet of the car next to my Irish racing colleague saying very few words to him, and watched the sun sink slowly towards the horizon. An hour later we were in complete darkness and the only passing traffic were the road trains coming from the Northern Territory, and they stopped for no one.

Thinking we were out in this semi-desert area for the night, I could suddenly see a lone vehicle's headlights in the distance heading towards us, coming from the Western Australian border. (In these regions you could see a vehicle approaching you from many, many kilometres away, especially if the surrounding area was completely flat.) After about ten minutes, it pulled up in front of us. Squinting my eyes through the glare of the headlights, I could see it was the family's Land Cruiser again. Stepping out of his vehicle and clutching two cans of Coke, a couple of Mars bars and two pies, the man walked towards us.

"How's it going fellas?" he said.

"We're okay," I replied. "Where's the pick-up truck?"

"They won't come out and get you at night as there's too many 'roos on the road," he informed us, as he handed us the cold drinks and food.

"Too many fucking kangaroos on the road! This is Australia isn't it? Surely they've got bull bars on their vehicles, haven't they?" Terry blurted out.

"I would have thought so," our one-man rescue service replied. "Anyway, I thought I couldn't leave you guys out in the desert for the night, so I put the wife and kids into a motel and here I am. Come on, I'll tow you in."

Grabbing a rope from the back of his vehicle, that is how we entered Western Australia – towed in by a complete stranger. Stopping briefly at the fruit, plant, and seed quarantine checkpoint on the border, we then carried on to Kununurra, where our saviour took us to the doorway of the garage he had initially visited. (This checkpoint is unique, as the state doesn't have the pests that the rest of the country has, so all fruit, plants and seeds have to be dumped in a bin before carrying on, unless you carry a permit.)

Thrusting fifty dollars into our rescuer's hand, I had to plead to him to take it, saying, "Buy something for the kids." And that's another amazing thing about this country. The openness and generosity of the people who live here is unsurpassable. From the time I met all the folk in Kiama, two and a half years previously, who had offered to put me up in their homes for nothing, to the gifts, advice and help offered by the Aboriginal people we met, this truly makes it a great nation to live in.

The next day we called at the garage, and when we asked what was wrong with the engine, the mechanic replied, "It's fucked!"

Now, if I was back home in Wales, I could probably get a replacement engine for my car within a hundred or so kilometres. Not in Kununurra. This town of just over two and a half thousand people only provided the basics, and that did not include car engines. The nearest place we could source an engine from was just down the road in the city of Perth. Three thousand, two hundred kilometres down the road – the equivalent of driving from London to Moscow.

Explaining that we needed an engine compatible for an automatic transmission, the owner of the engine suppliers informed us that it would take three days to transport it up to us after we had deposited a thousand dollars in cash into his account. Putting the cash into his bank, we waited for the three days, knocking all the doors of this little outpost and securing just two orders. The rest of the time I stayed in the pub while Terry stayed in our room watching videos or briefly joining me at a drinking den. The friction between us was now clearly visible, so we kept our distance as much as possible. The humidity had now given way to the dry north-western Australian heat and temperatures were now in the high thirties to low forties on a daily basis.

Three days later, I picked up the motel room's telephone and heard the voice of the mechanic.

"I've got some good news and I've got some bad news," I heard him say.

"What's the good news?" I asked.

"The engine's arrived."

"And the bad news?"

"They've sent the wrong one."

The suppliers had indeed sent an engine for a Mitsubishi, but one that was compatible with a manual gearbox and not an automatic. Complaining to the owner that he had sent the wrong one, he was adamant that it was me that had made the mistake. Realising that he had our money, I kept my cool and asked how he could solve our problem. Listening to him, my heart began to sink; he would send the right engine providing we would pay the transportation costs, but would only send another once he had received the other back. That was another six days in this furnace and the date for meeting Anna was getting ever closer. With no other choice, we had to wait it out.

One morning I decided to take a scenic flight over the Argyle Mining Dam and the Bungle Bungle Range – strange rock formations that lie in the Purnululu National Park. With the receptionist at the motel advising me to take the earliest flight available as the thermals rising from the baking ground during the day would make the little plane bounce all over the place, I found myself at the aerodrome at five thirty in the morning.

Racing down the runway in a six-seater Cessna, the drama began almost immediately. With the pilot finding that the intercom speaker system would not work, he informed us that he would relay his commentary by shouting over the sound of the engine. With a woman in her late fifties who had obvious hearing difficulties, this turned out to be quite comical, as during the flight she would often say "What did you say?" or "Can you speak up!"

In front of me were two young German girls in their twenties who spoke only basic English, and with them occasionally saying "Please" to certain words they did not understand, the pilot probably wished he had stayed in bed that morning. Sitting next to me at the back of the plane was an Australian man in his early thirties who remained incredibly quiet. After almost an hour into our two-hour flight, the pilot once again asked if we were all okay. The passenger sitting next to him almost took his ears off by shouting, "Yes, I'm fine thank you."

The two girls responded with a "Yes" as well, and he then shouted to the two of us at the back.

"You okay at the back, fellas?"

"Yes," I replied.

"What about you, fella?" he asked the passenger next to me.

Turning towards him, I could see he was perspiring heavily, and asking if he was okay, he replied, "No, I don't feel well."

"He doesn't feel well," I shouted back towards the cockpit.

"What's wrong with him?" the pilot called back again.

Now, the next answer I heard from him, I had to think – had I misheard him when his reply came?

"I'm afraid of flying!" he said.

Seeing the whites of his knuckles as he clutched the top of the seat that one of the girls was sitting on, I shouted back his problem.

The pilot momentarily digested this information and then said, "Well what the hell is he doing on a plane then?"

Asking him this valid question, he replied with his voice stuttering, "I have never flown before and I thought I would like it, but I don't. I want to get out."

Now fortunately the girls were sitting by the door, and even to this day I think that if he had been sitting where one of them was now sitting, he would have gone sky-diving without a parachute.

And what about the flight? Brilliant! Flying over the man-made water surface that is Lake Argyle, eight times the size of Sydney Harbour, I looked down onto the Argyle Mining Dam facility that was and still does, mine more rare pink diamonds than anywhere else in the world. Flying over the Bungle Bungles, as they are more commonly known, these weird beehive-shaped little mountains that were formed over three hundred and fifty million years ago through a process of the harsh desert winds blowing from the Tanami Desert and the rain driving into the sandstone rock presented a unique formation I had never seen before or since. The national park's name – Purnululu – means sandstone in the local Aboriginal language.

Now, here comes this other amazing fact. Kununurra lies just two hundred and fifty kilometres by road from this little range of rocks, but have a guess when they were discovered by European Australians?

It was 1983! Yep, that's nineteen eighty-three.

Apparently, a film crew flying back to Perth decided to take a different flight path from their usual one and stumbled onto the Bungles. Is this country remote or what?

The engine that was successfully to take us down the coast of Western Australia arrived six days later, as promised, and ten days later after arriving in Kununurra, we finally left.

Driving next to the town of Wyndham, we roasted there on two consecutive days in forty-five degree heat. On the second day I was amazed to see a group of Aboriginal people walking on a road that was about to melt, with some walking barefoot. Driving through the Kimberley region, we stopped on two consecutive nights to work the little inland towns of Halls Creek and Fitzroy Crossing before heading back to the coast and the town of

Derby (pronounced as spelt and not Darby). Derby boasts some of highest tides in the world with its tidal range of over eleven metres. Watching the speed of the tide come in (and go out) is an incredible sight to see. From there, we headed to the pearling town of Broome, and spying some nice little pearl earrings in one of the many jewellery shops, I bought them to give to Anna on her birthday.

Deciding to drive through the night (again not a wise thing to do), we witnessed an awesome spectacle of Mother Nature as we carried on down the Great Northern Highway. To the right of us, far out to sea above the Indian Ocean, raged two enormous separate electrical storms. To the left of us, and somewhere over the Great Sandy Desert, raged another, and behind us somewhere over Broome, yet another. Stopping at the Sandfire Roadhouse, we watched this fantastic light show without any sound of thunder. It reminded me of a space battle in one of the science fiction films I had seen in the past, but without the spaceships.

The six hundred kilometre drive to Port Hedland saw us arrive in this large port and town of fourteen thousand at three in the morning, and finding a lay-by, we grabbed some sleep in the car till dawn broke.

Waking and looking down at my right leg, I could see that several yellow sores had developed on my right calf and thigh. Booking into a motel, I drove to the town's medical centre because the pain in my leg had become excruciating by just pressing the accelerator. The doctor who examined me informed me that I had caught a sort of malarial skin infection. Giving me some iodine to put on the sores and a course of antibiotics, he told me to rest up for a couple of days. Within forty-eight hours my leg had healed and we were soon hurtling down to Perth. I still have the scars on my leg to this day.

Arriving in the capital city of Western Australia, we booked into a hotel in the suburb of North Cottesloe, overlooking the Indian Ocean. Explaining to Terry that I was to meet up and stay with my fictitious relatives and that I needed the car for the duration, he surprisingly agreed. I could never have revealed that I was meeting a girl that I had flown all the way from Sydney, or otherwise he may have thought I would drive off over the continent back to the east coast and leave him stranded, though this was never my intention. The reason I also wanted the car was the flip side of the coin, where while I was with her, he could have left me in the lurch and buggered off to another state.

Driving to the airport to pick her up, my mood was a mixture of excitement and apprehension as to whether she had changed since I had last seen her.

Scanning the crowd filling the arrivals lounge, I looked for her photogenic face. When a large Samoan man moved aside, there she was. Her hair had now been lightened to almost a blonde colour, and as she walked towards me smiling with her pink rosy-coloured lips, I looked deep into her piercing blue eyes. What happened next was to throw me completely. Taking her hand luggage and suitcase, I leaned forwards to kiss her on the lips, and as I reached her, she very quickly moved her head to one side to offer me her cheek. Over the next few days her body language told me that things had changed between us, and when she informed me that she needed time to think about what she wanted to do with regards to us, I decided to keep my status as an illegal immigrant secret.

Exploring the city and taking the ferry the twenty-odd kilometres over to visit Rottnest Island, we acted like old school friends and not lovers. The devil sat on my shoulder with his arms crossed, his legs swinging in the air and with a face like thunder, while the angel wagged her finger at him saying "No you don't!"

By the time her birthday arrived, the light that had ignited our passion for one another had been extinguished for good, and my only thought when I handed her the pearl earrings was that of returning home. Leaving her at the airport with another kiss on the cheek, she disappeared around the corner and I was never to see her again.

Perth is my favourite of all the Australian cities. The clean white sandy beaches that lead into the warm waters of the Indian Ocean meant I spent a large part of my day alone on the beach drinking cold sodas and swimming in safer waters than the ones up in box jellyfish and crocodile territory.

It was the fact we had booked our hotel rooms on the seafront that made me momentarily forget about returning home, and heading inland to work the towns of Katanning, Wagin and Narrogin, we booked back into the same hotel to spend Christmas in Perth.

Christmas Day was spent giving the folks a call back home, and then with a little knapsack of beers, I walked from the beach of Cottesloe, through the beaches of Swanbourne, City Beach and Scarborough, before catching a bus back for some Christmas drinks with Terry.

January was spent working back inland up to three hundred kilometres east of the city in places like Northam, York, Kellerberrin, Merredin, Narembeen and Mukinbudin.

By the end of January, I was getting bored with the job, and the thought of staying in a car with Terry for the three and a half thousand kilometre journey back to Melbourne, with the thought that if something happened to the car in the meantime, anything could happen, I decided we should part ways.

Selling the car, Terry decided he would buy a smaller vehicle and stay in the city. Calling the boss and informing him that I was coming to Melbourne via the bus, he asked why I didn't just catch a plane, as it was a two-day journey by road. The crazy logic I had put into my head was that I could then say I had travelled right around the continent by road. Telling me I was mad, I went and bought a ticket, and after being on the bus for twenty-four hours, with another twenty-two to go, I started to question my sanity as well!

Arriving in Melbourne, I told him of my intentions of returning home, and although the offer of more money was made, I couldn't think of anything worse than driving through turf I had driven through many times before. Then he came up with Plan B – Tasmania.

Flying me to the capital of this island state better known as "Tassie",

I was to run two teams in the city of Hobart for a month or so. Five weeks later, I brought the teams back to the mainland via the ferry, and by now I had decided I was going home no matter what!

Arriving at immigration, I was worried that they would question the fact that my intermediate visa had lasted so long. With the officer glancing at my visa stamp showing the date when I had entered the country and stamping it, he snapped my passport closed and said, "You've had a good stay. Did you enjoy it?"

"You bet! You have a great country here," I replied.

"Cheers mate, hope you come back soon," he said, with a big beaming smile.

Flying back home, I had time to reflect on my little adventure that had lasted three years and just over one month. It was now March 1994. I had travelled the length and breadth of the country and seen events that most tourists or backpackers, and indeed most Australians, would never see first hand. The outback that I had travelled extensively throughout had been absolutely amazing! I mentioned before that I had been born and bred on a coastal town, and for that reason I still had that invisible affinity that pulled me inland as much as possible.

I think the Aboriginal people have a culture most people would never begin to understand unless they have met them and been invited into their homes. Their superficial image and the dark side of seeing them drunk, with the violence that came with it, hid their true personalities and proud heritage that showed affection, care, and general generosity from what we saw. Many Aborigines choose not to go on that path of self-destruction, and for that reason I take my hat off to them. As I said before, to wake up each morning knowing you have no job to go to, or that the same mundane routine has started each and every day the sun rises, it must be difficult not to pick up a bottle or two and try to forget the hopelessness some of these people felt.

As you now know, the communities that gave their people a purpose in life functioned far better and without as much violence as what we had experienced in the places where the "sit-down" money led them to the pub each day.

Boredom leads towards the grog, as well as substance abuse from sniffing petrol or whatever was available from a young age to alleviate the tedium. I know there are ongoing programmes which have been implemented to get more Aboriginal people into the workforce and get them better educated. For example, I read that the mining giant Rio Tinto now actively looks to employ and train these indigenous people so that they can earn good money and provide themselves with a better standard of living and quality of life for their families – and that's great!

For places like Wilcannia, where there are no mines or industry, it is much more difficult to find a job as the place really is out on a limb. Successful projects that have been set up projecting and marketing the colourful Aboriginal art in remote places like Central Australia and the Kimberly have achieved considerable success by shipping these unique works of art to tourist areas for sale, so to generate some income for these people and give them a meaning to their lives. The people really have to travel to find jobs, but because they are culturally attached to their land, it is difficult for them to do so.

I said to you in chapter one of this book that a lot of my friends moved to find jobs after they had left education as the jobs that were suitable for them were just not in the town. My own little brother currently works in Scotland nearly seven hundred kilometres away, and obviously does not see his family as much as he would like. Though from making this sacrifice, he knows that from the money he is earning he can provide his family with a good living and give his little son, Euen, the best possible education he can afford.

Wilcannia and the other outback towns that have these problems are obviously for the Australian government to tackle, and again I know they are constantly looking at issues all over the country to improve the welfare, housing, education, healthcare and employment for these people, which is not just unique to Australia but the entire world.

Here is an interesting question a woman once asked me in a bar in Perth one evening, after we told of our success in the Aboriginal communities:

"How do you sleep at night when you have been ripping off the Abos?"

Replying to the person concerned, I informed her that, like the gentleman that had asked the same question to me in the supermarket in the town of Katherine, each package was the same price to anyone that purchased them. Furthermore, and to rub salt into her wound, I said that if only just one Aboriginal child benefits from those books from their parent's income and goes on to achieve a degree or scholarship that sees them go on to greater things, I will be pleased for that person and would think – Hey I sold a great product!

Onto the product itself. At the time, I didn't realise that the birth of the World Wide Web, coming online that very year, while we were going from Aboriginal community to Aboriginal community, would in turn give birth to the mighty powerful search engines such as Google.

I was working in an industry where the encyclopedia in book form was in its twilight years, and would very soon be redundant. In 1996, the company that produced the *Encyclopedia Britannica* sacked its entire door-to-door sales staff. With companies such as Google, there was no need to have a bookcase full of knowledge when you could now turn on the computer and at your fingertips have a wealth of information that easily surpassed what you would have had on a shelf.

Arriving at Heathrow Airport, I was picked up by another good friend of mine – Chris Hughes. Having been up in London to watch a rugby international match, I had timed it perfectly and he gave me a lift back to Tenby. Asking him to drop me at the foot of the road, I entered a telephone kiosk and rang home. With my mother sitting in her armchair by the window, not more than three hundred metres away and still not knowing when I was coming home, she picked it up.

"Hi Mum ,it's me!" I said. "What's the weather like?"

"Oh it's cold and damp," she replied.

"I'll be home soon," I said.

"How soon?" she asked.

"Very soon," I replied.

Having a quick chat, I replaced the receiver and walked the long way round, knowing that she would see me coming from around the corner. Putting the key into the lock, I quietly turned it and let myself in. Opening the living room door, there she was, sitting in the same green armchair, with the Dachshund on the left arm and the Corgi on the right. Both dogs now looked ancient, and whereas in the past they would have jumped off to greet me, they just sat there and probably thought, "Oh, he's home."

With tears of joy, she hugged and kissed me. My Australian adventure was over, but many other adventures to other parts of the world were to come.

For now though, The Encyclopedia Man was home!